The Data Analytics Advantage

The Data Analytics Advantage

Strategies and Insights to Understand Social Media Content and Audiences

LAEEQ KHAN

OXFORD

UNIVERSITY PRESS

OXFORD
UNIVERSITY PRESS

Oxford University Press is a department of the University of Oxford.
It furthers the University's objective of excellence in research, scholarship,
and education by publishing worldwide. Oxford is a registered trademark of
Oxford University Press in the UK and in certain other countries.

Published in the United States of America by Oxford University Press
198 Madison Avenue, New York, NY 10016, United States of America.

CIP data is on file at the Library of Congress

ISBN 9780197814239

9780197814222 (hbk.)

DOI: 10.1093/oso/9780197814222.001.0001

Paperback printed by Integrated Books International, United States of America

Hardback printed by Lightning Source, Inc., United States of America

The manufacturer's authorized representative in the EU for product safety is
Oxford University Press España S.A., Parque Empresarial San Fernando de Henares,
Avenida de Castilla, 2 – 28830 Madrid (www.oup.es/en).

Contents

Preface

Introduction

In the ever-evolving landscape of the digital era, businesses and organizations are dedicating their resources to establish a strong online presence. In this modern age, metrics such as views, likes, comments, and shares have emerged as the new currency, playing a crucial role in shaping a brand's success. This is why social media analytics, the study of translating these digital clues into useful information, is so important.

The digital revolution necessitates more than just having an online presence; it calls for businesses and organizations to skillfully utilize social media data as a strategic asset. This evolution has had a profound impact on educational fields, particularly for students studying communication, business and marketing, information technology, sociology, and data science. It highlights the importance of learners being able to effectively navigate the vast world of social media analytics, allowing them to gain a competitive advantage and improve their academic and professional endeavors.

Understanding the intricacies of digital behavior through quantitative analysis presents its own set of challenges. The use of social media analytics extends from lively discussions in corporate boardrooms to dynamic interactions in academic classrooms. For many, especially students in the social sciences, the world of analytics can seem intimidating, hidden behind a curtain of numerical intricacy.

Throughout my years of teaching social media analytics, I've noticed a common hesitation among students when it comes to quantitative disciplines. There seems to be a misunderstanding that these areas are inherently intimidating, less applicable, or excessively difficult. This sentiment is especially evident among students in business, education, and communication, who may perceive the unpredictability of digital behavior and the idea of quantifying such actions as challenging.

Furthermore, there is a common belief that the measurement of online activities is primarily performed by individuals in the field of computer science. This can be attributed to the comprehensive training in quantitative analysis, coding, and data manipulation that computer science students usually receive. Nevertheless, the ever-changing landscape of social media analytics requires a diverse range of skills that go beyond the confines of traditional academia.

To address these challenges, this textbook is specifically designed to break down these obstacles. It presents social media analytics as a field that brings together various disciplines such as business, communications, sociology, and more. This book presents itself as a thorough and easily understandable resource, with the goal of making the subject more approachable.

By emphasizing comprehension over intricate calculations, the book focuses on building a strong knowledge base in essential technical skills. It is designed to make sure that students can easily engage with data discovery, analysis, and visualization without needing any prior coding knowledge. Our aim is to make analytics accessible for social science students, highlighting the importance of their skills in understanding human behavior, societal trends, and communication patterns in the field of analytics.

The book focuses on real-world application, simplifying complex analytics concepts into easily understandable lessons. It empowers students to confidently analyze online activity data, transforming numbers into meaningful insights and stories that can influence strategies in different industries. Designed to cater to the interests of social science students, the book provides an engaging and approachable introduction to social media analytics, making it useful for both academic and professional purposes.

In the end, this book encourages students to thrive in social media analytics, highlighting the distinct and valuable viewpoints they contribute to the field. With a wealth of knowledge gained through years of academic pursuits and consulting in the industry, I have developed a guide that brings social media analytics to life, making it both approachable and captivating. Students will delve deeper into numerical data, analyzing human behavior, sentiment, and trends.

The book provides a comprehensive guide for students to navigate industry standards. It helps them in formulating pertinent questions, choosing appropriate metrics, and utilizing advanced tools and techniques for data collection, analysis, and visualization. The goal is to empower students to utilize social data in comprehending, analyzing, and predicting digital behaviors and trends that influence our society. This book encourages the cultivation of skills to unravel the numerical and computational aspects of social media analytics, turning them into practical, useful knowledge.

Why a Book on Social Media Analytics?

In the ever-changing world of social media, each like, comment, and share contributes to a broader narrative. As these platforms continue to shape our methods of communication, education, and decision-making, the mastery of social media analytics becomes an essential skill. This holds true for individuals across various fields, ranging from entrepreneurs to community organizers. The data that initially appear anecdotal may possess significant influence. This book is an essential resource for unleashing your full potential.

Designed to cater to the needs of scholars, professionals, and learners in fields such as marketing, business, communication, and sociology, this publication explores the most recent studies and developments in the realm of social media analytics. It provides readers with the information to stay ahead of current trends and practices by simplifying complex topics into easily understandable insights. It is a top-notch educational resource for students pursuing both undergraduate and graduate studies.

Imagine a situation where a company aims to improve its presence on social media platforms. The objective is to gain a deeper understanding of consumer behavior in order to enhance customer service, optimize marketing strategies, and uncover potential avenues for expansion. This undertaking requires a profound grasp of big data analytics and its implementation across various social media platforms. Our book takes readers on a thoughtful journey, demonstrating techniques for successful data collection and analysis.

Mastering this journey requires overcoming obstacles such as deciphering data, analyzing sentiments, and grasping the intricacies of hashtags and temporal patterns. The book presents readers with essential analytical techniques, including text and social network analysis, as well as data visualization. It offers strategies to overcome these challenges. And it delves deeper into the application of image, video, and spatial analytics as well as social monitoring to track and analyze activities across social channels.

Utilizing social media analytics can greatly improve a brand's online presence, strengthening customer satisfaction, loyalty, and retention. In order for businesses to fully harness these advantages, they need data scientists who can generate insightful, data-driven recommendations. This book provides a comprehensive examination of different data visualization tools and explores the effective dissemination of insights through reports and dashboards.

Divided into different sections, the book explores important aspects of social media analytics, ranging from establishing specific goals to comprehending metrics and KPIs. It also covers important aspects like data privacy and ethics, giving readers a thorough framework for analyzing social media data and making well-informed choices. With its collection of case studies and practical tutorials, this book is a valuable resource for students, social media managers, marketers, and data analysts. It provides the necessary expertise to effectively interpret and leverage social media data.

Why This Book Deserves Your Attention

Drawing from my extensive tenure as both an industry consultant and a university professor, this book is a synthesis of rigorous academic research and invaluable practical experience. With a perspective that bridges the gap between academia and the real-world demands of business, I possess a valuable understanding of the intricacies of social media analytics. This insight has been further enriched by my role as the director of an analytics lab, where my efforts in spearheading a consortium for institutions with specialized analytics or social media labs underscored the acute need for high-quality educational materials in social sciences such as business, communication, and sociology.

My journey began in the nascent stages of social media analytics, a field that has since witnessed exponential growth in both its importance and complexity. This book captures this evolution, offering a comprehensive exploration of social media analytics from its foundational principles to the latest innovations. It is designed to demystify the vast array of data types, analytical methods, and key performance metrics integral to understanding and leveraging social media for marketing success.

Motivated by a deep-seated desire to bridge a critical educational gap, this book is crafted to make the nuanced world of social media analytics accessible to a broad audience. Whether you are exploring the complexities of technical analysis or diving into qualitative assessments, this work strives to bring together these approaches, offering a cohesive, interdisciplinary viewpoint. It also serves as a reflection of my academic journey and professional engagements, aiming to empower readers by debunking misconceptions about quantitative analysis and providing them with valuable skills.

As we stand at the crossroads of the digital revolution, this book serves as a beacon for students and professionals alike, guiding them through the digital landscape's opportunities and challenges. Emphasizing practical application, the text is filled with real-world examples and case studies that showcase the concrete effects of social media analytics in different industries, based on personal experiences.

Regardless of your background— whether you're a professor looking to enhance your curriculum, a researcher keeping up with the latest trends, a student hoping to enter the field, or a professional wanting to sharpen your analytical skills, this book provides a wealth of valuable insights. This guide is essential for those who want to become experts in analyzing social media data. It presents complex concepts in a way that is both interesting and easy to understand.

In essence, this book is essential for anyone interested in mastering social media analytics and staying ahead in this ever-evolving field. If you're seeking guidance in navigating the vast seas of data generated by social media platforms, this book serves as your compass, directing you toward informed decision-making and strategic insight.

What's in the Book?

This book offers readers with a thorough overview of the most critical topics, methods, and tools utilized in social media analytics. It is a vital resource for both beginning and advanced learners due to its use of understandable language and visuals.

The book's content is organized in a way that effectively leads you through the steps of question formulation, data collection, and tool utilization to help you reach your objectives.

- This book offers a wide-ranging exploration of social media analytics, encompassing the principles, frameworks, and techniques necessary for analyzing and interpreting social media data. It delves into various types of social media analytics, including text, image, video, and network analysis, with a particular emphasis on the Discovery, Analysis, and Visualization (DAV) framework for understanding social media data.
- Building on the fundamentals of social media, the book guides readers through setting SMART goals (Specific, Measurable, Achievable, Relevant, and Time-bound), monitoring the efficacy of social media plans using various metrics and KPIs, and navigating social media strategically for effective digital marketing and communication. It then transitions to advanced topics, such as sentiment analysis, return on investment, and measurement, introducing various text analytics techniques such as content analysis, hashtag analysis, and topic modeling.
- The book also covers the significance of social network analysis (SNA), detailing its theoretical foundations, practical applications, and the various methods and tools used to collect and visualize network data within social media platforms. Additionally, spatial analytics is introduced, explaining how to harness spatial or location data and represent it within social media contexts.
- For those interested in the technical aspects, the book delves into data science and big data, focusing on how social media data is obtained from sources such as public APIs and web scraping, cleaned, and prepared for analysis. Ethical and legal considerations are also discussed to ensure

readers understand the responsibilities and potential challenges in working with social media data.

- A portion of the book is dedicated to image and video analytics, providing readers with a deeper understanding of how visual content is analyzed. The role of artificial intelligence in the future of social media analytics is also covered, highlighting AI's applications in data discovery, analysis, and visualization, along with current trends and future developments.
- Data visualization is emphasized as a crucial element in making social media data comprehensible and actionable. The book covers the history and evolution of data visualization, types of charts, principles of effective visualization, and challenges specific to visualizing social media data. It also integrates design thinking into the creation of dashboards and reports, showcasing how effective visualization applies across various careers.
- Finally, the book includes case studies to illustrate essential topics and help readers apply the knowledge to their own enterprises. It serves as an essential resource for students, academics, and professionals in strategic communication, advertising and marketing, public relations, business, data science, and media studies, and education offering insights and strategies to effectively understand and leverage social media audiences.

How the Book Is Organized

This book is carefully organized into three distinct parts, each intended to progressively build on the previous one, providing a thorough understanding of social media analytics. This methodical approach makes the book an essential read for individuals seeking to harness the vast potential of social media analytics.

Part 1: Discovery

The journey begins with Data Discovery, the cornerstone of social media analytics.

With "Introduction: Analytics Overview" in Chapter 1, the journey into social media analytics begins. This chapter lays the groundwork, covering data-driven organizations, the essence of big data, and the specifics of social media data. It also introduces various types of social media analytics and their practitioners, demystifying the field's jargon. Chapter 2, "Social Media Analytics Framework," presents the DAV (Discovery, Analysis, Visualization) framework, which forms the backbone of social media analytics strategies. This chapter also touches on the challenges encountered and strategies for navigating social media analytics effectively. In Chapter 3, "Goals, Metric, and Measurement," the focus shifts to setting and measuring goals using the SMART framework and SWOT analysis (Strengths, Weaknesses, Opportunities, and Threats). It delves into the importance of metrics, KPIs, and how to benchmark and explore audience engagement effectively. The final chapter of this part, Chapter 4, "Data Gathering, Organizing, and Cleaning," covers the practical aspects of accessing and handling social media data. From using public APIs to ethical considerations and the nitty-gritty of data wrangling, this chapter equips readers with the necessary tools for data preparation.

Part 2: Analysis

The second section of this book, titled "Analysis," digs more deeply into the ins and outs of social media analytics. The Analysis stage begins with an in-depth discussion of text analytics and the analysis process.

Chapter 5, "Textual Data Structuring," opens this section with an exploration of text analytics. It covers everything from text parsing and filtering to more advanced topics like named entity recognition and relationship extraction, providing insights into the tools available for textual data structuring. In Chapter 6, "Text Analytics Interpretative Methods and Tools," the book delves deeper into interpretative methods such as sentiment analysis and temporal analysis, offering an overview of various text analytics tools. Chapter 7, "Social Network Analysis," examines the connections within social networks, from the theoretical foundations to the visualization of these networks, offering insights into the tools and software used in SNA. Chapter 8, "Image and Video Analytics," concludes this section, discussing the significance of visual content in social media analytics and the challenges and tools associated with these types of analytics.

Part 3: Visualization and Storytelling

This book's third and final stage, "Visualization and Storytelling," demonstrates how data visualization can be used to tell compelling stories. I begin by discussing the origins and development of data visualization, as well as its fundamentals and advantages. Readers are guided through the evaluation of data visualization tools and the selection of the most suitable chart or graph. In addition, I will discuss the significance of data visualization in any profession.

Chapter 9, "Data Visualization," introduces the importance and history of data visualization, detailing the types of charts and key principles for effectively visualizing social media data. In Chapter 10, "Spatial Analytics for Social Media," the discussion extends to spatial analytics, showcasing its application in social media, techniques, and the types of maps useful for visualizing social media data. Chapter 11, "Integrating Design Thinking into Dashboards and Reports," explores how design thinking can enhance dashboards and reports, discussing the value of data visualization across different careers and the role of social media analytics centers and labs. The book culminates in Chapter 12, "Artificial Intelligence and the Future of Social Media Analytics," projecting into the future of the field. It covers current and anticipated developments, focusing on the role of AI in discovery, analysis, and visualization, offering a conclusive outlook on the evolving landscape of social media analytics.

Acknowledgments

I express my gratitude to The All-Knowing for providing me with wisdom, strength, and inspiration throughout this journey.

The journey of writing this book has been enriched and illuminated by the contributions of an exceptional group of individuals, to whom I owe a profound debt of gratitude. Over the years, as I have taught the Social Media Analytics course and other related courses at Ohio University since 2015, I have been fortunate to engage with a number of students whose curiosity and innovative projects have enriched my own understanding of the field. I am deeply grateful to all of them for their inquisitiveness, dedication, and the valuable insights they have shared along the way.

Foremost, the backing from our Dean, Dr. Scott Titsworth, at Scripps College of Communication, Ohio University, in establishing and supporting my Social Media Analytics Research Team (SMART) Lab, has been foundational to nearly a decade of profound learning and insights in the realm of data analytics, culminating in the writing of this book. I must also extend my appreciation to all the colleagues and graduate and undergraduate students whose inquisitive questions helped refine my ideas.

Furthermore, I extend my heartfelt thanks to Dr. Adil Albusaidi at Sultan Qaboos University in Oman. Our extensive discussions over coffee concerning the multifaceted domain of social media analytics were not only intellectually enriching but also pivotal in creating an environment of inspiration throughout my sabbatical. Special thanks to Dr. Aqdas Malik, whose exceptional collaboration since his days at Aalto University in Finland, provided critical insights. I am also profoundly grateful to Dr. Umar Ruhi of the Telfer School of Management at the University of Ottawa in Canada. My collaborative research efforts during the summer at Ottawa were instrumental in refining various sections of this book.

Additionally, I offer my special appreciation to Dr. Howard Welser at Ohio University and Dr. Ika Idris at Monash University Indonesia, whose profound research insights have significantly deepened my understanding of social network analysis over the years. Likewise, the influential work of Dr. Marc Smith at the Social Media Research Foundation in the United States has greatly expanded my comprehension of social networks, introducing new paradigms and perspectives that have enriched this manuscript. I must recognize the earliest text in social media analytics by Dr. Gohar Khan from the University of Waikato in New Zealand.

My father, Dr. Mahmood Khan, has been an unwavering source of inspiration and motivation from my earliest days. Since childhood, our discussions, spanning the breadth of life's experiences, were met with his patient listening, sage advice, and nurturing spirit. Since the start of this book project, his encouragement to distill my thoughts into written form has been a guiding light.

I am profoundly grateful to my wife, Hina, whose steadfast support and love have been the cornerstone of this endeavor. Her patience and understanding allowed me to devote countless hours to this work, and her insightful suggestions enriched its pages. This book owes much to her presence in my life, and for that, I am eternally grateful.

The collective wisdom, encouragement, and inspiration provided by these distinguished individuals have been the bedrock on which this book was constructed. Their contributions not only have advanced my knowledge but also have been a source of continuous motivation, for which my gratitude is immeasurable.

About the Companion Website

www.oup.com/us/dataanalyticsadvantage

    This book includes a companion website offering supplementary materials that extend beyond the scope of the printed text. These resources include brief tutorials related to key concepts and tools discussed throughout the chapters. Readers are encouraged to explore the website alongside the corresponding chapters for a deeper understanding. Online examples are referenced in the text using Oxford's designated web icon

1

Introduction

Analytics Overview

Chapter Outline

Have you ever wondered how successful organizations can make informed decisions, accomplish their goals, and maintain a competitive advantage? Chances are that you have witnessed the power of data in action. Whether it is businesses like Apple, Walmart, GoPro, Ben & Jerry's, Pepsi, Marriott, Netflix, or Nike, all have successfully harnessed the dynamic landscape of social media, where every engagement metric, such as a view, like, comment, or share, has left a data trail. Whether you are a small business owner, a rising influencer, or a student aspiring to acquire a skill set that would prove beneficial in the job market, learning about social media analytics (SMA) is vital.

In a world characterized by technological dependence, success is rooted in decision-making that is guided by insights derived from data. In the contemporary, fast-paced business landscape, being data-driven is not merely advantageous but essential for survival. Organizations and businesses can obtain significant insights into their operations, customer behavior, and market trends by collecting and analyzing data (Guellil & Boukhalfa, 2015).

The Data Analytics Advantage. Laeeq Khan, Oxford University Press. © Oxford University Press (2025).
DOI: 10.1093/oso/9780197814222.003.0001

A data-driven approach can be immensely beneficial, especially for businesses seeking to optimize their social media strategies. For example, a supermarket can employ a data-driven strategy to analyze social media data to shed light on the factors that influence the volume of posts and sentiment toward the retail business. This can help its decision-makers make more informed choices when faced with comparable situations (Li et al., 2023).

This chapter serves as an introduction to the complex world of SMA. We start by shedding light on the role of data in organizations and explaining what it means to be a data-driven organization. We will understand how data-driven decision-making may assist firms in achieving their business objectives related to social media, the importance of being data-driven, and the kind of value that can be derived from social data. We will delve into various ways SMA has been defined and elaborate on the various types of SMA, from descriptive to prescriptive analytics. Considering the disciplines where SMA has been discussed, we will also untangle the terminologies surrounding SMA, demystifying the concepts that cloud and complicate our understanding of this field. We will build on the premise that SMA is not merely about collecting data but also about discerning patterns, trends, and sentiments and telling an effective data story, besides forming a data-driven culture.

1.1 Data-Driven Organizations

Today, it is unimaginable for any household, an organization, or a business to function without the internet. The basis of this connectivity is the exchange of massive amounts of data and information. The true potential of this data can only be unlocked when organizations embrace a data-driven culture, leveraging insights to drive informed decisions and strategic growth. Being data-driven means basing decisions and actions on the conclusions and confirmation gained from data analysis (Korherr et al., 2022). Such an approach is informed and rational. Instead of relying on instinct, opinion, or tradition, a data-driven approach is based on numbers. It can improve an organization's efficiency and effectiveness, reduce costs, lead to better customer engagement and relationship building, and offer an advantage over competitors. A *Harvard Business Review* article emphasizes that companies must become data driven to catch up (Bean & Davenport, 2019).

A data-driven strategy is not a stand-alone but a comprehensive approach. In a data-driven approach, data are gathered, processed, and evaluated to provide insights that can guide decision-making at each stage (Szukits & Moricz, 2024): from the data acquisition stage, when data is gathered from social platforms, to data processing, when data is transformed (cleaned, organized, filtered, and analyzed), to visualization and insights, whereby specific questions are answered. This process is ongoing, as social media data is constantly obtained over time, thus developing a feedback loop that leads to real-time agility and flexibility to deal with emerging issues and crises. Hence, a data-driven approach permits firms to monitor and analyze performance over time, discover trends, and alter their overall strategy as necessary.

A practical data-driven approach is grounded in business objectives and goals, driving well-aligned business outcomes. Such an approach includes creating key performance indicators (KPIs) and utilizing data to track progress and quantify success. Consider a tech company that adopts a data-driven approach based on clear goals like increasing market share. The company can employ analytics techniques on customer data obtained from a loyal online user community in a Facebook group, leading to better customer insights and more realistic KPIs. This can be an ongoing process that helps improve business strategy for maximum customer growth and a data-driven cognizance of customer needs. We will unpack this further in the chapters ahead.

Developing a data-driven culture is essential for enterprises to be successful in today's data-driven world (Patil & Mason, 2015). Simply being "present" on social media can be detrimental. On the other hand, proactively employing a data-driven strategy as part of the wider organizational culture can yield immense dividends. For example, a travel agency built a robust social media presence to increase brand awareness, engage with customers, and achieve business results. It transformed its culture from a reliance on paper brochures to a real-time pulse of social media. They cultivated a strong presence on TikTok and Instagram and analyzed trending hashtags and influencer hotspots. This entailed uncovering hidden insights and assigning dollar values to interactions through likes, comments, and shares, gauging the impact on bookings. The travel agency unearthed its hidden brand perceptions by analyzing the sentiment behind user comments. It also engaged in proactive reputation management by tracking social media conversations to identify emerging trends and rewarded influential customers, finding them through network analysis (detailed discussion about social network analysis is available in Chapter 7). Furthermore, by quantifying qualitative data such as brand awareness, impressions, and referral traffic, the travel agency could better understand its social initiatives, strategically allocate resources, and make informed decisions aligned with specific goals. Hence, a data-driven approach was not a stand-alone thing, it was woven into the very ethos and culture of the travel agency.

Businesses can use analytics-based decision-making to gain an advantage over their competitors while ensuring that the organization possesses the appropriate people, technology, and culture (Davenport & Harris, 2007), which all complement each other for combined strength. Such organizations have a hive-mindset, a sort of collective consciousness, where data analytics is not something alien or a fad. Rather, organizations having a strong analytics cultures value data-driven thinking and decision-making. They have a certain level of data literacy, data integration, and a leadership commitment to employ data in their everyday decision-making.

For example, a clothing brand can employ a data-driven strategy for their social media. They can employ a dedicated chief data analytics officer to oversee the efficient implementation of a data-driven social media strategy. By evaluating social media data, the clothing brand determines what styles and fabrics resonate with its customers. Data may also reveal which type of content (text, image, video) resonates most with their audience, the optimal posting times, and the most efficient customer engagement strategies. The clothing retailer can also discover new markets and increase their operational efficiency through the insights derived from social data. All this becomes possible with a well-thought-out, data-driven culture that aligns with the company's unique needs and requirements.

A survey of senior executives in 116 Fortune 1000 companies by NewVantage Partners (2023) reflected an increasing commitment to data despite the obstacles to embracing a data-driven approach. Leading organizations within healthcare (such as Cardinal Health, Humana, Novartis), financial services (such as AIG, USAA, Fidelity Investments, CitiGroup), retail (such as Best Buy, Procter & Gamble, Albertsons), and media/entertainment (such as Bloomberg, McGraw-Hill, Consumer Reports) found a need for more clarity in goals and objectives, resulting in a delayed adoption of digital transformation. Only 23.9% of companies characterized themselves as being data-driven. Furthermore, a mere 40.5% of companies reported that the role of a chief data analytics officer is well-understood within their organization. Approximately 80% of participants cited cultural issues within the organization, resistance to change, and people and process concerns as the most significant hurdles on the way to becoming entirely data-driven. These findings further illuminate the need for a data-driven desire and a data-driven culture that can propel an organization to success. Through this example, we understand that impediments such as organizational misalignment with objectives and opposition to a change in culture are the primary contributors to a company's failure to adopt a data-driven approach to decision-making.

It has been observed that many well-established and newly founded small and medium-sized organizations are also hesitant to invest in analytics because they are still determining whether the investment will yield a significant return. There is a common misconception among business owners that big data projects have failed to provide significant returns on investment. This may be true when a data-driven culture is absent; however, several success stories justify the efficient utilization of data analytics for meaningful insights, effective decision-making, and success in a competitive market.

Despite the challenges and resistance to change in adopting a data-driven approach, various small and medium-sized organizations and businesses have successfully utilized analytics in diverse fields such as healthcare, politics, tourism, finance, services, and media. By utilizing data insights, these companies have improved the quality of their customer experiences, crisis management, branding, and identifying audience behaviors, preferences, and emotions. These success stories have motivated even more businesses to invest in analytics projects to realize the full potential of a data-driven approach to their social media presence.

The process of getting value from analytics is complex. It requires careful thought at each level, beginning with the collecting of data and continuing through to the gaining of insights and the formulation of decisions. Moreover, the value of each step is dependent on the value of the other stages, and a holistic approach is required for success. Companies can generate significant value from their investments in analytics if they acknowledge each stage's significance and ensure that it operates seamlessly with the others.

The success of analytics can vary significantly from business to business, leaving some organizations confused about whether they will ever see a return on their investment. This gap might be caused by how "value" is attributed to the various steps of the analytics process at different points in time. While each stage is essential to deriving value from data, the stages themselves do not produce any value on their own; instead, value can only be recognized once the whole process has been carried out.

1.2 Understanding Big Data

Before the advent of the digital age, data generation was limited. Most of the work was manual, and without widespread computing, data was relatively small and straightforward to manage. There were rudimentary handwritten methods of documentation, limited communication and collaboration, and a dearth of data analysis tools. Advancements in computing technologies and communication networks transformed everything. The volume of data produced increased exponentially due to increased digitization. Businesses and organizations were soon faced with the new reality, where the overwhelming volume of data presented immense challenges in storing it, managing it, and, most importantly, extracting meaning from it. The era of big data had begun.

Almost all industries that interact with customers—dealing with content, goods, and services—are involved in financial transactions that are already being impacted by big data (Davenport, 2014). Data also comes from numerous sources, including social media, sensors, and mobile devices. The big data revolution has impacted companies directly or indirectly involved with marketing, supply chain management, human resources, manufacturing, finance, and information technology. The ubiquitous use of social media also led to the generation of a treasure trove of audience, customer, or user data rich in hidden insights waiting to be extracted. The widespread use of the internet and social media has made big data more significant and impacted the economy at a global level. Hence, with the exponential increase in the quantity of data in all fields, businesses were challenged to make sense of it all (Khan, 2020).

Businesses and organizations gradually became aware that the large volumes of data held deep insights that might assist them in making better business decisions. However, they needed to learn how to extract those insights. They thus looked toward modern computing technologies that could handle vast amounts of data, evaluate it quickly, and identify patterns and trends so that they might find a solution to this challenge. For example, Hadoop, MapReduce, and Spark are some technologies that enable businesses to store, process, and analyze vast volumes of data to derive insights that can be put into practice. Moreover, companies such as IBM and SAS offer advanced data analytics solutions.

Big data has certain qualities that make its analysis complex. First, big data tends to be nonstatic; thus, we can notice the constant, ongoing, and rapid flow of data from various sources, including social media (Khan, 2020). Second, big data, or data in general, is often unstructured. For example, organizations can collect web data (such as page views, the amount of time spent on a website, etc.) and data from social platforms such as YouTube, Facebook, TikTok, and Instagram (in the form of text, images, and videos). Data can also include location information (through GPS coordinates or IP addresses). Despite the challenges of volume, velocity, variety, and veracity (see Figure 1.1), data can be analyzed to assist businesses and organizations in better comprehending customer behavior, likes, and dislikes (Puschmann & Burgess, 2014).

In the era of big data, other issues have also emerged. Organizations face concerns about data privacy, the obligation to keep data protected, and the responsibility to observe various regulations. Furthermore, there are heightened concerns around the credibility of data. Fake news, misinformation, and disinformation are major challenges facing individuals, organizations, and government entities. It is becoming hard to differentiate between what is true and original. Advancements in artificial intelligence (AI) have provided various benefits but also have given rise to challenges in terms of veracity of information and data.

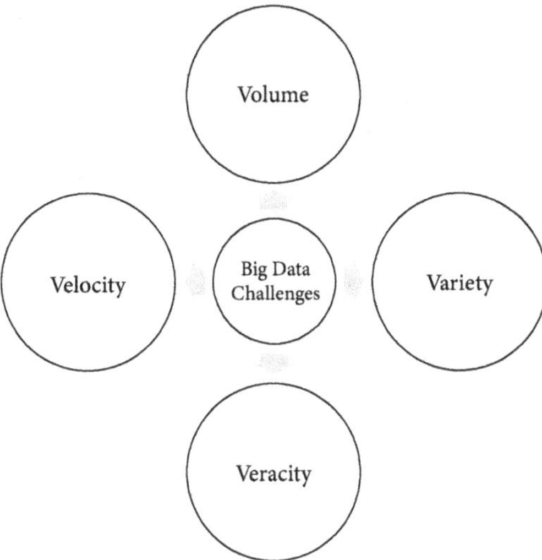

Figure 1.1 Big data challenges

Despite these obstacles, the era of big data has fundamentally altered how we think about information. Data and information are a powerful resources increasingly being utilized across various industries. One thing is abundantly clear: data will continue molding our environment in ways beyond our comprehension.

1.3 Making Sense of Social Media Data

"Social media" is a broad term that comprises various digital platforms where anyone with an internet connection and skills can access and share diverse forms of content, such as text, images, and video, to entertain, inform, learn, collaborate, and build relationships. This content shared by users, known as user-generated content (UGC), is exciting to organizations, businesses, and governments. UGC can provide precious insights into what users or customers think and what they enjoy and dislike about a product or service. Monitoring social media can help organizations uncover opportunities to increase consumer engagement and enhance customer experience. Most importantly, gathering and analyzing UGC can assist organizations in identifying possible opportunities and even negative feedback before it becomes a significant problem.

The data generated by social media platforms must also contend with issues relating to volume, variety, velocity, and veracity. In 2023, there were approximately 4.8 billion social media users worldwide, equaling about half of the global population (Dixon, 2023). Because of the extensive use of social media and its status as a driver of discourse on a global scale, the term "big data" has essentially become synonymous with "social media."

Understanding UGC from social media involves gathering, analyzing, and visualizing data to understand user behavior, preferences, and emotions. This data is rich in information. It can contain their likes, dislikes, emotions, comments, and other activities. Gathering and analyzing data from social media platforms to derive insights about users, brands, organizations, and government interactions to make informed decisions is what comes under the domain of SMA. This process may require the use of a variety of data analytics techniques and methodologies.

Over the years, SMA has matured as a separate subfield of broader data analytics due to the immense volume of data generated on social media platforms. There is thus a need to engage in data analytics to derive meaning from this vast social media data. The following section will delve deeper into SMA.

1.4 Social Media Analytics Overview

Social media is in a perpetual state of change. The changing user demographics, global subcultures of online social interaction, technological disruption and innovation, internet regulation, content delivery algorithms, AI, and mobile technology all add to the dynamic nature of the field. These developments mandate that individuals and organizations keep themselves updated about SMA.

Effective SMA can be recognized by their capacity to sift through the clutter of online conversations in search of actionable market, competitive, and consumer intelligence. SMA also comprises constantly monitoring social media interactions and audience conversations over time. Utilizing social media data as a resource, SMA aims to facilitate the formation of well-informed and intelligent decisions (Lynn et al., 2015).

When conducting analysis of social media data, the most critical questions are "Who? What? Where? When? Why? and How?" These questions help choose the appropriate data sources to assess which might impact the kinds of analyses that can be carried out. For example, each question addresses a distinct aspect of data. By answering the question about "Who," we can identify user demographics; "What" for examining the social media content; "Where" for determining the platform or user location or status within the network; "When" for analyzing the temporal patterns or time-related aspects of posts; "Why" for understandings the motives for engagement; and "How" for choosing the right analytical approach (e.g., network analysis or engagement analysis?).

SMA applications in diverse industries have been central to research in marketing, hospitality, tourism, and disaster management domains. For example, Twitter (now known as X) has been a major source of social media data (mainly due to the relatively easy data availability) and hence various research studies employing sentiment and content analyses have been published (Zachlod et al., 2022). However, data access has become increasingly challenging as various social media platforms have curtailed access.

1.4.1 What Is Social Media Analytics?

SMA is "the use of varied tools and techniques to make sense of online activities and conversations by obtaining, refining, analyzing, and visualizing social media data" (Khan & Malik, 2022, p. 651). SMA refers to gathering information from social media websites and blogs and using that information to inform business choices. This method goes beyond the typical monitoring or simple examination of retweets or "likes" to establish a comprehensive concept of the social consumer.

The field of SMA has developed into a distinct academic discipline that can assist businesses in formulating and putting into practice measurement strategies for gleaning insights from social media. In a nutshell, SMA is the process of applying the necessary analytics capabilities to user-generated content on social media platforms to accomplish a particular purpose (s).

Another helpful definition of SMA describes it as follows:

> the art and science of extracting valuable hidden insights from vast amounts of semi-structured and unstructured social media data to enable informed and insightful decision making.
>
> (G. Khan, 2015, p. 1)

It is an art because it requires creativity, design, and interpretative skills. It is a science because it entails rigorous analysis of data from social media platforms using various cutting-edge tools and methods. The following is another comprehensive definition of SMA:

> SMA is an interdisciplinary research area that is concerned with developing, adapting and extending informatics tools, frameworks and methods to track, collect and analyze a large amount of structured, semi-structured and unstructured social media data to extract useful patterns and information.
>
> (Zachlod et al., 2022, p. 1066)

"SMA" is thus a broad term that includes a wide range of activities and methods as diverse as the many websites that make up the social media landscape. Social media is not limited to well-known social platforms like Facebook, YouTube, and X, but includes all online sites where humans interact. Social media allows users to participate, build communities, and connect, leading to content generation (Sinha et al., 2012). Such content can be found on blogs and microblogs (such as Blogger and Twitter), professional social networking sites (such as LinkedIn), wikis (such as Wikipedia), social bookmarking sites (such as Delicious), social news sites (such as Digg), review sites (such as Yelp), and multimedia sharing sites (such as Yelp, and YouTube) (Sinha, et al., 2012).

It is worth noting that SMA is not just about understanding metrics or performance measures for organizational success. Ruhi (2014) very aptly differentiates between social media metrics and analytics, where SMA is a "higher-order construct," helping to generate insights (p. 3). Hence, SMA transforms user data into a veritable treasure trove of unique insights into your target audience that you will not find anywhere else.

SMA has become a popular tool for gaining knowledge of social media user interactions in various sectors. Organizations and brands require SMA because, rather than relying on assumptions, there is an effort to acquire information about the target population to customize content to the audience's requirements more effectively. The breadth and depth of social media, measured in terms of the volume of user-generated material and the speed with which it is disseminated, is one of the critical reasons for the growing interest in SMA.

The research landscape in the realm of SMA and related studies in digital humanities, social sciences, new media studies, and informatics offer rich insights that help understand human interactions on social media. Several studies have used SMA to investigate diverse topics, such as perceptions of genetically modified foods on Twitter (Whittingham et al., 2020), the use of social networks by tourists during crises (Park et al., 2019), and the reputation of Australian universities based on Google reviews (Shah et al., 2020). SMA has been employed to understand discourse on COVID-19 pandemic (Khan et al., 2022) and public health agencies outreach through Instagram (Malik et al., 2021). SMA has also been utilized in government research, such as analyzing social media data to shed light on India's government policies (Singh et al., 2020) and in public diplomacy by the German embassy in Pakistan (Khan et al., 2021).

Additional research has investigated public views toward wildlife management and culling in Australia using Facebook data (Mehmet & Simmons, 2018); spatial patterns of visitor feelings in Disneyland (Park et al., 2020); charity-related communication in Afghanistan, Iran, and Pakistan (Khan et al.,

2018); and how libraries might use social listening techniques to meet community needs (Pomputius, 2019). In addition, social media mining methods have been employed to evaluate service quality in the airline industry (Tian et al., 2020) and to analyze YouTube dance videos (Thelwall, 2018). These studies illustrate the breadth of issues that may be investigated using SMA approaches and emphasize the usefulness of this methodology for gaining significant insights into social media user behavior.

Many terms related to SMA may seem confusing for some readers. The following section clarifies the varied yet related and often overlapping terms that have emerged over the years.

1.4.2 Demystifying Varied Social Media Analytics Terms

Keeping up with the latest developments in SMA might sometimes feel like traversing a maze. Social media is employed in various fields such as computer science, communication, politics, business, education, and sociology, and different disciplines use varied methodological approaches when studying human interactions. SMA is built on a wide variety of analytical methods, such as opinion mining and sentiment analysis, insight mining, trend analysis, topic modeling, social network analysis, influence analysis, and visual analytics. For this fundamental reason, a consolidated methodological approach that guides the nascent field of SMA is much needed. Compared to the more established quantitative and qualitative research techniques, analyzing social media data is a relatively young field. Several researchers have argued for a structured and consolidated approach to SMA (Stieglitz et al., 2014, 2018).

It is not unusual to encounter situations where SMA, listening, and monitoring are used synonymously. I would argue that "social media analytics" is an umbrella term that incorporates a variety of methods for studying social media data. Included are social media monitoring, social media listening, social media intelligence, social media analysis, and social competitive analysis. Generally, social media analysis is the practice of evaluating social media data to get insights and inform business decisions. Let us unpack these terms to understand better how they fit the broader realm of SMA.

- **Social media monitoring**: This may be considered the most rudimentary form of SMA, as it involves tracking and studying social media platforms for brand mentions, customer feedback, and consumer mood. Social media monitoring has been defined as tracking the effectiveness of advertising campaigns (Baur, 2017), finding information about competitors (Arnaboldi et al., 2017), and seeing online activity to determine the reaction to events (Lepkowska-White & Parsons, 2019). Monitoring entails observing social media channels for changes in activity about a particular issue or brand. Such real-time information is vital for companies to address any issues as soon as they arise and before they can spread. Based on this understanding, it is evident that the term "social monitoring" has similarities with "social media listening"—the two are similar in scope are often used interchangeably (Avery, 2017).

- **Social media listening**: Listening is about keeping tabs on various social channels for issues and potential possibilities. Listening on social media is generally included as part of a more comprehensive reporting system in SMA tools. While most argue that monitoring and listening are the same, others are of the view that listening on social media goes beyond social media monitoring because it involves not just tracking but also some basic form of analysis and interpretation of the data to acquire a deeper insight into client behavior and attitude (Williams, 2024). What is clear is that social listening is an essential part of SMA (Micera & Crispino, 2017). Nevertheless, SMA takes the approach of "listening" to UCG, and different tools offer varied functionalities regarding social listening and monitoring. Commonly used social media listening tools are Sprout Social, Brandwatch, Hootsuite, Talkwalker, and HubSpot.

- **Social media intelligence**: This covers a wide range of tools and techniques for tracking activity in online communities and identifying new trends as they emerge. Social media intelligence entails collecting and analyzing data from numerous sources, including social media platforms, to gain insights into audience behavior.

- **Social competitive analysis**: A competitive analysis based on social media data is a type of social media analysis that focuses on studying competitors' social media presence and actions. Organizations can learn about the competition's strengths and weaknesses on social media through competitive analysis. For example, using SMA tools, a social competitive analysis offers insights and comparisons into product offerings, social mentions, and related consumer sentiment.

- **Social analytics**: SMA and "social analytics" are often interchangeable terms that are used to refer to the analysis of data from social media platforms to acquire insights into the behavior and trends prevalent on social media. "Social media analytics" mainly refers to evaluating data from social media platforms like YouTube, Facebook, and TikTok to derive insights about user behavior, liking, and opinions. "Social analytics" also refers to analyzing data from other social platforms such as blogs, forums, and

Reddit online communities. Hence, it may be argued that "social analytics" is a more inclusive term than "social media analytics." Moreover, analyzing data obtained from non-social-media sources, such as consumer feedback or surveys, is another component that can be included in social analytics. Understanding customer behavior, tastes, and opinions is the objective of social analytics, with the end goal being to improve decision-making. Both terms are commonplace in the industry and can thus be used interchangeably depending on the nature of the situation and the extent of the investigation.

These terms refer to several facets of SMA. These facets are often connected and utilized to understand social media trends, audience behaviors, and industry insights. Thus, social media analysis is a multifaceted and complex field requiring expertise with diverse analytical techniques and approaches. It is vital to employ these tools cohesively and strategically to accomplish particular objectives. Gaining expertise in SMA requires a methodical and integrated approach using diverse analytical tools and procedures.

1.5 Social Media Analytics versus Business Analytics

"Social media analytics" and "business analytics" are commonly used terms in the industry, and both are crucial for businesses to make data-driven decisions and maintain a competitive advantage. Although they both have distinct roots, their methodologies have often overlapped. In the simplest terms, business analytics is a broader phrase about applying analytics to business data to understand business performance. Business analytics guides business decisions across finance, marketing, human resources, and management. It involves collecting and analyzing data from sales, customer service, and supply chain management sources to comprehend business trends, identify growth opportunities, and optimize business operations. Typical business analytics employs structured, historical data (Liere-Netheler et al., 2019).

On the other hand, SMA refers to data analytics applied solely to social media data. SMA focuses on data obtained from social media platforms, such as social networks, microblogs, forums, and review sites, which is predominantly unstructured data (Liere-Netheler et al., 2019). SMA entails collecting, monitoring, and analyzing social media data to comprehend customer behavior, brand reputation, and product and service sentiment.

1.6 Digital Humanities, New Media Studies, and Social Computing

Other terms that need to be elaborated on are "digital humanities" and "new media studies." Digital humanities as an academic field illuminates how digital communication is both a product and a reflection of human culture, history, and society. Over the years, digital humanities scholarship, which combines technology with humanities, has also helped us understand user interactions on social media. Scholars within the digital humanities realm have been analyzing social media data using computing techniques to reveal cultural and social trends in diverse areas such as language, digital norms, social media's ethical and societal impacts, privacy, the digital divide, and algorithmic decision-making.

The evolution of research in digital humanities has been characterized by an interdisciplinary approach, which draws from various fields, including computer science, linguistics, psychology, and cultural studies (Warwick et al., 2012). This cross-disciplinary integration has been pivotal in navigating and making sense of social media data, a journey of exploration enriched by established methods of inquiry (Felt, 2016). To a significant extent, the imperative to decipher human interactions on social media platforms has been the driving force behind the progress made in humanities and social sciences. This evolution has given rise to various terms, including "new media studies" and "social computing," which reflect the rapidly expanding nature of these technological advancements. Consequently, it is recognized that this amalgamation of distinct but related disciplines has significantly contributed to the emergence and growth of what we now understand as SMA.

1.7 Types of Social Media Analytics

Big data and analytics are inseparably intertwined (Watson, 2014). Analyzing large amounts of data can help businesses and other organizations derive value and better meet the needs of their customers. SMA can be divided into three subfields: descriptive, predictive, and prescriptive analytics.

1.7.1 Descriptive Analytics

This is the most common form of analytics. Descriptive analytics involves collecting and studying past and current data. Data about customer or user interactions on social media in the form of posts, mentions, followers, and so on, and related information are all included in descriptive data analytics. The focus is on providing a helpful summary of what has already happened and identifying patterns (Davenport & Harris, 2017). Descriptive analytics can serve as a meaningful foundation for further analyses. The following is a list of the types of descriptive analytics that can be found in the realm of SMA:

- **Engagement analysis.** Managers of social media platforms can utilize descriptive analytics to acquire insights into their engagement metrics, such as the number of likes, comments, shares, and followers their platforms have. Furthermore, engagement metrics can show which content received the most user attention.
- **Content analysis.** Content analysis is a research method whereby information is methodically coded and analyzed. Social media content can be analyzed to derive descriptive information and enrich the data. Content analyses can analyze text, images, and even videos.
- **Audience demographics.** As descriptive information, audience demographics on social media in age, gender, location, and user interests can help get a bigger picture of the audience. Such demographic information can also help target different audience segments, offer customized solutions, and enhance social media campaigns. Some content analysis techniques need to be applied to social media data to uncover audience demographics.
- **Sentiment analysis.** Sentiment analysis is about gauging audience opinions. For example, user comments in text on social media platforms are analyzed to understand what users feel about the brand. Sentiment can be positive, negative, and neutral.
- **Competitor analysis.** As evident from its name, competitor analysis is an essential technique within SMA to understand how competitors perform on social media and study their online presence. This is especially useful for businesses competing on social media. Such an analysis can help identify competitors and learn about their products and services and how they engage with audiences on social media.

In general, descriptive analytics in SMA can provide significant insights into historical performance and user behavior, which can drive future marketing plans and increase social media engagement. These insights can also help boost social media engagement. Descriptive analytics can be presented in the form of graphs and charts. Based on clear goals, descriptive analytics provides a better understanding of business concerns or opportunities by compiling and characterizing data gathered from social media in the form of reports, comparisons, and visualizations. Descriptive analytics can also provide a summary of online activities based on the straightforward counting of certain events. With descriptive analytics, for instance, it is now possible to get a numerical count of the number of likes, mentions, posts, fans, and followers on a social media platform. Descriptive analytics continues to receive attention as a method for problem-solving and understanding social media activity.

Descriptive analytics is readily available and widely utilized by businesses. Simple statistical software, such as Microsoft Excel, can assist with data parsing and correlations between variables. Specialized data visualization tools like DataWrapper and Tableau can help identify trends and display information visually. Descriptive analytics is particularly beneficial for describing change over time and using patterns as a launching point for further analysis to inform decision-making.

Popular streaming service Netflix serves as a suitable illustration of how descriptive analytics may be applied. Netflix's data-driven team collects and analyzes data on users' in-platform behavior to determine which TV series and films are currently popular. This information is subsequently presented in a designated portion of the platform's home screen, enabling consumers quick access to popular content.

1.7.2 Predictive Analytics

Predictive analytics enables the forecasting of future outcomes with data-driven insights. Using statistical techniques (such as regression), forecasting, and machine learning approaches, predictive analytics in SMA analyzes enormous volumes of social media data to predict future events and outcomes (Davenport & Harris, 2017). It answers queries to the "What" and "Why" of things.

Predictive analytics focuses on recognizing patterns and trends in data to obtain future predictions. Predictive analytics can predict audience behavior, such as their interactions with the product and services. In the field of SMA, some examples of predictive analytics are as follows:

- **Predicting novel trends**: Predictive analytics in social media can uncover popular trends based on hashtags. Moreover, trends can be forecasted through a sentiment analysis of UGC in textual data. It is also possible to predict how a specific content will perform while considering variables such as content type, the time of day, and the audience's demographics.
- **Identifying influencers**: Predictive analytics can help identify potential customers based on demographics, social media engagement, and online

behavior. Moreover, predictive analytics can help identify key influential individuals so they can be better engaged for maximum benefit.

- **Crisis management**: Predictive analytics can identify social media crises, such as negative sentiment or conversations toward a brand or an issue likely to cause future controversy. This can facilitate the preparation of a mitigation strategy and a response plan.

Hence, predictive analytics in SMA can provide valuable insights into future user behavior and trends. It can also help brands to stay ahead of the competition. With the advancement of technology, predictive analytics applications will become even more potent in guiding business success.

1.7.3 Prescriptive Analytics

This may be viewed as the most advanced form of analytics, as it goes beyond describing social media activity and forecasting to suggest and prescribe the best course of action (Davenport & Harris, 2017). Using advanced analytic approaches, prescriptive analytics in SMA entails recommending the optimal action for a specific situation. Prescriptive analytics suggests what actions should be taken to attain a desired outcome. For example, based on a recommender system, prescriptive analytics can suggest an optimal social media content strategy, identifying the best content format and post timing for maximum reach and impact.

Prescriptive analytics works through sophisticated algorithms that can scan large social media datasets to discover patterns and then provide suggestions for effective decision-making. This can also prove helpful in reputation and crisis management, as algorithms can suggest the best response tactics. Thus, by delivering customized recommendations and actionable insights, prescriptive analytics can help organizations make better decisions. Prescriptive analytics is set to gain further prominence with the rise of artificial intelligence.

In SMA, prescriptive analytics can enhance social media performance. Some applications of prescriptive analytics in SMA are as follows:

- **Prescribing post timings**: Prescriptive analytics can identify the best times to post content on social media. This analysis can be done by analyzing the historical performance of previous social media posts, current events, and other factors related to content type. Such measures can ensure maximum engagement with audiences.
- **Increasing content engagement**: Based on specific goals within the company, prescriptive analytics can suggest strategies such as influencer

identification, engaging in trending conversations, and running events that grab audience attention.

- **Customer service recommendations**: Prescriptive models can anticipate customer queries and suggest appropriate responses depending on the type of customer and his/her preferences.
- **Collaboration with influencers**: Prescriptive analytics can help find and provide targeted recommendations for the most effective influencers. Such targeted engagement can prove fruitful in expanding content reach and creating a more significant impact.

1.8 Who Does Social Media Analytics?

SMA comprises a diverse range of individuals and organizations. It can be performed by professionals within organizations as in-house teams. Depending on the financial prowess of an organization, large corporations can invest significantly in an in-house analytics team. Alternatively, SMA can be sourced out to outside vendors and companies.

Professionals who engage in SMA can have distinct roles and responsibilities, which can depend on the type of organization and the overall needs and requirements of a social media project. You might have heard of titles such as social media analyst, social media manager, digital marketing analyst, data analyst, and data scientist. These are all interrelated terms and serve as good examples of professionals who perform SMA. What is common to all these roles is that these professionals possess the skills to make sense of social media data. It is worth noting that some roles require a more advanced skill set and understanding of tools and methodologies to conduct sophisticated analyses. Some would have advanced programming know-how in computer languages such as R and Python, while others would make detailed analyses using specialized tools for data analysis (such as SPSS). Yet others will specialize in data visualization and storytelling employing tools such as PowerBI and Tableau. The following are a few professional roles in SMA and their details:

- **Social media analyst**: A social media analyst is responsible for evaluating social media data to assist organizations in understanding the performance of social media strategies. Such professionals analyze social media market trends and identify opportunities for business growth. A career as a social media analyst can be rewarding, and it requires a solid grasp of social media systems and sound analytical and creative abilities.
- **Social media manager**: A social media manager is responsible for implementing social media initiatives and engaging with the organization's

audience on social media platforms. They also develop and organize content on social media platforms, manage marketing and advertising efforts, and handle audience engagement strategies. A social media manager may have some data analytics know-how but can have strengths in employing social listening tools.

- **Social media strategist**: These are usually experienced professionals who develop social media plans and strategies and utilize analytics to measure performance and suggest solutions to problems. Social media strategists also understand and successfully manage an organization's social media in a competitive environment.
- **Data scientist**: A data scientist is a professional expert extracting insights from large datasets. They have skills in statistical modeling and machine learning to make predictions. They usually possess descriptive, predictive, and prescriptive know-how to offer detailed insights. Additional professionals include data engineers, business intelligence specialists, and data architects, each performing specialized tasks. With high earnings, becoming a data scientist or data analyst is a highly desirable professional choice.
- **Academic researcher**: Academic researchers specialized in SMA not only are expected to have greater depth in understanding SMA but also contribute to an empirically based understanding of human behavior in online settings and of human communication patterns, and when needed, they apply a theoretical lens to the what, how, and why of the social media landscape. Such researchers are in an ideal position to advance the field of SMA by synthesizing the developments in different industries and disciplines.

The evolving nature of social media means that SMA professional roles will also continue to adapt to meet the emerging needs of the industry. There is an increasing emphasis on an interdisciplinary set of skills to transform data insights into effective business strategies.

1.8.1 The Global Nature of Social Data

Modern media technology and social media platforms have become essential elements of the global economic and political environment. When exploring SMA, we analyze data from a particular location and access a comprehensive and globally interconnected information collection. The global scope of social media data exemplifies these platforms' worldwide reach and impact.

The overwhelming majority of enterprises in this digital domain serve an international clientele. The global audience is consuming information and generating data encompassing diverse cultures and geographical locations. Hence, the data extracted from social media platforms is fundamentally global, comprising various consumer behaviors, interests, and interactions from various parts of the planet. Moreover, there are platforms that are more common in other parts of the world such as China (WeChat, Douyin, Baidu) and Russia (VKontakte, Telegram). It can be argued that SMA principles are equally applicable to those platforms as well.

The global aspect of social media data presents distinct possibilities and challenges. It enables organizations and researchers to learn about worldwide market trends, cultural dynamics, and global communication patterns. However, it also requires a refined comprehension of various cultural settings and the capacity to analyze data within the framework of worldwide variety. Essentially, the global expansion of social media data demonstrates the broad reach of these platforms and emphasizes the importance of internationally aware approaches in assessing and utilizing this information.

Chapter Summary

- Businesses can use data to make more informed decisions, achieve their goals, and remain ahead of the competition.
- Data-driven decision-making refers to using data analysis as the basis for making decisions rather than relying solely on intuition or observation.
- Big data is often unstructured and nonstatic, but when handled and analyzed, it can assist businesses in better understanding audience behavior.
- SMA is the systematic collection and examination of data derived from social media platforms to provide insights that guide business decision-making.
- SMA encompasses descriptive analytics, which analyzes historical and current data to outline past and present scenarios; predictive analytics, which uses statistical methods and machine learning to anticipate future trends and behaviors; and prescriptive analytics, which leverages vast volumes of social media data to recommend optimal actions to achieve specific outcomes.
- User-generated content (UGC) refers to content produced and distributed by individuals on various online platforms, including social media, blogs, and websites.
- Professionals like social media analysts, managers, digital marketing analysts, and data scientists perform SMA to provide insights and recommendations, driving a business's online strategy.
- The global nature of social media data pertains to the international extent and consequences of the data produced by social media platforms.

Questions for Review

1. How does a data-driven approach help businesses make better decisions and stay ahead of the competition, especially regarding social media strategies?
2. What are the main differences between using data and the old ways of making business decisions?
3. Explain the three types of SMA: descriptive, predictive, and prescriptive. Then, give some business examples of how these types of analytics are employed in organizations or businesses.
4. Identify the key individuals in SMA and describe how they use data to make business choices.
5. Discuss the global implications of social media data on businesses, highlighting both opportunities and challenges.

2

Social Media Analytics Framework

Chapter Outline

In the previous chapter, we focused on understanding the importance of data-driven decision-making, the power of big data, defining social media analytics (SMA), types of SMA, and the various job roles related to SMA. It has been established that social media has transformed everyday communication and that organizations must fully embrace a data-driven approach to compete effectively and not be left in the dark about their audience's perceptions. We will now pivot to a discussion about the importance of deriving value from SMA.

The Cambridge Dictionary defines "value" as "importance, worth, or benefit" (Cambridge, 2024). Measuring social media performance helps individuals, organizations, and businesses see the latest trends, gauge the level of efficacy in their social media initiatives, and understand the benefit or value they derive from their online efforts. Just as in our everyday lives, we want to know what something is worth in the marketplace and how much we should be paid for our work effort; it makes sense that we would also like to know how successful our social media initiatives have been in terms of the value they provide.

In this chapter, I will introduce a framework that will prove helpful in deriving value from SMA. This comprehensive SMA framework comprises three key stages: Discovery, Analysis, and Visualization. It provides a roadmap for organizations to utilize the potential of social media data and make informed decisions. This comprehensive framework will also set the course for the rest of the chapters in this book, where each stage will be discussed in greater detail.

The Data Analytics Advantage. Laeeq Khan, Oxford University Press. © Oxford University Press (2025).
DOI: 10.1093/oso/9780197814222.003.0002

Gaining value from SMA emerges as a potent means for accomplishing various strategic objectives. Organizations can gain insights into their social media activities that lead to better and informed decision-making and enhanced customer experiences if they apply the three stages: Discovery, Analysis, and Visualization. These three stages serve as integral components of the wider SMA. As you may recall from the previous chapter, SMA is "the use of varied tools and techniques to make sense of online activities and conversations by obtaining, refining, analyzing, and visualizing social media data" (Khan & Malik, 2022, p. 651).

In the following section, we will delve deeper into how these three analytics stages or components of SMA contribute to the generation of value. Making sense of online activities through the lens of the DAV Framework can ultimately lead to tangible and intangible benefits and outcomes for businesses and organizations.

2.1 Deriving Value from Social Media Analytics

The human mind naturally tends to seek patterns and establish order from disorder. This drive for structure is necessary for making sense of the world, especially involving the massive volumes of data that organizations must handle. Fragmented or unstructured data might make it challenging to comprehend and make decisions. However, extracting valuable insights and making educated decisions becomes much more straightforward when data is organized and presented logically and intuitively.

Analytics value refers to the advantage that a company gains from the insights produced from the analytics projects it undertakes (Saggi & Jain, 2018). In social media, value refers to the perceived worth, benefit, or usefulness that an individual or organization derives from a social media activity. For example, when an organization employs SMA to measure social media activity, it can gain valuable insights into its audience behavior. Based on these insights, companies can enhance the quality of customer experience, boost loyalty, and propel revenue growth (Verhoef et al., 2016).

Such value can only be derived when organizations are able to make sense of the vast amounts of social data (Arora & Malik, 2015). However, such data is usually found raw and must be processed, analyzed, and visualized to derive value. There are a variety of methods available for determining value. The monetary return an investment generates is value that can be quantified in finance. When it comes to marketing, the value may be measured in terms of either the satisfaction of customers or their loyalty to a brand. Value can be analyzed regarding an organization's efficiency or productivity when assessing operations.

Value can be either tangible or intangible. Tangible value refers to benefits that can be measured or quantified, such as improved financial performance. On the other hand, intangible value refers to benefits or gains from social media activity that are difficult to quantify, such as a brand's reputation or the level of happiness experienced by employees (McCann & Barlow, 2015).

Organizations are often faced with challenges. Here are some examples of ways SMA can help derive value:

1. **Understanding the target market.** One of the advantages is that it enables companies to have a better understanding of their target market. Organizations can gain insight into their audience's demographics, interests, and behaviors by analyzing data collected through social media platforms (An et al., 2018). This information can be used to modify marketing campaigns and content to communicate more effectively with the target demographic.

2. **Identifying influencers and key opinion leaders.** The field of influencer marketing contains a considerable amount of untapped potential; however, identifying these influencers consistently from large datasets is a challenge that must be overcome (Harrigan et al., 2021). A framework can help identify influential users within a specific niche or industry. Engaging with these individuals can help businesses amplify their message and reach a wider audience.

3. **Identifying patterns and trends.** SMA can assist businesses in recognizing patterns and trends within their respective industries. They remain current on the most recent trends and alter their strategy accordingly if they analyze data gathered from their competitors and influencers. Analytics can support businesses in identifying new business opportunities by revealing patterns and trends in the data that were not previously recognized (Marjani et al., 2017).

4. **Improve marketing strategy and competitiveness.** Review websites, social networks, blogs, and forums are good sources of data about customers, product, and service experiences. Such data can be analyzed to develop and refine marketing and sales initiatives. To make informed judgments that can reveal new opportunities or identify possible market disruptors, it is also vital to be aware of actions by competitors (Bekmamedova & Shanks, 2014). Using SMA, organizations and businesses may also measure and evaluate the success of their social media activities. Measurements such as engagement, reach, and conversions can help assess which efforts resonate with the target audience and which do not. In turn, this data can help maximize their return on investment (ROI).

5. **Reputation management.** SMA can also be used to monitor and manage or improve the internal and/or external reputation of a brand,

product/service. Traditionally, this can be achieved by observing reputation and conducting surveys and focus groups. With SMA, data can be used to perform sentiment analysis. By measuring audience perceptions, organizations and even governments can continuously monitor whether people have favorable or adverse views toward a brand, product, services, or initiatives. Such intelligence can help alter the positioning of their social media presence. For example, the airline industry (and most big retail brands) keep a constant check on their social media pulse to evaluate their performance and safeguard their brand's reputation through SMA.

6. **Crisis management.** SMA can especially be beneficial in crisis and disaster scenarios. Before, during, and after a crisis, companies and agencies can use SMA to be better informed about issues and respond to them promptly (Wang & Ye, 2018). In crisis situations like hurricanes and earthquakes, organizations can use SMA to understand whether evacuation information, risk mitigation strategies, and overall support and rescue in affected areas were effective enough. For example, in 2012, during Hurricane Sandy, SMA was employed by officials to make sense of Twitter data for identifying and mapping disaster-hit areas. For organizations and businesses, in various crisis scenarios, a company's reputation may be in jeopardy, and understanding among whom and where a connected conversation is occurring on social media can enable prompt corrective action. Similarly, the dissemination of incorrect or fake information requires analysis and the development of countermeasures. By monitoring brand mentions and evaluating sentiment, firms may respond swiftly to unfavorable comments and complaints, enhancing their reputation.

7. **Informed decision-making.** Effective decision-making hinges on insights that are backed by solid numbers. A structured approach to social media analysis can provide valuable insights that inform business strategies, product development, and other vital decisions (Ruhi, 2014). In addition to improved decision-making, the value of analytics can be evident in increased revenue, decreased expenses, improved customer satisfaction, and more effective operations, among other benefits (Kitchens et al., 2018).

As discussed above, organizations can employ a structured approach to SMA to help derive immense value by being responsive to the needs of their audiences, identifying trends, managing reputation, and dealing with crises. Building on this understanding, I present the DAV Framework of SMA, a systematic framework for assisting organizations in effectively navigating the vast expanse of social media data. This paradigm simplifies the process by dividing it into manageable stages, allowing for a systematic and focused analysis of social media presence. The following section will examine each stage in depth, focusing on their function in translating raw data into actionable insights that drive corporate growth and reputation management.

2.2 The DAV Framework for SMA

At the heart of SMA is the process of gathering, analyzing, and interpreting data from social media. This implies that it is a structured and comprehensive approach. From data gathering to discovery, various types of analyses and interpretation are included in this process. For example, it is not enough to discover raw data. Data must be processed, cleaned, and then analyzed. Similarly, data analysis is not the end goal, but the insights gleaned through the analysis are essential in telling a compelling data story.

Consider a local coffee shop wanting to expand its footprint and compete against established brands. The coffee shop needs SMA to first understand its current footprint and the needs of its clientele to be able to tailor its offerings and market accordingly. SMA can help the coffee shop to evaluate its social media presence. This would entail a comprehensive and structured approach, from data collection to analysis in the form of sentiment and thematic analyses. The coffee shop can gain clarity on customer perceptions of and feelings toward its own brand and that of its competitors by conducting a sentiment analysis using social media data. The coffee shop cannot ignore trends such as increasing demand for ethically sourced coffee and brands that believe in justice and equality for all. It also needs to be able to see these numbers and analyses as visualizations so that it can make sense of it all. Hence, gaining a deeper understanding of client tastes and preferences via SMA is not a one-step but a multilayered approach. It is here that the need for a robust framework for sense-making becomes evident. A structured pathway for SMA ensures that no detail is left out and that every strategic decision is carefully considered throughout and distilled within a robust framework.

A framework represents a structured way of thinking. It serves as a guide, providing a scaffolding that ensures that best practices and past know-how support the navigation of complex issues. Frameworks also provide clarity, direction, and a common language that individuals at different levels of understanding can relate to and use to find their way through the intricacies of data. Using a framework can ensure that important details and steps are not missed, thus saving time and providing a logical structure.

Scholars in different domains have presented roadmaps or frameworks to solve the mysteries of data analytics. Drawing from the literature on information systems, Stieglitz et al. (2014) proposed a three-stage framework for SMA, comprising tracking, preparation, and analysis. Likewise, Fan and Gordon (2014) suggested three crucial stages for SMA: capture, understand, and present. In his pioneering work on SMA, Gohar Khan presented a seven-layer framework. The novel framework included different elements such as text, networks, actions, mobile, hyperlinks, location, and search engines (G. Khan, 2015).

In 2018, Stieglitz and colleagues presented an SMA framework by integrating analytics insights from various fields such as computer science, statistics, computational linguistics, communication science, and sociology. They proposed a four-step SMA framework, which includes discovery, tracking, preparation, and analysis. The discovery stage was incorporated as an enhancement to the original framework, addressing the challenges of event and topic identification, reflecting the interdisciplinary nature of social media research (Stieglitz et al., 2018). While recognizing the importance of visualization, their framework formulation lacks an explicit mention of data visualization and storytelling within the four-step framework.

Given the complexity of each phase and the diverse application domains, standardizing the process of SMA using a framework is crucial. This book presents the DAV Framework for SMA, a streamlined and parsimonious framework for understanding SMA. It consolidates various technologies and techniques to make sense of social media data, grounding them in empirical research

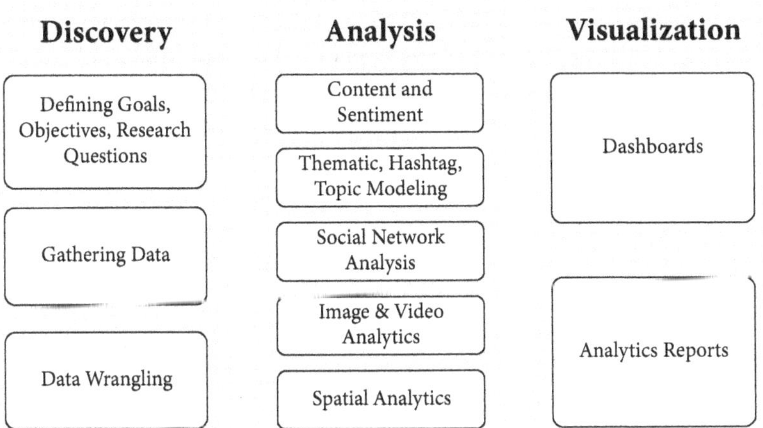

Figure 2.1 Discovery (left), Analysis (center), and Visualization (right). DAV framework for social media analytics

to form an all-encompassing framework. This framework details the steps required for comprehensive social media analysis. The DAV Framework for SMA comprises three main components, which are described in the following sections (see Figure 2.1).

2.2.1 Discovery

The first part of the DAV framework is the discovery phase, which entails discovering and gathering pertinent data from various social media platforms. Data is collected from several social media networks, such as YouTube, X, Instagram, TikTok, and others, in the first part of the process. This stage entails defining goals and metrics, identifying, locating, and obtaining suitable data for analytical purposes, data cleaning and organizing. In the Discovery stage, we first find, organize, and clean datasets by identifying patterns, trends, and insights. The Discovery stage comprises the following key elements:

1. Defining goals, objectives, and research questions

Creating a strategy for SMA begins with setting clear goals and objectives and defining specific research questions. Identifying specific questions that can be answered using SMA forms the basis of any analysis (Gao, 2018). This process requires a consistent alignment between the goals and objectives of the business and the capabilities of the social media platform (Hassan Zadeh & Jeyaraj, 2018).

The goals for social media engagement have a significant role in guiding the source and selection of data. Therefore, it is vital to craft pertinent questions and connect them to the relevant objectives and goals. Objectives might include enhancing user engagement and increasing brand awareness. For example, a university using TikTok to connect with current and prospective students could set a goal to boost engagement on the platform. It could employ SMA to analyze data like views, likes, comments, and shares, to understand which videos resonate most with this audience. Based on the intelligence derived from TikTok data, the university can modify its content to feature more of the elements that enhance engagement numbers, such as campus life events and student success stories.

During the Discovery phase of SMA the effectiveness of obtaining valuable insights is contingent on posing insightful and pertinent questions. These questions should be aligned with the organization's objectives and aims and should be specific enough to elicit insightful responses. By asking the right questions, businesses can identify growth opportunities, potential hazards, and areas requiring modification. For example, a corporation wishes to boost engagement on its social media pages. The organization might ask more specific questions, such as "How can we increase engagement in terms of comments on Instagram?" rather than asking a general question, such as "Which types of content generate the most engagement among our target audience?" Social media objectives are clarified when these more specific questions are asked, and the insights gathered can be leveraged to build more targeted strategies for enhancing engagement. Therefore, an organization will be able to discover the precise issues that lead to poor engagement and design-focused solutions to improve the quality of its content if it asks more specific questions to do so.

2. Gathering relevant data

The next step entails collecting pertinent information from various social media networks. To make this procedure more manageable, it is necessary to conceive a complete strategy for the collection of data, as well as the identification of essential data sources. An organization's social media channels, such as Instagram, TikTok, Facebook pages, blogs, and YouTube channels, will source most of the data required for analytics.

The volume and type of data (text, numerical, or network data) will determine the strategic approach that will be taken and the instruments that will be used for data collection. On a smaller scale, numerical data can be retrieved manually, for instance, by perusing a Facebook fan page, calculating the number of likes, and transcribing comments in a spreadsheet. On the other hand, numerical data may be automatically gathered at a larger scale using an Application Programming Interface (API). APIs are sets of processes and protocols provided by social media service providers to simplify users' access to their stored data. Social media platforms may enable access to user data through their APIs. We will discuss data-gathering techniques, including the use of APIs, in greater detail in Chapter 4.

3. Data wrangling

Due to the unstructured nature of social media data, multiple phases of data preparation are required before the dataset can be deemed suitable for analysis. Following the data-gathering phase, the information must be processed and cleaned to correct any errors or inconsistencies within the data. The process of transforming data to be analytically ready is called "data wrangling" (Rattenbury et al., 2017).

Data wrangling involves sorting, filtering, and summarizing information to make the data more manageable and relevant to the study. This stage includes cleansing the data to ensure it is high quality and consistent throughout. Typically, it entails filling in any gaps in the data, removing any duplicates, and standardizing the format of the data.

In the data wrangling part of the Discovery stage, the information automatically extracted is subjected to a process that removes unnecessary information. While some data items could be immediately ready for instant inspection, other datasets might require considerable data cleaning. For example, irrelevant or spam content may need to be filtered out from textual data. Furthermore, coding and filtering are two examples of tasks that may be carried out automatically by computer algorithms or manually by a human (more details about data wrangling in Chapter 4).

2.2.2 Analysis

Following the Discovery phase, the Analysis phase aims to recognize patterns, trends, and insights. Analyzing the data obtained from social media platforms makes it possible to extract hidden value from data. In the DAV framework for SMA, the Analysis phase helps derive insights from the social media data. The analysis includes content, sentiment, hashtag, social network, image, video, and spatial analyses. We will discuss these in detail in the following chapters under the following categories: analyzing text for what is being said (content and sentiment analysis), topic modeling and thematic analysis (image, video, and spatial analytics), how much is being said (engagement levels), and who and where it is being said (network analysis).

1. Content and sentiment analyses
   Content and sentiment analysis are vital when comprehending the dynamics of conversations on social media. Analyzing the subjects, themes, and keywords that appear most frequently in a piece of content (text, image, video) can provide valuable information about the interests and concerns of the target audience. On the other hand, the primary goal of sentiment analysis is to ascertain the tone of the audience's feelings regarding the subject matter. For example, sentiment analysis enables firms to track public opinion, predict possible issues, and evaluate the success of marketing initiatives by classifying information as positive, negative, or neutral.

2. Thematic analysis, hashtags, and topic modeling
   A qualitative research method known as *thematic analysis* can be used to locate, investigate, and report on recurring themes or patterns within textual data (Braun & Clarke, 2006). When applied to data from social media platforms, thematic analysis can provide insight into user behavior and their preferences and interests. For example, health agencies use thematic analysis for COVID-19 messaging on social media by systematically finding and analyzing data patterns. This entails coding social media data

into categories or themes such as "vaccine safety," "efficacy," and "side effects." With this insight, health agencies can tailor their messaging on social platforms.

Examining *hashtags* is another essential component of understanding what is being discussed on social media. Hashtags are vital in understanding a conversation (Laucuka, 2018). Organizations can find current topics, participate in relevant discussions, and improve their exposure across platforms by researching which hashtags are used most frequently and have the most influence.

Topic modeling uses statistics to find themes in big-text corpora (Sandhiya et al., 2022). Topic modeling produces a list of topics with related keywords and a weight representing their corpus importance. Topic modeling and thematic analysis overlap as methods and can discover themes or patterns in social media data to reveal the most-discussed subjects or events. Topic modeling focuses on co-occurring terms, while theme analysis focuses on meaning. These are discussed in greater detail in Chapter 6.

3. Engagement analysis

   When evaluating the impact of content shared on social media platforms, it is essential to have a solid understanding of engagement levels (Kietzmann et al., 2011). Organizations can determine interest and engagement levels among their target audience by analyzing the number of likes, shares, comments, and retweets. Compared to lower engagement levels, which may call for reevaluating the content or message approach, higher engagement levels typically imply a more significant impact and resonance with the audience.

4. Social network analysis

   By using the social network analysis technique, organizations can identify essential people on their social networks within their target audience, such as opinion leaders, influencers, and advocates for their brand (Marin & Wellman, 2011). Organizations can acquire insights into the structure and dynamics of their online communities if they analyze the connections, interactions, and relationships between their members. This information may be used to target the users who have the most influence, cultivate relationships with people who are champions of the brand, and understand how information moves around the network.

5. Image and video analytics

   Image and video analytics studies visual data like images and videos to gain insights. This can be accomplished by using machine and deep learning to analyze data. Computer models are trained on massive datasets of tagged photos or videos to recognize objects, actions, and behaviors in data. In some instances, computer vision is used to identify persons, emotions, and objects in social media photos. For example, in social media marketing, firms can employ image analytics to evaluate user-generated content (UGC) and find their most associated products, activities, and locations.

Video analytics can assess social media videos' objects and activities, tone and sentiment, and users' demographics. Image and video analytics can both aid businesses and organizations better understand their audience, optimize their social media operations, and stay ahead of industry trends. Image and video analytics is also applicable in social media monitoring and analysis to analyze brand mentions, trends, and sentiment around particular themes or events. Image and video analytics are discussed in greater detail in Chapter 8.

6. Spatial analytics

Spatial analytics involves interpreting data that has a geographic component. Spatial analysis uses spatial data to find patterns and relationships to inform decision-making in areas such as environment science, retail, marketing, and logistics. Spatial analysis of social media data analyzes user locations and the places and events they post about.

Social media data can be analyzed using several spatial methods. Geospatial data can map social media posts and find trends, such as concentrations of posts surrounding specific areas or events. This can assist in detecting patterns and issues of interest and tracking information and opinions across locations. Spatial analysis can find links between social media data and other geographic data, including population demographics, environmental conditions, and transportation patterns. This can also discover correlations between social media activity and real-world occurrences and assist policy and decision-making in urban planning, public health, and disaster response.

Geographic or spatial analysis can also discover social media communities based on shared interests, places, or behaviors. This can identify community influencers and essential opinion leaders for focused marketing and outreach. Overall, spatial analysis of social media data can help businesses, organizations, and governments make better decisions and respond to real-time data by revealing geographic trends and relationships.

2.2.3 Visualization

Data visualization forms the third component of the DAV Framework for SMA. The science of effective visualization or visual analytics is a central component of effective decision-making and visual data storytelling. Effective visualization techniques can uncover previously hidden patterns, correlations, and trends in vast and complicated datasets, making them a particularly valuable aspect of SMA. Data storytelling may help drive effective decision-making as data is presented in an engaging manner that is easy to understand.

In the digital age, the adage "A picture is worth a thousand words" has taken on new meaning. The impact of computing is so visible in everyday lives that data visualization has become a cultural phenomenon and a primary language of sense-making from numbers. For example, PowerPoint presentations, newspaper graphics, charts, and infographics, have become the usual way to communicate information. In our contemporary societies, we are conditioned to make sense of data through visualizations. It can thus be said that the cultural history of visual learning has laid the groundwork for SMA as a specialized tool that fulfills this important need for data interpretation.

Data visualization can vary in complexity from simple bar charts to sophisticated choropleth maps. Depending on the nature of the data, various data visualization styles are feasible, each with its strengths and objectives. For instance, scatterplots can highlight correlations between variables, whereas heat maps can illustrate the distribution of user activity throughout a geographic area. Similarly, network diagrams can show the relationships between social media users and the issues they are discussing as communities. Visualization in the realm of SMA is thus a natural extension of evolved human visual literacy, rooted in the human urge to understand and uncover something hidden in images, shapes, and patterns.

SMA builds on these historical precedents, incorporating and building on visual storytelling to translate social media data into actionable insights. Going beyond traditional visualizations, the DAV framework embraces structure, comprehensiveness, and interactivity. Users are now able to not only see a standalone visualization but also engage with it in real time, hence attaining a deeper understanding and a sense of agency.

Successful data storytelling through visualizations requires a certain level of technical expertise and an awareness of effectively communicating data to various audiences. It requires selecting relevant visualization approaches and producing easily understood and interpretable visualizations. Furthermore, modern interactive visualizations are especially valuable since these enable users to study data more deeply, experience it, and discover new insights beyond two-dimensional plots.

Data storytelling through visualizations is an integral component of visual analytics, allowing businesses, organizations, and governments to make educated decisions based on real-time data. Visualizing the insights gathered by SMA comprises presenting those insights through reports and visuals that communicate significant results and inform action plans. Following are some examples of Visualization that could be used in SMA:

1. Developing graphs and charts to visualize engagement data over time (temporal analysis).
2. Creating reports that summarize the most valuable insights gleaned through analysis of social media data.
3. Developing interactive dashboards that offer real-time insights into the functioning of social media platforms to derive new knowledge from previously collected data.

By focusing on these three key components—Discovery, Analysis, and Visualization—organizations and businesses can gain valuable insights into user behavior, trends, and preferences and develop strategies and tactics to improve social media performance, achieve business goals, and derive value. Chapters 9 through 11 discuss different aspects of compelling data visualizations in greater detail.

Despite the apparent advantages of adopting a comprehensive SMA framework, it is vital to identify and address any implementation-related obstacles. In the following section, we will examine the challenges of accessing social media data, including privacy problems, platform limits, data volume and diversity, ethical considerations, and data quality and dependability. By recognizing and overcoming these obstacles, businesses may successfully navigate the complexities of SMA and harness their power to improve decision-making, optimize strategies, and achieve desired objectives.

2.3 Social Media Analytics Challenges

Data has immense potential for research, marketing, and decision-making. The emergence of big data and analytics has provided organizations and businesses with various benefits. However, these organizations must also address the various data-related challenges that need to be addressed. Some of these multifaceted challenges include privacy concerns, platform restrictions in data access, data volume and variety, and ethical considerations.

- **User privacy concerns**: Protecting user privacy is one of the most challenging aspects of gathering social media data. Social media users frequently post sensitive personal information, interests, and opinions. So, there is a possibility of violating the privacy of consumers when collecting and analyzing their data. For example, in the Cambridge Analytica incident, data of millions of Facebook users were taken for political advertising reasons without their consent (Hinds et al., 2020). This incident increased global awareness of safeguarding user privacy on social media platforms.

- **Platform restrictions**: Social media networks have established a variety of data access limitations to safeguard their users and commercial interests. These constraints frequently limit the quantity and variety of data available to researchers and enterprises. For example, X (formerly Twitter) largely restricted access to its data through its API, which previously allowed limited access to tweets. Similarly, Facebook had also imposed restrictions on data access.
- **Data volume and variety**: The sheer volume and variety of data produced by social media platforms provide formidable obstacles for collection, storage, and analysis. As the volume of data increases, handling and analyzing it promptly and effectively becomes more challenging. Facebook has almost 3 billion monthly users and generates millions of daily posts, comments, and replies (Statista, 2024). Such vast amounts of data demand sophisticated data processing techniques and specialized software for analysis.
- **Ethical considerations**: Obtaining and utilizing social media data involves several ethical concerns, including informed permission, data anonymization, and potential research biases. Researchers using social media data must carefully evaluate these ethical issues. In the Facebook emotional contagion study, researchers modified users' news feeds to determine the impact of happy and negative information on users' emotions (Hunter & Evans, 2016). Because the study was done without the explicit knowledge of the participants, it created controversy and highlighted questions about the ethical implications of altering the emotions of users for research reasons.
- **Quality and reliability of data**: Social media data can often be noisy, unstructured, and untrustworthy. Spam, fake accounts, and bots compromise the data quality and precision of analysis. During the 2016 US presidential election, it was uncovered that many Twitter accounts were bots created to spread misinformation and sway public opinion (Bovet & Makse, 2019). These bots can distort data and make recognizing human interactions on social media networks difficult. Accessing data from social media networks creates several obstacles that researchers and enterprises must address. Furthermore, it is also possible for social media users to have more than one account on the same platform, thus skewing understanding of communication patterns. When utilizing social media data for research or commercial objectives, it is essential to balance user privacy, platform limits, data quality, and ethical considerations.
- **Staffing and skills**: Implementing SMA effectively can be challenging for some organizations and businesses due to a lack of personnel skilled in this domain. To realize the full potential of the DAV Framework for SMA, it is vital to have a dedicated team of specialists well versed in various facets of social media analysis.

- ◦ Consider a family-run bakery in Michigan, United States, aiming to improve its social media presence. It may struggle to fully benefit from SMA because many of the available tools are unaffordable and their team lacks specialized expertise in data analytics. To address this challenge, they could invest in training of their team members with specialized skills thereby enhancing their social media efforts.
- **Rapid change**: Keeping up with the ever-evolving algorithms that determine what users see in their feeds is important. Social media platforms are constantly upgrading their algorithms, and such information is kept confidential by the platforms. This ongoing change can impact the accuracy of the analytics and poses a challenge for businesses in keeping up with the latest updates and accurate data interpretations. For instance, a fashion retailer based in Istanbul, Turkey, uses Instagram to market its products. They witness a sudden drop in engagement despite a consistent posting strategy. This could be explained by an Instagram algorithm update that impacted content visibility in user feeds. To deal with this unforeseen challenge, the retailer needs to study engagement trends and adapt their strategy accordingly to realign their approach with the platform dynamics.

Paying attention to and dealing with the various challenges is important in deriving value from SMA. As part of the overarching DAV Framework, organizations must be conscious of elements such as defining goals, asking the right questions, using the correct data, and generating the proper measures or metrics especially in a dynamic social media environment rife with challenges.

After establishing the significance of a complete SMA framework (DAV Framework), the next step is to build a strategic implementation and maintenance plan for SMA practices. By navigating SMA successfully, firms can more effectively allocate resources, optimize tactics, and accomplish desired results. The following section will cover how to lay the groundwork for success in SMA, addressing problems such as staffing, tools, budgeting, and establishing a data-driven organizational culture. This strategic approach will enable firms to realize the full potential of their SMA initiatives, fostering growth and improving decision-making (see Case Study 2.1).

Case Study 2.1 Maximizing Brand Value Through Social Media Analytics—The Journey of Bien Parfum

Bien Parfum, a luxury perfume brand based in Paris, France, has been a famous fragrance in Europe for two decades. Known for its sophisticated scents and elegant packaging, Bien's clientele is a mix of fashion-forward individuals and fragrance enthusiasts. However, with the rise of digital marketing, Bien found itself struggling to keep pace with competitors in the fast-moving world of social media.

In a bid to increase brand visibility, engagement, and customer loyalty, Bien's marketing team decided to embrace SMA. The goal was clear: to leverage insights from social media to fine-tune their content strategy, increase engagement, and strengthen their brand presence across platforms like Instagram, Facebook, and YouTube.

Step 1: Discovery—Uncovering Key Insights

The first phase of Bien's social media strategy was Discovery. This involved tapping into the wealth of data available from social media platforms to uncover critical insights about their audience and brand performance. Using Instagram Insights and Facebook Analytics, the team collected data on engagement metrics (likes, comments, shares), audience demographics (age, gender, location, with a particular focus on key markets like France, the United Kingdom, and the United States); brand mentions and sentiment (listening tools like Brandwatch were used to track what people were saying about Bien and its competitors).

Step 2: Analysis—Turning Data into Actionable Insights

Once the key data had been gathered, the next step was Analysis. The goal was to identify trends and patterns that would guide the brand's social media strategy.

Step 3: Visualization—Making Data Actionable

The final phase was Visualization. To make sense of the data and make it actionable for the team, Bien used tools like DataWrapper and Tableau to create dashboards that illustrated key metrics. One key visualization was a heatmap showing the most effective posting times, which helped the brand schedule posts to maximize engagement. Another was a sentiment trend graph, which showed a positive spike in brand sentiment whenever they posted about sustainability initiatives or eco-friendly packaging. These visualizations allowed Bien's team to easily track what was working and make data-driven decisions.

Navigating Social Media Strategically

Through the data analysis, various vital insights emerged. Videos showcasing luxurious, real-life experiences featuring Bien perfumes (e.g., influencers using the scent at fashion events) received the highest engagement—30% more likes and shares than standard product posts. The brand's posts received the highest engagement in the evening hours, between 7 p.m. and 9 p.m. CET. This indicated that Bien's target audience, especially in key markets, was most active online during those times. Moreover, posts featuring collaborations with well-known French influencers or perfume bloggers received significantly higher engagement. Analysis of customer comments revealed that people were particularly interested in sustainability—many asked about the brand's use of eco-friendly materials for packaging.

Conclusion: A Data-Driven Approach to Growth

By implementing a structured approach to SMA, Bien Parfum was able to transform its digital presence. Through the Discovery, Analysis, and Visualization phases of the DAV Framework, the brand gained valuable insights into its audience, content performance, and customer sentiment. This data-driven approach helped the brand refine its social media strategy, increase engagement, and improve customer relationships.

With a better understanding of what their audience wanted—luxurious, sustainable, and relatable content—Bien Parfum positioned itself to continue growing and thriving in the competitive luxury fragrance market. Through careful analysis and adaptation, Bien's social media journey proves that data-driven decisions can be the key to successfully navigating the ever-evolving digital landscape.

2.4 Navigating Social Media Analytics Strategically

Individuals and organizations must strategize and optimize resource allocation to maximize benefits in a world with limited resources. The significance of SMA in guiding these strategies and assisting enterprises in achieving their objectives is crucial. For example, it has been observed that while some news organizations have entire teams devoted to digital analytics, the vast majority have a few minutes each week to devote to data analysis. The time and focus dedicated to digital analytics are contingent on available resources, the extent of social media operations, and the desired outcomes.

Companies should maintain the following minimum standards for effective SMA:

- A designated analyst with at least two hours each week to devote to data analysis.
- A desktop or portable computer with an Internet connection.

- A tool for creating spreadsheets, such as Excel, OpenOffice, or Google Sheets.
- Goals and benchmarks for social media activities that are well-stated.
- A decision-maker who can act based on the findings of analytical studies.
- A predetermined frequency of reporting, such as monthly reports.

It is understandable that decisions and behaviors supported by data analytics continue to have a significant advantage over those grounded only in guesswork or intuition. SMA can be of tremendous value to businesses and organizations, and that value can be realized by implementing the DAV framework offered in this book.

There is tremendous potential for advantages from investment in SMA. These benefits include greater operational efficiency, improved customer experiences, and more revenue. Hence, for businesses to get the most value out of the money they invest, they need to have a solid understanding of the interdependencies that exist across the various stages of the analytics process.

Chapter Summary

- In the context of social media, value refers to the perceived worth, benefit, or usefulness that an individual or organization derives from a social media activity.
- The DAV Framework (Discovery, Analysis, Visualization) of SMA offers a structured and comprehensive approach to extracting value from social media data.
- The Discovery phase involves collecting and preparing social media data for analysis.
- Data is analyzed and interpreted in the Analysis phase to uncover hidden trends and inform strategies.
- The Visualization phase presents data in an accessible, compelling format for decision-making.
- Challenges such as data privacy, ethical considerations, and platform data restrictions need a thorough consideration.
- A strategic approach to SMA is essential for operational efficiency and competitive advantage.
- Implementing the DAV Framework for SMA can lead to improved audience experiences and the success of an organization.

Questions for Review

1. What is social media value, and how can it be derived from SMA?
2. What are the three key stages of the DAV Framework for SMA?
3. How does Analysis in the DAV Framework help organizations make informed decisions?
4. In what ways does Visualization play a critical role in SMA?
5. Discuss the challenges businesses might face when implementing SMA.

3

Goals, Metrics, and Measurement

Fluency in numbers, or numeracy, is not merely an academic skill. It is an indispensable expertise in the modern-day business. The ability to assess, decipher, and extract insights from data provides a clear competitive advantage within the increasingly data-driven corporate world. As we begin this chapter about goals, metrics, and measurement, we explore how the strategic application of numeracy shapes the promotion of informed decision-making and the broader success of an organization. Numeracy spans different functional areas of an organization, including financial management, marketing, operations, and human resource management. Therefore, having a comprehensive grasp of numbers is essential to the decision-making processes, highlighting the necessity of this skill set in today's modern business operations.

The power to derive value from numbers is the cornerstone of social media analytics (SMA). This is primarily because social media platforms generate massive volumes of data, which may include metrics such as the number of likes, shares, comments, follows, impressions, and engagement rates. To develop successful social media strategies, understand online user behavior, and measure the impact of marketing and engagement activities, it is necessary to possess the capacity to evaluate and examine this data accurately. Furthermore, the ability to work with numbers lays the groundwork for strategic decision-making, including formulating goals and their subsequent evaluation. Hence, by analyzing social media data, businesses can acquire significant insights into user/client behavior and preferences (Wieneke & Lehrer, 2016), enabling them

The Data Analytics Advantage. Laeeq Khan, Oxford University Press. © Oxford University Press (2025).
DOI: 10.1093/oso/9780197814222.003.0003

to target their social media efforts more effectively, improve sales or revenues, and engage with customers. Moving on from numerical prowess to goal setting, the commencement of every successful project, including SMA, requires the creation of clear goals and subsequent metrics.

3.1 The Value of Goals

Any project's path to success, including SMA, begins with established goals. Deciding which data to collect, which metrics to analyze, and how to interpret the results without precise and detailed goals becomes challenging. According to Sterne (2010), three key business goals are raising revenue, lowering costs, and increasing customer satisfaction. These business/organization goals are broader and somewhat different from specific social media goals, which may include creating brand awareness and loyalty, driving traffic to the company's website, or enhancing audience engagement. It must also be understood that the overall business goals cannot be effectively realized if any of the social media goals are not addressed.

Here, it needs to be clarified that "goals" and "objectives" are two terms often used in social media and marketing vernacular. These terms are subtly distinct but used interchangeably for simplicity. Goals are often general targets that provide a sense of direction for organizations and are more abstract and less measurable. In contrast, objectives or tactics are somewhat specific and more quantifiable actions. I believe in parsimony and the simplification of the use of varied terms that emerge due to the interaction between different disciplines. From a practical communication perspective, in this book, the terms "goals" and "objectives" are used synonymously for streamlining strategic social media planning.

Reconciling technology or social media goals with the broader organization's goals is daunting (Hassan Zadeh & Jeyaraj, 2018). This gap may emerge when the organization's goals for social media are detached from its overall business plans. Because of this, the value of analytics for social media can be reduced, and the organization may need help to fully reap the benefits that are potentially available from using social media.

Establishing social media goals or objectives is an essential aspect of business strategy that requires careful consideration. More than a simple task, it is a fundamental procedure that determines the direction of social media efforts. It may be advantageous to begin this process with a broad, overarching goal that aligns with the business's mission and vision. For instance, a newly established business may seek to cultivate relationships with its target market to expand its presence in the community. In contrast, a small local business pursuing market penetration may concentrate on generating leads for an existing product to boost its visibility and reach. After articulating this broad goal, the next stage is to develop specific, actionable goals or objectives that serve as a road map for daily social media activities. Some have referred to these daily social media activities as tactics. These granular objectives or tactics are integral to the overall strategy, influencing and aligning social media efforts with the organization's core goals. Businesses can create a cohesive and effective social media strategy that resonates with their audience and generates measurable results by establishing specific and purpose-driven social media goals.

There are numerous compelling arguments in favor of social media administrators establishing goals. Here are three principal reasons that underscore the importance of setting specific goals:

1. **Accountability**: Social media goals are necessary for ensuring accountability, allocating resources, and encouraging marketers to concentrate on the data they obtain. Businesses can track their advancement and evaluate their effort outcomes by designating specific and measurable goals. Accountability ensures that the organization moves in the right direction and utilizes its resources efficiently.

2. **Budget management**: Well-articulated goals can guide how resources should be allocated, resulting in efficiencies in time and costs. For example, a company aiming to increase brand awareness might invest in paid advertising campaigns. On the other hand, if the objective is to increase audience engagement, the focus may shift toward developing and curating engaging content.

3. **Decision-making informed by data**: Establishing social media goals assists organizations in focusing on data. Data is the foundation of social media analytics, and organizations can ensure their success by setting measurable goals. For example, based on carefully crafted goals, a university communication department can increase prospective student engagement through an analysis of data through social media.

3.2 Defining Social Media Goals Using the SMART Goals Framework

The first step in defining social media analytics goals is to determine the primary purpose of the analysis. Whether the intent is to grow brand awareness, boost engagement, or assess the effectiveness of a marketing campaign, the chosen goals will guide the selection of relevant social media channels and suitable analytic tools. Most importantly, the choice of goals will affect the metrics selected for monitoring progress and the nature of the data that must be collected.

When setting specific and measurable goals in social media analytics, the focus shifts to the widely accepted framework for goal setting that exemplifies these principles: SMART goals. This concept originated in the middle of the 20th century and has garnered significant attention in numerous disciplines, including communication, business, engineering, and education.

The SMART goals framework represents a systematic goal-setting approach (Morrison, 2010). Each letter in the acronym highlights a distinct characteristic of a well-defined objective: Specific, Measurable, Achievable, Relevant, and Time-bound. The SMART goals framework provides a robust structure for achieving social media success (Rubin, 2002), offering clarity, focus, and drive to achieve objectives. It increases the likelihood of success by encouraging organizations to define their goals within a set time frame.

The SMART goals framework is appropriate for realizing insightful and quantifiable results (see Figure 3.1). Let's understand how the SMART goals framework can be applied to social media analytics.

- **Specific.** The enormity and diversity of social media can make it challenging to establish which data are pertinent for analysis. A particular goal has to be articulated and clearly defined. For instance, the goal "increase brand awareness on social media" is vague, whereas "increase comments on Instagram by 15% within the next quarter" is precise and well-defined.

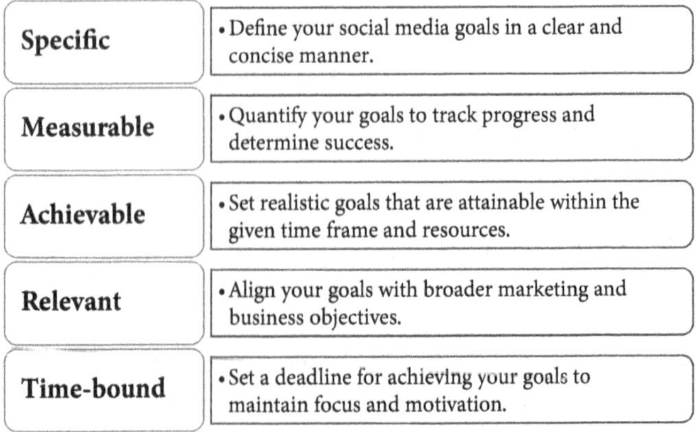

Figure 3.1 SMART goals for social media measurement

- **Measurable**. The second component of SMART goals prioritizes the ability to quantify and, consequently, monitor and evaluate progress. Consider the goal to "increase mentions of the brand on X (formerly Twitter) by 15%." This goal is measurable, as the number of brands mentioned on X can be systematically tracked to measure success. This measurement uses brand mentions and engagement rates. These metrics help ascertain whether the established goals have been achieved and provide data-driven insights that can inform future decisions regarding social media strategy.

- **Attainable**. The "A" in SMART goals stands for attainability, emphasizing the need for the goals to be achievable and realistic, given the constraints of available resources. For example, an objective to "increase brand mentions on Facebook by 1000% in two weeks" may be unattainable due to its enormous size and the constraints imposed by existing resources. If an organization lacks the resources to conduct a comprehensive analysis across all social media platforms, it would be prudent to concentrate on the few platforms that most closely align with its objectives. This focused approach circumvents the impracticality associated with overstretching the analytics efforts and ensures that objectives are established with a realistic understanding of achievable goals.

- **Relevant**. The fourth criterion of the SMART goals framework is relevance. A goal must be aligned and relevant to the organization's values, vital long-term objectives, and strategy. Every action should move you closer to the primary goal. Hence, the action should be appropriate and focused. For instance, if the primary goal of an organization is to increase customer retention, an aim such as "reduce customer service response time by 30%" would be more pertinent. Conversely, a target of "boosting brand mentions on X by 17%" could be misaligned and even off the mark if it does not directly serve the primary objective of improving customer retention.

- **Time-bound**. A final characteristic of SMART goals is to adhere to a timeline. A goal must have a distinct and specific completion date. For example, a goal to "increase customer engagement on LinkedIn by 20% within the next six months" is time-bound because it specifies a specific time frame: "within the next six months." Given the dynamic character of the social media landscape, setting time-bound goals is necessary. A clear-cut deadline also ensures that the analysis will be completed on time.

By incorporating the SMART goals framework into the social media analytics mix, organizations, and businesses can define clear and realistic objectives,

Table 3.1 Examples of SMART goals in social media analytics

	Criteria	Goal	SMART goal
1	Specific	Increase Instagram followers	Increase Instagram followers by 15% within three months
2	Measurable	Improve engagement on Facebook	Increase Facebook engagement rate by 10%
3	Attainable	Increase website traffic from X	Drive 500 clicks from X to the main website in April
4	Relevant	High engagement on YouTube videos	Increase dialogue on YouTube from 7 p.m. to 9 p.m., raising comments from 2% to 7% of views on premiere videos
5	Time-bound	Increase brand awareness on social media	Increase brand mentions on TikTok by 20% in the third quarter.

thereby improving the effectiveness and precision of their efforts. The following table illustrates how general goals can be transformed into SMART goals:

In Table 3.1, the objectives in the general "goal" column are imprecise and do not adhere to the SMART criteria. For example, "Increase Instagram Followers" fails to specify the goal's scope, timeline, or relevance. In contrast, the SMART goal column contains well-defined objectives that adhere to the SMART framework. For example, the objective "Increase Instagram followers by 15% within three months" is specific and measurable, allowing for the observation of progress. Additionally, it is deemed achievable and pertinent to the overall social media strategy. The same attributes apply to the other SMART goals, such as "Increase the Facebook engagement rate by 10%" and "Drive 500 clicks from X to the website in April." The fifth general goal, "increase brand awareness on social media," is neither specific nor measurable due to the absence of distinct metrics, targets, or platforms. However, the corresponding SMART goal, "increase brand mentions on TikTok by 20% in Q3," satisfies all SMART criteria, making it a compelling goal.

Utilizing the SMART goals framework enables organizations to track progress and adjust strategies as needed quickly. Understanding that social media platforms have unique goals reflective of their business strategy is vital. For instance, YouTube may prioritize views and channel growth. In contrast, TikTok may prioritize video views and followers, Facebook may prioritize post reach and website traffic, Instagram may prioritize follower growth, and X may prioritize tweet impressions and engagement. Moreover, each platform offers something unique. TikTok is for short-form videos, and X mainly addresses the motivation for information sharing in the form of brief text. Understanding these distinctions ensures that SMART objectives are well-crafted and aligned with each platform's unique characteristics.

Case Study 3.1 Building Community and Engagement Using SMART Goals—A Strategic Approach to Increasing YouTube Video Comments for an Etsy Handmade Jewelry Business in Lansing, Michigan

---

The background

In the expanding world of online entrepreneurship, Sarah, a small business owner in Lansing, Michigan, USA, embarked on a journey to promote her handcrafted jewelry products via her newly launched YouTube channel. Despite the aesthetic appeal of the jewelry-showcasing videos, the channel suffered from a lack of engagement, especially in the form of comments. Recognizing the potential for comments to cultivate a sense of community and engagement with the target demographic, Sarah sought to strengthen this aspect of her social media presence.

SMART Goal Development

The goal was to "Increase the number of comments on YouTube videos by 50% in the third quarter." This goal was formulated using the SMART framework:

- **Specific**: The goal identified the precise engagement metric to be enhanced, namely the number of comments on YouTube videos, providing a clear and focused target.
- **Measurable**: The goal was quantified by specifying a 50% increase by the end of the third quarter, allowing for precise monitoring and evaluation.
- **Achievable**: The goal was grounded, considering the current comment rate and recognizing that it was within the scope of possibility.
- **Relevant**: The goal's alignment with broader objectives of enhancing audience interaction and cultivating a brand-centered community highlighted its relevance.
- **Time-bound**: A specific time frame, the third quarter, was established, creating a sense of urgency and a transparent window for accomplishment.

Action strategy

To achieve this goal, a strategic action plan was formulated:

1. **Stimulate Audience Participation**: Sarah sought to encourage audience participation by including queries or calls to action after the videos, thereby inviting comments.
2. **Respond to Feedback**: Sarah fostered a sense of community by actively responding to viewer comments and demonstrating a sincere appreciation for their input.
3. **Promote the Videos**: The videos were advertised on other social media platforms, such as Facebook and Instagram, to increase their visibility and likelihood of engagement.

The Outcome

At the end of the third quarter, a comprehensive analysis revealed a 60% increase in YouTube video comments, surpassing the initial SMART goal of 50%. This success was not merely a numerical achievement; it resulted in tangible benefits. The increased engagement fostered a robust brand community and increased brand awareness, substantially contributing to the business's overall growth and success.

Key Takeaway

This case study demonstrates the effectiveness of well-defined SMART goals in the context of social media analytics. By aligning specific, measurable, attainable, pertinent, and time-bound goals with strategic actions, the hand-crafted jewelry business not only met but also surpassed its objective. This case highlights the significance of goal setting as a dynamic and integral component of social media strategy, with far-reaching implications for community building, brand development, and business success.

Setting precise and attainable social media goals, especially SMART goals, is crucial to a successful marketing strategy (Case Study 3.1). But how do we navigate the complex social media landscape to guarantee these goals are set and achieved? This brings us to the timeless concept of SWOT analysis. Let's explore this further.

3.3 Understanding the SWOT Analysis in Social Media Strategy

The SWOT analysis framework serves as a valuable method for informed decision-making. It is an essential tool in strategic business analysis (Gurel & Tat, 2017). It involves the examination of strengths, weaknesses, opportunities,

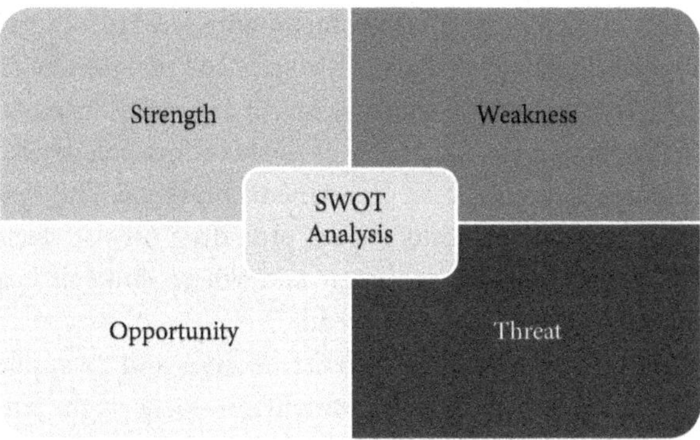

Figure 3.2 SWOT analysis

and threats. Tracing its origins in the early 1950s at Harvard Business School, the SWOT analysis has been widely used in various fields (Benzaghta et al., 2021). This framework's versatility and enduring significance are exemplified by its utilization in both academia and industry. The field of social media analytics is also benefiting from the organized approach that SWOT analysis offers.

Simplicity and depth of understanding characterize the core premise of SWOT analysis. It entails employing a four-quadrant framework (see Figure 3.2) comparable to a compass, where each direction gives insights into the obstacles and possibilities ahead to evaluate plans for every campaign or endeavor. This systematic approach enables a thorough comprehension of the internal and external variables that might affect success.

When examining social media, a SWOT analysis necessitates careful and thorough deliberation. Brands frequently have the task of striking a balance between what is seen as "realistic" and what is considered "ambitious." The SWOT analysis serves as a valuable tool for navigation, identifying prospective challenges, and clarifying the presence of impediments. The strategic map functions as a navigational tool, preventing obstacles that impede achieving goals.

In the dynamic realm of social media, where the perception of one's reputation is important and every choice is scrutinized, the SWOT analysis plays an essential and indispensable function. It provides insights into how well different strategies worked, highlighting what exceeded expectations and what needs improvement. By incorporating frequent reporting with SWOT analysis, a more detailed comprehension of social media efforts is attained. This strategy goes beyond merely observing trends, highlighting the need for data-driven decision-making.

Consider the decision to pursue social advertising on Facebook. The SWOT analysis allows for a comprehensive evaluation, contrasting *strengths*, such as compelling posts and consistent engagement, with *weaknesses*, such as limited historical data or budget constraints. This balanced perspective allows for the identification of *opportunities* to increase brand awareness using artificial intelligence (AI) for content creation, as well as the identification of potential *threats* in the form of a competitor's robust social media presence. The SWOT analysis, therefore, converts ambiguity into clarity, providing precise decision-making guidance. The key is recognizing when and where strategic engagement is merited instead of chasing every new trend.

After examining the intricacies of SWOT analysis and its application to the development of social media strategies, we will now focus on the tangible aspects of monitoring and quantifying success. How do we quantify the effectiveness of our strategy? The following section will introduce us to concepts of key performance indicators (KPIs), metrics, and measurement.

3.4 Metrics, KPIs, and Measurement

Measuring social media presents its unique set of challenges (Grave, 2019). From the four Vs (volume, variety, variety, and veracity) to the quantifying of intangible numbers, a concerted effort is required. In various fields, the terms "metrics" and "key performance indicators (KPIs)" are frequently used interchangeably. This can lead to ambiguity and confusion in understanding what these terms mean and how they are applied to measuring social media strategies. In this book, I'd like to elucidate this distinction, which makes sense from a social media analytics perspective. By clarifying the functions of metrics and KPIs, we can better understand their significance in strategic decision-making and performance evaluation.

Metrics

Metrics are quantitative measurements that monitor aspects of business activity and evaluate the success or failure of that activity's performance. They are usually tactical, enabling specific results to be stated to demonstrate the performance of actual activities concerning predetermined goals or objectives. Metrics are specific data points or indicators necessary for measuring progress, diagnosing problems, and implementing enhancements (Farris et al., 2006).

You may recall that social media analytics is the process of collecting, analyzing, and interpreting these metrics to gain insights. For example, metrics provide insight into user engagement (likes, comments, and shares), content effectiveness, and overall performance in social media. Simple metrics include the number of times a piece of content was downloaded. In contrast, complex metrics include the conversion rates and calculation of social media strategies' return on investment (ROI) (discussed below). For predictive analytics, historical metrics can be used to forecast future trends on social media.

Key Performance Indicators

KPIs are strategic measurements that reveal a business's success in attaining a particular aim or objective. In contrast with metrics, KPIs define values against which metrics are measured. KPIs are quantifiable and require precise definitions. Examples of KPIs include the targeted percentage increase in market share over a specific period. For example, a KPI could be a quarterly increase in engagement rate or the number of followers over social media.

KPIs are at the apex of strategic planning, whereas metrics form the tactical base. Metrics support KPIs, supporting the business's overarching strategic aims and objectives. Metrics are the measurements that offer granular insights into operations, while KPIs are the measurements that reflect the success of the business in achieving its high-level strategic goals. In social media, metrics provide the necessary data for determining whether the strategic KPI is being met. Metrics and KPIs are thus related indispensable tools for quantifying and evaluating social media activity.

Case Study 3.2 Decoding Instagram Engagement with Fitness Influencer Sami

---

Sami had always been passionate about fitness. What started as a personal journey to get in shape eventually turned into a full-fledged Instagram career. With a growing following of 500,000 fitness enthusiasts, Sami's Instagram account became a platform where he shared workout routines, nutritional tips, motivational quotes, and glimpses into his daily life. But as his follower count grew, so did his desire to refine his content and engage more effectively with his audience.

Like many influencers, Sami had been posting regularly—sometimes daily—and yet he wasn't seeing the level of engagement he had hoped for. Sure, his posts got likes and comments, but there was always that nagging question: What type of content truly resonates with his followers? And more importantly, How could he measure and improve his engagement rate? That's when Sami decided to dive deeper into the numbers.

Understanding Metrics and KPIs

Sami knew that to truly understand how his content was performing, he needed to look beyond the obvious likes and comments. It was time to dig into metrics and KPIs. Metrics are the quantifiable measures that provide a snapshot of activity. These are the number of likes, comments, and shares a post receives on Instagram. Despite their apparent simplicity, these numbers can serve as the foundation of a deeper analysis. While metrics provide us with bare numbers, KPIs offer context. Sami quickly realized that KPIs— which offer context to these raw numbers—were much more insightful. The primary KPI he focused on was the engagement rate. The engagement rate is a percentage that reveals how much a post resonates with followers. It's calculated by dividing the total number of engagements (likes, comments, shares) by the number of followers, then multiplying by 100. A high engagement rate signals strong audience interest, while a low rate indicates the need for improvement.

For example, if Sami's post receives:

500 likes
100 comments
50 shares

And he has 5,000 Instagram followers, his engagement rate is:

$$\text{Engagement Rate} = (500 + 100 + 50) / 5000 \times 100 = 12\%$$

This formula would give Sami a tangible way to evaluate how well his posts were performing.

Diving into Instagram Analytics

With a clearer understanding of metrics and KPIs, Sami turned to Instagram's native analytics tool, Instagram Insights, which provides valuable data on engagement. His goal was to gather insights into the type of content his followers engaged with the most. Sami's first step was to segment his posts by content type. He categorized his posts into the following types:

- Images—Fitness tips, before-and-after transformation photos, and motivational quotes.
- Videos—Short workout tutorials and long-form fitness advice.
- Reels—Quick workout challenges and behind-the-scenes glimpses of his training routine.
- Stories—Real-time updates, Q&A sessions, and interactive polls.

By examining the engagement data for each content type, Sami was able to identify trends. He noticed that his reels (quick, engaging workout videos) were consistently driving the highest engagement, with an average engagement rate of 14%. On the other hand, static images—despite being popular—had the lowest engagement rate, hovering around 4%. Sami's immediate takeaway was clear: reels were where the action was.

The Role of Audience Interaction
Sami also noticed that comments played a significant role in boosting engagement. Posts that encouraged conversation, such as Q&A sessions or polls, received more comments—and therefore higher engagement rates—than posts that were purely informational or promotional.

For example, in one post, Sami asked his followers, "What's your biggest challenge when it comes to staying consistent with your workouts?" This sparked a conversation, and within a few hours, the post had over 300 comments, far higher than the average 50–60 comments on his regular fitness tips posts.

This revealed an important insight: Engagement wasn't just about the content Sami posted, but also about how much he actively encouraged his followers to engage with him. Posts that fostered conversation created a deeper connection with his audience.

After just a month of refining his Instagram strategy, Sami noticed a significant improvement in his engagement rate. His overall engagement rate increased by 30%, and his follower count grew by 15%. The number of comments per post also skyrocketed, and his DMs were flooded with brand offers from fitness companies interested in sponsoring his posts.

Conclusion: Data-Driven Success
Sami's story is a testament to the power of data-driven decision-making. By diving into Instagram's native analytics tools, organizing data by content type, and analyzing engagement metrics (likes, comments, shares), Sami was able to make informed decisions about his content strategy. His approach helped him align his content with his audience's preferences, leading to increased engagement, a growing following, and even lucrative sponsorship deals.

For any influencer, brand, or content creator on Instagram, understanding the metrics and KPIs that drive engagement is crucial for success. By analyzing and responding to data, Sami turned his Instagram account into a thriving platform for fitness inspiration, turning numbers into genuine connections with his audience.

> By organizing and making sense of data, brands and influencers can gain valuable insights that enable them to modify their Instagram content strategy to what genuinely resonates with their audience. This systematic approach demystifies organization's success on Instagram and provides a roadmap for continuous improvement.

It can be challenging to navigate the world of social media analytics, particularly when terms like "metrics" and "KPIs" are frequently used interchangeably. This ambiguity may result in misunderstandings and misaligned strategies. However, understanding their distinct functions and implementations can provide clarity and guidance when assessing social media performance. As we progress through this chapter, we will further demystify these concepts by illustrating their significance in social media. Case Study 3.2 provides a practical example differentiating between metrics for engagement and KPIs on Instagram. We now delve into different types of commonly used metrics and KPIs.

Commonly Used Metrics and KPIs

Audience Profile/Persona Metrics

Audience metrics humanize your followers by revealing information related to audience demographics, psychographics, and online activities. These metrics help create a detailed profile of your audience. By understanding your audience, you can modify your content strategy to resonate with them more effectively. Key audience metrics are as follows:

- **Demographic information**: Age, gender, income, education, occupation.
- **Psychographic information**: Interests, hobbies, values, attitudes, lifestyle preferences, challenges.
- **Online behavior**: Preferred social platforms, time spent online, content preferences (e.g., reels, posts), devices used (e.g., smartphones, tablets, desktops), frequency of communication (daily, weekly, monthly), and brands they follow.

Awareness Metrics (Tactical)

Awareness metrics help measure your brand's visibility on platforms such as Instagram. They are essential for businesses seeking to increase brand awareness. Key awareness metrics include:

- **Follower count**: While a primary metric, combining it with engagement data offers a clearer picture of brand strength.

- **Impressions**: How often content appears on someone's screen.
- **Content reach**: The unique viewers of a post or ad.
- **Visitor frequency rate**: Differentiates new from returning visitors, indicating content resonance and loyalty.
- **Audience growth rate**: Measures the pace of gaining new followers.

Engagement Metrics (Tactical)

Engagement metrics reveal how audiences interact with your content, indicating the attractiveness of the content with audiences on social media. Engagement metrics are the number of likes, comments, shares, and other types of participation on a social media platform. The following are further details about the vital engagement metrics:

- **Likes, reactions, favorites**: Often termed the "applause rate," it usually signifies positive user feedback (YouTube also offers a video dislike option).
- **Comments and replies**: Termed the "comment rate," it measures user-generated responses.
- **Shares and retweets**: Known as the "amplification rate," it indicates content virality.
- **Sentiment**: Gauges the tone of conversations around a brand, categorized as positive, negative, or neutral.

Conversion Metrics (Strategic KPIs)

Conversion metrics track the effectiveness of social media in encouraging users to take actions aligned with business goals. Conversions can be understood as actions that users take as a result of the campaign, and thus a conversion metric can provide tangible evidence of the success or failure of a campaign. Conversions can be measured through various methods.

- **Combined/overall engagement rate**: A holistic view of user interaction, considering likes, comments, shares, and so forth. The average engagement rate is the percentage of your overall audience that engaged with your content in any manner on a social channel during the reporting period.
- **Click-through rate (CTR)**: The ratio of users who click a link in a post to its total viewers.
- **Conversion rate**: Measures the effectiveness of a call-to-action, be it liking a post, following a page, or clicking a link.
- **Return on investment (ROI)**: Assesses the value derived from social media campaigns, considering costs and returns. A high ROI indicates that the investment's returns offset its costs. ROI is used as a performance KPI to

evaluate the success of an investment. The ROI for a social media campaign is the ratio of benefits obtained from the campaign, such as increased sales or enhanced brand awareness, to the expenses associated with the campaign, which include the amount of time and money devoted to the creation of content and its promotion. The formula for computing ROI within social media is as follows:

$$ROI = \frac{\text{Estimated Media Value} - \text{Cost of Investment}}{\text{Cost of Investment}} \times 100$$

Customer Advocacy Metrics (Strategic KPIs)

Customer advocacy metrics evaluate the extent to which a brand's customers become promoters, recommenders, or ambassadors, advocating the brand to others through their social media activity. These KPIs are crucial for businesses aiming to foster loyalty and harness the power of word-of-mouth (WOM) or electronic WOM marketing. Key customer advocacy metrics include:

- **Brand mentions**: Indicates brand popularity and share of voice.
- **Net promoter score (NPS)**: A loyalty metric gauging the likelihood of customers recommending or promoting the brand. The calculation of NPS is straightforward. Customer loyalty or satisfaction is gauged based on a simple question: "On a scale from 0 to 10, how likely are you to recommend our company/product/service to a friend or colleague?" Respondents can be classified in three categories: Promoters (scores 9 to 10) as loyal enthusiasts, Passives (scores 7 to 8) as satisfied but passive and could be swayed by competitors, and Detractors (score 0 to 6) as unhappy customers who can generate negative word-of mouth. Hence the formula to calculate is as follows:

$$NPS = (\%\ \text{Promoters}) - (\%\ \text{Detractors})$$

The results can range from −100 (all detractors) to +100 (all promoters).

- **User-generated content (UGC)**: Reflects customer satisfaction through reviews, testimonials, or brand-centric posts. UGC includes any form of content such as videos, text posts and reviews, and images created by audiences reflecting their opinion. UGC can be analyzed through measures such as sentiment and content analyses.
- **Referral traffic**: Tracks visitors coming from shared links on social media.
- **Leads**: Potential customers showing interest in the brand or its offerings.

Table 3.2 Alignment between business goals, social media goals, metrics, and KPIs

Business goal	Social media goal	Metrics (tactical)	KPIs (strategic)
Increase customer satisfaction	Engender brand loyalty	Audience sentiment of text testimonials	Net Promoter Score (NPS)
Boost sales revenue	Drive product purchases	Click-through rate (CTR), conversion rate	Monthly revenue growth
Expand market reach	Increase brand awareness	Follower count, impressions, reach	Audience growth rate
Enhance customer engagement	Foster audience interaction	Likes, shares, comments, click-through rates	Overall engagement rate
Improve customer retention	Strengthen community ties	Repeat visits, returning visitor rate	Customer lifetime value (CLV)
Increase brand advocacy	Cultivate customer advocacy	Brand mentions, user-generated content (UGC)	Referral traffic, NPS

Definitions:

- Metrics (tactical): Quantitative data points used to measure specific activities on social media (e.g., likes, shares, impressions).
- KPIs (strategic): High-level indicators that assess the success of achieving business objectives (e.g., revenue growth, customer loyalty).

Monitoring and analyzing these audience advocacy data can help organizations identify their most committed and vocal advocates, adjust their social media efforts to encourage further advocacy, and eventually enhance their brand's reputation and foster long-term audience connections. While metrics provide a tactical view of specific activities, KPIs offer a strategic perspective, aligning with broader business goals. This distinction is vital for a realistic understanding of social media analytics. When metrics and KPIs are analyzed, it enables organizations to adjust their strategies, ensuring that social media initiatives are not only reverberating with the audiences but also contributing tangibly to the overarching business goals.

Table 3.2 provides a snapshot of the alignment between business goals, social media goals, metrics, and KPIs. For example, in the case of the business goal to increase customer satisfaction, the social media goal is to engender brand loyalty, monitored through metrics like audience sentiment of text testimonials, with the NPS serving as the KPI.

3.5 Exploring Audience Engagement

Engagement of online users or audiences is how individuals interact with digital content and platforms. This interaction can range from passive to active, with each type of engagement involving the user to varying degrees (Khan, 2017).

1. Passive Engagement:

The most typical form of online interaction is passive engagement. It consists of consumers merely ingesting content without taking any additional steps. Examples include:

- **Reading**: Reading is a fundamental passive engagement activity, regardless of whether the reader is perusing a news article, blog post, or lengthy social media status update.
- **Watching**: This includes watching videos, livestreams, and even GIFs. With the proliferation of platforms such as YouTube, Netflix, and TikTok, passive viewing has become the main form of engagement.
- **Viewing**: Looking at images on social media.

Passive engagement may appear less significant because it does not always result in an overt response, but it is essential for content creators and marketers. Higher passive engagement can indicate that a piece of content is appealing to a large audience and consumed by many individuals.

2. **Active Engagement**: Far less common than passive engagement (see Figure 3.3), active engagement involves users taking explicit actions in response to content. Examples include:

- **Liking**: Click the Like or React button to express approval or emotion toward content.
- **Commenting**: Commenters leave a text response to provide feedback, pose a query, or participate in a discussion.
- **Sharing**: Sharing is distributing content to one's network, thus expanding its reach.

Figure 3.3 Typical audience engagement distribution

- **Uploading or creating**: Contributing additional content, such as posting images, composing evaluations, or creating or uploading videos.
- **Purchasing or subscribing**: committing financially by buying a product or subscribing to a service.

Active engagements indicate a user's strong interest in or connection to the content. Frequently, audiences demonstrate a deeper level of dedication indicative of loyalty or advocacy. Even though most online engagement may be passive, active engagements, albeit infrequent, are significant for determining the extent of users' connections with content or platforms. Recognizing and leveraging both forms of engagement is essential for businesses, influencers, and other digital content creators to create meaningful and sustainable online relationships.

3.6 Benchmarking

After defining its goals and selecting the relevant KPIs and metrics, an organization must develop success criteria based on data benchmarks. This data includes information about the company's historical and social media accomplishments and the performance of its primary industry competitors. Benchmarking provides the required context for making educated decisions based on the chosen metrics, as it enables a firm to examine and analyze its social media performance according to its own historical records and industry norms.

Social media benchmarking is comparing the social media performance of an organization to that of its competitors or industry peers. This procedure collects and analyzes data from multiple social media networks, including X, Facebook, TikTok, Reddit, Instagram, and LinkedIn, to find trends and best practices. Organizations can measure their social media performance and identify areas for growth by utilizing benchmarking. For example, benchmarking can be done in terms of engagement rates (comparing the average number of likes, comments, and shares a company receives for each social media post to those of its competitors), reach (comparing the average number of impressions obtained by a company's postings to those of its competitors); followers (evaluating a company's total number of followers on each social media platform in comparison to its competitors), and ad spend (comparing the amount of money a company spends on advertising across social media platforms to that of its competitors, to determine how well a company utilizes its advertising budget).

An essential point in benchmarking is to ensure correct and pertinent data utilization. While social media data can be complicated and unstructured, acquiring and analyzing relevant data from social media platforms is vital. This entails identifying suitable data sources, such as social media sites, and employing appropriate data processing and visualization techniques. Businesses may assure the reliability and applicability of their insights by utilizing precise and reliable data.

After establishing a foundational comprehension of goals, metrics, KPIs, engagement, and benchmarking within social media, discussing the data and tools that facilitate their measurement is crucial. Each social media platform has native analytics tools to provide insights about its features and user behaviors.

In the next chapter, we will delve into the specifics of native analytics tools, examining their features, benefits, and how they can optimize social media strategies. More specifically, you will learn about data gathering, organizing, and cleaning, a step within the Discovery stage of the DAV framework for SMA.

Chapter Summary

Businesses can use data to make more informed decisions, achieve their goals, and remain ahead of the competition.

- Data-driven decision-making refers to using data analysis as the basis for making decisions rather than relying solely on intuition or observation.
- Big data is often unstructured and nonstatic, but when handled and analyzed, it can assist businesses in understanding audience behavior better.
- Social media analytics is the systematic collection and examination of data derived from social media.

Questions for Review

1. How does a data-driven approach help businesses make better decisions and stay ahead of the competition, especially regarding social media strategies?
2. What is the significance of the SMART goals framework?
3. What are the different types of engagement metrics?
4. Why is audience engagement mostly passive?

4

Data Gathering, Organizing, and Cleaning

Chapter Outline

The global proliferation of social media has led to the generation of immense data repositories that provide deep insights into human behavior, preferences, and interactions. The massive volumes of data created by social media platforms are analogous to raw gold. Although intrinsically valuable, this data, like unpolished gold, requires a complete extraction, organizing, and cleaning process to realize its full value. This comparison is especially appropriate when considering social media's position as a large reservoir of unprocessed knowledge. Just as gold ore takes rigorous refinement to generate pure, precious gold, social media data requires methodical processing to translate into useful insights.

This chapter begins with the realization that, while the sheer volume of data available via social channels is tremendous, its inherent worth, like that of unrefined gold, remains dormant until properly purified. We go into the basic techniques of social media data processing, drawing parallels to how raw gold is cleaned and refined to show its true worth. As raw gold moves through different phases of refining before becoming an asset, raw data from these platforms must be carefully vetted and evaluated. We will look at the important approaches and

The Data Analytics Advantage. Laeeq Khan, Oxford University Press. © Oxford University Press (2025).
DOI: 10.1093/oso/9780197814222.003.0004

tactics for refining this digital gold, that is, social media data, so that stakeholders like academics, corporations, and individuals may use it to get in-depth insights into human behavior, social patterns, and engagement.

The massive amounts of data produced on social media sites is in the form of text, images, and video. Such data is critically important across various fields such as sociology, business, psychology, statistics, entertainment, politics, computer science, and other areas. Data mining, also known as "knowledge discovery," is a subfield within data science, situated at the crossroads of computer science and statistics (Han, 2006).

With the increasing use of social media, the need for applying mining techniques to extract valuable and hidden insights from data has increased manifold (Barbier & Liu, 2011). Data from social media platforms has become fundamental for individuals, institutions, and researchers aiming to gain a complete understanding of their target demographics and refine their social media strategies accordingly. However, the data collection process is marred by obstacles. On one hand, user privacy concerns guided by platform "terms of service," take center stage. On the other hand, social media platforms are increasingly reluctant to allow access to their data, thus impeding researchers in making sense of social media activity. Moreover, the sheer volume of daily content can overwhelm efforts to locate relevant data. These challenges illustrate the complexities of data collection from social media platforms, where privacy and data accessibility concerns intersect.

Data accessibility is a fundamental aspect of data analytics. It is essential to distinguish between public and private data, particularly in the domain of social media. While public data is accessible to everyone, private data remains safeguarded and confidential. Access to public data is essential for conducting competitive analysis and benchmarking, both of which are essential for enhancing social media strategies. Researching public data enables an evaluation of the competitor's activity on social media. However, it is essential to recognize the boundaries of privacy: confidential data cannot be subjected to the same level of inquiry as public data. This understanding serves as the ethical foundation of social media analytics (SMA).

This chapter unravels the complexities of social media data, providing readers with the necessary insights to navigate this complex domain ethically and effectively. We will learn about the methods, sources, and categories of data collection as well as the ethical considerations involved. In addition, we will investigate various methods for extracting data from social media platforms such as Reddit, X, and YouTube. We will then discuss data preprocessing, a crucial phase in the framework for social media analytics. This procedure, which is integral to the phase of discovery, ensures the accuracy and consistency of the data, preparing it for subsequent analysis.

4.1 Types of Data on Social Media Platforms

In 2023, Facebook had a staggering 3.03 billion active users, followed by YouTube at 2.4 billion active users, and WhatsApp and Instagram at 2 billion active users worldwide (Statista, 2024). In the same year, TikTok had a fast-growing user base at 1.2 billion active users and Telegram at 800 million (Statista, 2024). With billions of active users throughout the world, social media platforms generate immense data that can be harnessed to gain insights into user behavior, interests, and social connections.

Social media data can be classified into several categories, each offering unique perspectives and opportunities for analysis. By examining these different data categories, it becomes possible to better understand the complex dynamics of social media and develop effective strategies to achieve overall business and social media objectives. We will delve into three key categories of social media data: user engagement or behavior data, demographic data, and network data.

1. **Audience engagement or behavior data (likes, posts, comments, shares)**: As discussed in Chapter 3, audience engagement is how individuals interact with digital content and platforms. This category encompasses various forms of user-generated content and interactions on social media platforms. These forms of user-generated content and interactions comprise likes, comments, shares, and other types of reactions. The analysis of these data helps businesses and researchers understand the preferences, interests, and trends of users. This knowledge can then be applied to the creation of tailored advertising and content and for the enhancement of the user experience.

2. **Demographic data (age, gender, location, education level)**: Demographic data refers to personal information that individuals provide or that can be inferred from their profiles and activities on social media platforms. Examples of demographic information include age, gender, occupation, and education levels. Surveys and interviews are commonly used to collect this type of data about audiences. However, content analysis of social media data can also reveal such information. For example, X/Twitter profile information that includes user name, image, and description can help enrich data and add depth. Furthermore, information such as location or other specifics that are relevant to the situation can also be deduced through social media data. Obtaining and analyzing demographic data can prove immensely beneficial for having a comprehensive understanding of target audiences. Such insights further help develop targeted marketing campaigns, and make educated judgments based on the characteristics of a particular user group.

3. **Network data (friend/follow relationships and status in the network):** Network data incorporates the connections and ties that exist between users on social media sites. This data can provide insights into the structure and dynamics of social networks, such as user status or influence inside the network, friend or follower relationships, group affiliations, and more. The analysis of network data provides businesses and researchers with the ability to comprehend the spread of information within social networks. Analysis of network data aids in finding influential users or communities, and to devise strategies for capitalizing on social connections. A clear understanding about who resides within a social network, and their level of influence, is vital in accomplishing objectives such as the promotion of products, the dissemination of messages, or the raising of brand awareness through influencers. We will delve deeper into the understanding of network characteristics in Chapter 7.

4.2 Accessing Social Media Data

The selection of a suitable data source is an important step in any analytics or research process. This is because accessing relevant data significantly influences its quality and relevance. The choice of where data is obtained is guided by three primary considerations: (1) the analytics goal or the research question, (2) the nature and characteristics of data sought, (3) and the available resources.

A data source is a point of origin or repository from which the data under consideration is obtained. For instance, a university researcher is interested in studying the spread of misinformation and user engagement patterns on Reddit. The specific question might be: "What type of misinformation trends on Reddit, and what is the nature of user engagement with such content?" To address this research question, data needs to be obtained from the Reddit website, as it contains the digital traces, footprints, or data about audience engagement such as user posts, comments, and even the time, date, and location of those who engaged. Hence, there needs to be a mechanism through which this data can be obtained from Reddit.

Typically, researchers and analysts can find and utilize the most appropriate data from social media platforms' own databases by utilizing their API (application programming interface). While APIs provide access to social media data, major platforms such as Facebook have restricted access to their raw data due to its commercial importance (Batrinca & Treleaven, 2015). Unfortunately, only a small number of social data sources provide academic and research institutions with cost-effective data solutions.

In addition to public APIs, web scraping is an alternative method to collect social media data. However, depending on the need, technical know-how, and the availability of resources, social media data can also be obtained from some public sources, native social platforms (such as YouTube analytics, Facebook insights, etc.), and social listening tools (which provide access to social data possibly through APIs). Native social analytics tools are built into the social media platform. Social listening tools help monitor trends, mentions, and reputation of a brand and provide a picture of how audiences perceive them. Social listening and native analytics tools are described in greater detail later in this chapter. First, let's delve into how APIs are used to access prime sources of data.

4.2.1 Public APIs

An API is a standard interface that aids data access by providing a clear and ordered structure of an application's data. APIs can be understood as sets of rules that enable communication between different applications. APIs serve as intermediaries that facilitate data transfer in a controlled and structured manner.

APIs streamline the data collection process by allowing developers to quickly identify and access the data they need (Janetzko, 2017). Numerous social media networks, like Facebook, have APIs that enable developers to pull data directly from the platform. For instance, a programmer may utilize YouTube's API to request specific data, such as the total number of likes, dislikes, comments as text, channel subscriber numbers, and views for a specific video. The API then specifies where the appropriate data can be located in their database, simplifying the retrieval process.

Using APIs simplifies the design of recurrent operations and establishes a safe link between two programs, assuring the transmission of consistent data (Ofoeda et al., 2019). Popular APIs include the X/Twitter API, the Facebook Graph API, and the Instagram Graph API. Typically, these APIs provide access to user profiles, postings, comments, and engagement data. Due to the rate limits and access restrictions typically imposed by these platforms, however, developers must conform to the platform's regulations and standards.

In circumstances where a website does not provide API access or has constraints such as fees, rate restrictions, or insufficient data access, web scraping can be used as a substitute (while complying with site's policies and procedures). Large platforms such as YouTube, X, Facebook, LinkedIn, and Google provide APIs for a variety of applications, but web scraping may be required when limits or APIs are unavailable.

4.2.2 Web Scraping

Web scraping refers to the process of using specialized programs called "scrapers" or "bots" to extract data from websites. Web scraping, or screen scraping, may also be referred to as a form of web harvesting, or web data extraction (Khder, 2021); and the process involves extracting the HTML code of web pages. When API access is limited, researchers may resort to web scraping to create datasets that can then be analyzed.

Although data can be scraped manually (by copying and pasting information into spreadsheets), a computer program completes the web scraping more efficiently and precisely than a person could. A written code or a program can automatically download, interpret, and arrange data from the internet. Content displayed on web browsers may be pleasing to the eye but is not organized or presented in a manner that allows for easy extraction and export in the structured rows-and-columns format for analysis in spreadsheets. Web scraping can transform unstructured data into structured data in a worksheet or a database for analysis.

Web scraping, or "screen scraping," as a data collection technique, was used in the early days of computing (between the 1960s and the 1980s) to extract data from text-based terminals. Scraping predates the internet, and is considered the precursor to the idea of automated data collection (Broucke & Baesens, 2017). For example, scraping started with manual efforts such as through newspapers, books, and hand-written and printed materials often involving cutting, pasting, and manually inputting information extracted from different sources. People, then as now, were interested in collecting data and storing it for eventual use. This interest continues to this day.

Data collection via this method can include things like user profiles, postings, and comments made on those profiles. It is very possible that while surfing the web, you come across websites containing data that you'd like to collect, save, and evaluate. The large amount of data that is currently accessible via the internet presents numerous opportunities for the field of data analytics. The following are some examples of these kinds of initiatives:

1. **Extraction of tables from Wikipedia as part of a statistical analysis**: Wikipedia is a rich source of information that is laid out in tables throughout the site's many pages. Data scientists can extract these tables and use them to carry out statistical studies, recognize trends, or create visualizations. For analyzing growth patterns over the course of time, a researcher can, for instance, acquire historical population statistics from the Wikipedia page of a city.

2. **Collecting user ratings and comments on movies for text mining, recommendation engines, or spotting fraudulent ratings**: Movie websites frequently include user-generated information on their pages, such as ratings and reviews. Data scientists can utilize this information to develop recommendation engines that propose films based on user tastes, do sentiment analysis to assess public opinion, or apply machine learning algorithms to detect fraudulent reviews.

3. **Collecting property listings from multiple websites pertaining to real estate**: Property information may be found on real estate websites in great detail, including the property's location, square footage, selling price, and list of included amenities. Data scientists are able to produce interactive visualizations, assess market patterns, and build prediction models for property valuation if they collect and aggregate property listings from different sources.

4. **Analyzing social networking profile pages in quest of new information**: User profiles, postings, and interactions are just some examples of the massive volumes of user-generated content that can be found on social networking platforms. Data scientists have the ability to evaluate this data in order to study human behavior, identify influencers, follow the flow of information, and even predict future trends. For instance, researchers may examine data from X to discover how public opinion shifts over time regarding a specific topic. Alternatively, they may use data from public Facebook pages to investigate the dynamics of social interactions.

5. **Examining online news sources for breaking stories**: Data scientists can benefit from the wealth of knowledge that can be found on news websites because these sites are often updated with articles covering a variety of subjects. Researchers can monitor current events, trace the creation of trends, or evaluate the impact of specific events on a public attitude if they scrape and analyze data from the news. For instance, a data scientist may examine news items to determine the impact that a political scandal has had on the approval ratings of a politician or to search for recurring themes in the manner in which a specific news topic has been covered.

4.2.3 Ethical and Legal Concerns About Web Scraping

Web scraping, screen scraping, or data scraping are not the most dependable methods of data collection. This is especially an issue with automated data scrapers, because websites may change or modify their source code. This requires programming a new scraping approach, which can be time-consuming. Web scraping also has the potential to violate the privacy limits that website owners have imposed.

Ethical and legal concerns often limit the potential of web scraping. For example, Facebook restricted access to its API in response to the Cambridge Analytica scandal (Mancosu & Vegetti, 2020). This modification hindered the ability of independent researchers to investigate pertinent political and social behavior topics. Nonetheless, researchers may collect Facebook data methodically using web scraping techniques.

In some cases, web scraping has become synonymous with stealing data from the websites of one's competitors. Such concerns have sometimes given a negative connotation to data scraping. While performing data scraping, it is crucial to ensure that you are adhering to any legal restrictions that may be in place. Many websites include disclaimers that ban the use of data extraction tools or scrapers.

Proponents of web scraping believe that the method only collects data that is already publicly available and does not gain access to any secret or confidential information on websites. It is also argued that web scraping is essentially the automation of a process that is otherwise performed manually by copying and pasting data into a spreadsheet. Since manual copying and pasting of data in spreadsheets can lead to significant time and effort, there is a motivation to rely on programming codes and online tools to engage in web scraping. Nevertheless, the bulk of analytics tools available today are API-based, and it may be thus argued that API access should be used whenever it is feasible to do so.

4.3 Insights and Data Through Embedded (Native) Social Media Tools

Many social media platforms include built-in, native, or embedded analytics tools that provide valuable insights into user activity, engagement, and other essential data points. Examples include Facebook Insights, Instagram Insights, TikTok Analytics, and YouTube Analytics. Embedded analytics tools within social media platforms serve as useful tools for knowing user engagement, reach, and overall performance on the social platform. These tools are intended to provide businesses, content creators, and marketers with a detailed view of the performance of their campaigns, enabling them to make data-driven decisions. Here is a list of some of the features commonly offered by these embedded tools:

- **Audience insights:** One of the most prominent features of native analytics tools is their capacity to provide comprehensive audience information.

These include demographic information (age, gender, location) and forms of engagement (likes, shares, remarks). By understanding their audience and how they interact with content, those running these pages or channels can tailor their campaigns to resonate with their target demographic more effectively.

- **Content optimization**: Beyond merely comprehending the audience, these instruments provide insights into the type of content that performs most effectively. This allows organizations to determine not only what type of content to post (videos, images, text) on their social media but also when to post it for maximal engagement.

- **Reach and engagement metrics**: Native analytics tools offer insights into the content's reach and engagement of social media content. This includes metrics such as impressions (how frequently content is shown), views (how frequently content is viewed), and interactions (likes, remarks, shares). Organizations and businesses can evaluate the success of individual posts and campaigns by analyzing these metrics.

- **Ad performance**: Native analytics tools are invaluable for organizations and businesses investing in paid advertising on social media platforms. They provide information regarding the effectiveness of advertisements in terms of click-through rates, conversion rates, and overall engagement. This enables them to modify their advertising strategies in real-time, maximizing their return on investment. Here is an overview of some of the well-known social media platforms' embedded or native analytics tools:

- **Facebook Insights**: Currently this resource is accessible to all Facebook pages with at least 100 followers or likes. Facebook Insights can assist page owners in understanding the performance of their content and identifying areas for improvement. It provides various forms of metrics, including page views, reach, post engagement, and demographics of the audience.

- **X/Twitter Analytics**: Provides insights on X account tweet performance, engagement, impressions, audience demographics, and more. Users can monitor tweet activity, recognize high-performing content, and comprehend audience interests. As of early 2025, X Analytics can only be accessed through a premium account.

- **Instagram Insights**: This tool provides data on post and story performance, audience demographics, reach, and engagement for Instagram business accounts. Users can monitor the performance of content and obtain insight into audience preferences.

- **LinkedIn Analytics:** This tool provides insights on post performance, engagement, follower demographics, and more for LinkedIn company pages. On the platform, users can identify high-performing content, monitor growth, and comprehend their audience.

- **YouTube Analytics:** YouTube Analytics is very useful for video content creators or channel owners. For YouTube channels, YouTube Analytics provides insights into areas such as video performance, views, watch time, top videos, user engagement, and audience demographics. This analytics tool provided to channel owners assists creators in identifying which of their videos resonate with their audience and why.
- **TikTok Analytics:** TikTok analytics provides insights into video engagement metrics such as views, likes, comments, shares, average watch time, and completion rate. It also offers traffic source information and audience demographics such as age, gender, location, and viewer interests. TikTok analytics can be accessed by those who have a Pro or business account on TikTok.
- **Exporting data through embedded tools**: The ability to export data increases the utility of these solutions. This functionality enables users to download their collected data in multiple forms, including CSV, Excel, and JSON, for additional analysis and reporting. Exporting data is a substantial advantage of many native analytics applications. We explore some of the advantages and applications of the data export capability below.

By exporting data, users can delve deeper into their social media performance. By capitalizing on raw data, users, analysts, and researchers can focus on what matters, gain deeper insights by going beyond the platform to discover hidden trends through advanced data visualization tools, and even apply statistical methods for predictive modeling. Native analytics platforms do provide valuable platform-specific insights, however, for an advanced analysis, data export and subsequent analysis using third-party tools can truly unlock the potential of data. For example, advanced data visualization tools can generate custom reports, concentrating on metrics that are most pertinent to their social media objectives to produce a more targeted and insightful analysis. By leveraging the unique strengths of native and non-native analytics tools, organizations and businesses can achieve data-driven precision and a better comprehension of social media performance.

4.4 Social Listening Tools

Social media listening, also known as social listening or social media surveillance, involves tracking brand-related conversations across multiple social media platforms. Social media listening tools are computer applications that enable organizations and businesses to understand social media activities more effectively across a variety of communication channels. Access to social listening solutions typically requires a subscription.

Social listening solutions provide a vast array of innovative capabilities that streamline the data access, analysis, and reporting procedures. These tools can assist in improving social media tactics and overall performance by giving comprehensive data and insights. It is difficult for an individual or a company to properly manage their social media presence, communicate with their audience, assess their performance, and schedule updates without the assistance of some specialized listening tools.

Utilizing analytics in this manner can provide actionable insights and facilitate automated feedback cycles, thereby optimizing operations based on the collected data. These tools assist businesses and organizations better comprehending public sentiment by analyzing the large amount of data created by users on social media. They also help businesses and organizations identify influencers and follow developing trends. The information that can be gathered from social listening can be utilized to drive product development, improve customer service, manage online reputation, and inform marketing initiatives.

The social listening process typically begins with a keyword search that captures mentions from both brand-owned channels and external sources. Social listening serves a greater purpose than simply monitoring brand mentions; it is a tool for broader market research. It provides organizations and businesses with a window into ongoing conversations about their products, allowing them to better comprehend consumer sentiments, requirements, and preferences.

Although the method resembles a Google search, social listening focuses on social media content. To provide a richer context, many applications take data from news websites, blogs, and other non-social platforms. These tools generally aggregate social media data from a number of platforms such as Facebook, Reddit, X, YouTube, and blogs in a single dashboard. The primary method for retrieving relevant data involves keyword searches; however, it is important to note that the results may not include every brand mention on the web. Most listening tools refine this data further by adding layers of information such as user demographics, interests, mention sentiment, and influencer metrics. Typically, this enrichment is performed automatically by the tool's underlying algorithms.

There are a variety of well-known tools available, each of which possesses exclusive capabilities and features. HubSpot, Brandwatch, Sprout Social, Falcon.io, Hootsuite, Buffer, TweetReach, BuzzSumo, and Keyhole are among the popular social listening tools. Beyond these, numerous organizations are developing custom analytics systems that integrate social media data, combining insights from various departments for specific objectives, such as product launches or digital initiatives. The following are some details about prominent social listening tools:

- **Hootsuite** is an all-inclusive social media management platform with social listening capabilities, such as monitoring and analyzing brand mentions, hashtags, and keywords across multiple social networks.
- **Sprout Social** is a social media management tool with robust social listening capabilities, such as monitoring keywords, hashtags, and mentions, as well as sentiment analysis and reporting.
- **Brand24** is a real-time social listening tool that monitors mentions, analyzes sentiment, and sends notifications when particular keywords are used on social media platforms, blogs, and forums.
- **Mention** is a social listening and media monitoring platform that enables users to observe and analyze brand mentions, competitors, and industry keywords across social media, blogs, and other online sources in real time.
- **Brandwatch** is a social media suite owned by Cision. Brandwatch offers two distinct offerings: consumer intelligence and social media management.
- **Buffer** is another social media management utility that enables users to schedule posts, evaluate the performance of those posts, and manage multiple accounts across multiple platforms.

4.5 Public Data Sources

Some organizations make social media datasets available to the public for research purposes. These datasets can be utilized to examine social media trends, sentiment, and other variables.

- **Google Dataset Search**: Various institutions, such as universities, government agencies, and research laboratories, often publish data related to their projects and on their websites. However, it can be challenging to directly locate this information using conventional search methods. Google Dataset Search is a Google search engine that assists researchers in locating freely accessible online data. It is an endeavor to aggregate online open-access data. Dataset search by Google offers a treasure trove data for data journalists and scientists.

By integrating open-source metadata identifiers into their web pages, organizations can make their data discoverable and accessible via Google Dataset Search. This innovative tool/search engine now includes a vast variety of data sets on diverse topics, such as skiing-related injuries, earthquakes, volcanic eruptions, penguin populations, global climate patterns, socioeconomic trends, and medical research advancements. By facilitating seamless access to such extensive datasets, Google's Dataset Search enables researchers, policymakers, and other stakeholders to make informed decisions and nurture new advances in various fields. Datasets by various organizations are usually available in a CSV file format. Datasets available as CSV files can be opened in spreadsheet software. Google Dataset Search can be accessed via the following link: https://datasetsearch.research.google.com/.

- **Kaggle**: Kaggle is a platform for users to discover and share datasets and is a subsidiary of Google. Kaggle gives users access to the data and code they need to work on data science projects. Kaggle was introduced in 2010 with machine learning competitions and now serves as a cloud-based public data platform. Kaggle can be access via the following link: https://www.kaggle.com/.
- **Stanford Large Network Dataset Collection (SNAP)**: SNAP is a library for network analysis and graph mining that can be used for various purposes. SNAP incorporates numerous datasets gleaned from a variety of social media networks for the purpose of doing network analysis. SNAP can be accessed via the following link: http://snap.stanford.edu/.
- **Dataverse**: The Dataverse Project is an open source web application for archiving research data. It contains social media datasets that have been submitted by academic academics. This resource grants access to a vast array of data that can be used for additional research. Researchers, data authors, publishers, data distributors, and affiliated institutions all receive proper credit via a data citation that includes a persistent identifier (e.g., doi or handle).

4.6 Data Wrangling

Raw data, also referred to as source data or primary data, is data that has not yet been processed for use. It is essential to make raw data analytically usable by processing it. Working with raw data can prove challenging since such data is frequently disorganized and inconsistent and may contain errors or values that are missing. It is said that data scientists spend a bulk of their time collecting, organizing, and cleaning their raw data before it can even be analyzed. To make data organized and consistent for analysis, we wrangle data.

Data wrangling is typically used in exploratory data analysis. Data wrangling is about transforming unstructured data into a more structured and usable format. In North America, the term derives from the practice of wrangling livestock, particularly horses on a range. The objective is to make manageable something that is otherwise dispersed, disorganized, or difficult to work with. This process is also known as data cleaning, data remediation, and data munging. Data wrangling involves removing errors in data, dealing with missing values, sorting, and addressing data inconsistencies. In addition to enhancing the reliability and credibility of data for analysis, omitting any superfluous or redundant data will reduce the time and effort required for analysis.

Hence, data wrangling is the process of identifying, cleaning, and integrating raw data in preparation for analysis (Furche et al., 2016). This ensures that data is correct, complete, and ready to be analyzed once it has been processed through the appropriate procedures. The precise data wrangling procedures vary from one project to the next and are determined by the type of data being utilized and the objectives that are being pursued.

Data wrangling can be performed manually or automatically. In situations involving exceptionally large datasets, automated data cleansing becomes essential. In organizations with a comprehensive data team, data collection and wrangling are typically the responsibility of a data scientist or another team member. In smaller organizations, where the size of data obtained from social media is relatively manageable, a person with analytics know-how can wrangle data prior to analysis.

4.6.1 Steps in Data Wrangling

Data wrangling is a crucial, iterative process designed to refine raw data into a clear analyzable format. This procedure is laborious but worthwhile, since it ensures the reliability and correctness of data analysis. Identifying and eliminating any errors or discrepancies in the data is a necessary step in the process of data wrangling. For instance, comments data from YouTube can contain information that is redundant and repetitive as comments often contain repeated phrases by certain users who post the same thing multiple times on various videos.

Identifying and removing these comments ensures that data is not skewed by overrepresented comments. Similarly, in an X/Twitter dataset, there may be duplicate tweets that need to be deleted for an accurate analysis. Incorrect results and conclusions may be reached due to duplicate data, which can be a source of difficulty while analyzing data. Additionally, tweets and YouTube comments may contain multilingual content due to the global nature of these platforms. Either such content needs to be translated or removed to include English-only content depending on the nature of the analysis objectives.

A Harvard Business School (HBS) article by Stobierski (2021) provides six steps and techniques of data wrangling. Each data project requires a unique approach to ensure its final dataset is reliable and accessible. The method is often informed by several different processes. These are the actions or activities that are typically referred to as "wrangling" the data. In this book, those steps are simplified into the following four steps as depicted in Figure 4.1. The steps are explained below.

1. **Familiarizing and contextualizing data.** This initial step is about becoming familiar with the data. Simply eyeballing or looking at the data for a broad overview can help identify any abnormalities. During exploration, you may identify data trends or patterns, as well as apparent issues, such as absent or incomplete values, that must be addressed. This is a crucial stage because it will inform all subsequent actions. It also needs to be ensured that one is aware of what the data is about, when it was gathered, and where it was gathered. Such additional information proves very helpful in understanding the dataset.

2. **Formatting, structuring, and organizing raw data.** In this step, raw data is transformed into a structured format. This could mean correctly naming the variables, fixing the formatting, parsing it and ensuring that there are headers, and sorting data in rows and columns. Raw data is verified

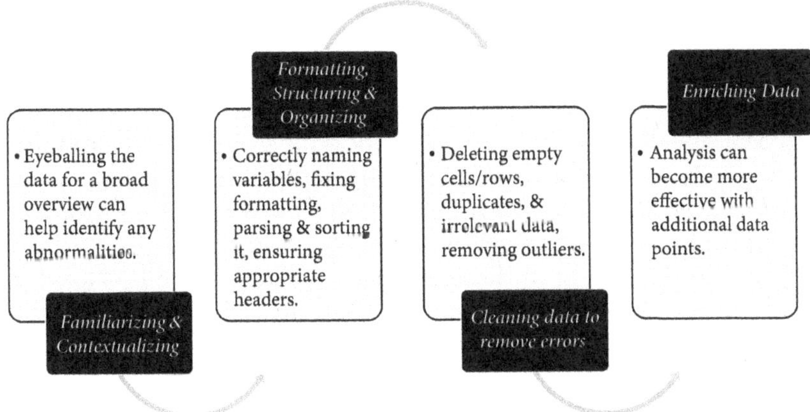

Figure 4.1 Data wrangling process

for consistency and quality through actions such as standardizing date and time formats, units of measurement, and currency symbols. It must be ensured that the data follows a standard structure, since consistent formatting makes it easier to analyze and compare data.

3. **Cleaning data to remove errors.** Data cleaning is an essential step within the data-wrangling process. There are various types of cleaning, such as deleting empty cells or rows, removing outliers, and standardizing inputs. The objective of data cleaning is to ensure that there are no errors (or as few as feasible) that could impact the final analysis. Identifying and removing faulty data has a significant impact on the remaining data manipulation processes. This may also include deleting irrelevant or superfluous data, identifying extreme data outliers, checking for duplicate records. Unfortunately, many data sets contain instances of poor quality information. It is essential to verify the data quality to ensure the veracity of your analysis.

4. **Enriching data.** Often a dataset may not include all the needed variables for a particular analysis. In such a scenario, data needs to be enriched with additional datasets. Analysis can become more effective with additional data points. For example, two data files can be combined into one, thereby enhancing the usability of the overall dataset. If you have data from multiple sources, combine them into a single dataset.

It is thus essential to make certain that the data is accurate and up to date. This means that any data that is lacking should be filled in, and any data that is no longer relevant should be updated. Hence, observing best practices when performing data wrangling is crucial for maintaining efficiency, accuracy, and dependability of the process. Other best practices in data wrangling should include the following:

- **Documenting the data wrangling process.** It is crucial to maintain thorough documentation of the data wrangling procedure, including any data modifications that have been done. Maintaining detailed records or notes of the step-by-step data wrangling process is beneficial. If any steps need to be traced back or corrected, this documentation would help save time and effort. Hence, documentation improves the reproducibility and transparency of the data, allowing others to comprehend the steps taken, replicate the procedure, and verify the results.
- **Adopting uniform naming standards.** Establishing a system for properly and consistently naming data files will ensure that data is well organized.

Such measures also ensure data comparability and consistency. This practice simplifies the process of comprehending and interpreting data more accessible and understandable for current and future users.

- **Ensuring a backup copy.** It is wise to always create and maintain a backup copy of the original data before performing any data transformation or cleaning. This precaution ensures that the original data remains intact and can be readily retrieved, if necessary, especially if errors occur during the data wrangling process or if there is a need to return to the original dataset.

Organizations and businesses can ensure that they will be able to derive the most value from their data and thus make informed decisions based on accurate and reliable data. This in turn is achieved when raw data is appropriately organized and cleaned. Data wrangling may prove to be a daunting task in addition to being time consuming. However, it is a necessary step in the overall process of data-driven decision-making. Advances in artificial intelligence (AI) are automating and speeding up the data wrangling process.

4.6.2 Data Wrangling Tools

There are many different tools that may be utilized to fulfill the requirements and applications of data wrangling. There are several automated and manual tools for data munging. Some of these tools are described here:

- **OpenRefine:** OpenRefine is an open-source desktop application for data cleaning and format conversion, also known as data refining. It resembles a spreadsheet application and supports spreadsheet file formats like CSV.
- **Google DataPrep:** Dataprep by Trifacta is an intelligent data service that visually explores, cleans, and prepares structured and unstructured data for analysis, reporting, and machine learning.
- **Tableau, Qlik:** Tableau can allow for data cleaning and its visualization.
- **Alteryx:** Alteryx analytics enables organizations to identify and clean data in a variety of ways—without the use of code—by providing a set of automation-building elements that are simple to use.
- **Spreadsheets:** Spreadsheets provide analysts with a practical and accessible solution for managing a modest to moderate amount of data. This solution enables users to easily store, alter, and analyze information in various ways. In this book, our focus is on building an understanding of data discovery using spreadsheets.

4.6.3 Let's Begin with Spreadsheets

A spreadsheet or worksheet is a file composed of rows and columns that facilitates the efficient sorting, organization, and arrangement of data and the calculation of numerical values (see Figure 4.2). Spreadsheet software is distinguished by its ability to compute values using mathematical formulas and cell data. Creating a summary of expenses and income, neatly organized in rows and columns is one way in which a spreadsheet may be utilized.

Spreadsheets are one of the most used software applications in the world. Every day, millions of people use spreadsheets, to compute numbers, organize information, and solve decision problems they regularly encounter at work. As a result, employers seek out candidates with experience and skills with spreadsheets. Spreadsheets enable users to manipulate massive, complex data in a familiar, collaborative, and controlled environment.

Many people prefer Microsoft Excel and Google Sheets when it comes to managing data. They are readily available, simple to learn, and compatible with all file types. It may be argued that most Excel users are entirely unaware of the program's potential to make monotonous and repetitive tasks easier and more efficient. With spreadsheets, individual analysts/researchers can explore their data rapidly, conduct simple arithmetic operations, and disseminate the spreadsheets to colleagues with ease and convenience.

In a spreadsheet application such as Google Sheets or Microsoft Excel, the interface includes tabs that are located at the bottom of a worksheet. Data is

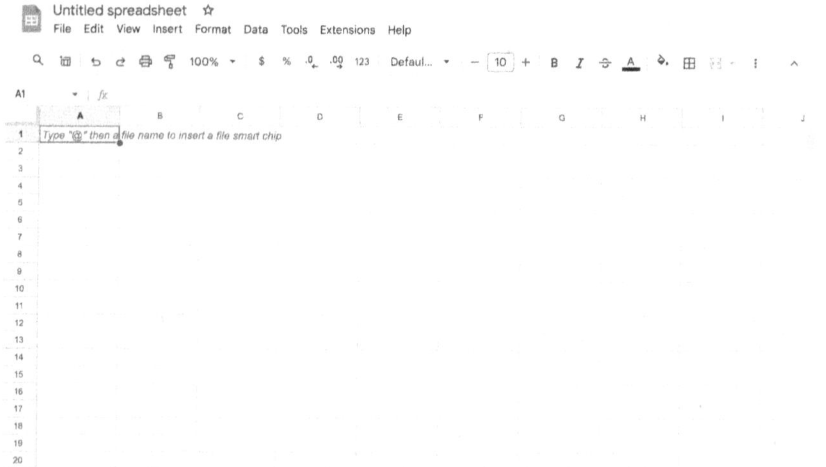

Figure 4.2 Sample spreadsheet. Google Sheets is a trademark of Google LLC.

inputted in one or more cells of a spreadsheet. The cell-based organization of a spreadsheet enables the organizing of data into different elements, by which the spreadsheet may subsequently be sorted.

In the realm of numerical data processing, spreadsheets like Google Sheets have a considerable advantage over word processors. Google Sheets is a free and powerful spreadsheet application that offers built-in features for rapid data analysis. Google Sheets facilitates data transformation and analysis with its graphical tools and built-in features. It is not feasible to perform calculations that involve multiple numbers using a word processor due to its inability to exhibit results immediately. Conversely, spreadsheets possess an inherent capacity for greater flexibility when faced with data. They provide capabilities for efficiently organizing large datasets, thereby significantly improving the experience of data processing. For example, common functions like SUM, AVERAGE, and COUNT are available in spreadsheet applications and tools. These fundamental capabilities suffice for most tasks.

Flat file. Another type of data storage is referred to as a flat file. In these, the records all adhere to the same format, but there are no indexing or linking mechanisms used. These files can be simple text files or binary files; in either case, they include a series of entries that follow a standard structure and have specific limits for the value types they can contain. The data contained within these flat files are organized in a flat structure, which makes it difficult to modify or inspect them without first importing them into another program. A comma-separated values file, also known as a CSV file, is a good illustration of a flat file. Tabular information is stored in a CSV file as lines of ASCII text; table cell values are delimited by commas, and each row is denoted by a new line when viewed in a text editor such as Notepad.

Databases. When dealing with big data, databases become an essential tool for ensuring proper adequate storage, retrieval, and management of information. Databases enable storage and retrieval of vast amounts of data in a manner that is structured and organized, allowing users to perform better analyses and make more informed decisions. There is a wide variety of database types available, each with its own design and set of features. Microsoft Access, Oracle, DB2, Informix, SQL, MySQL, and Amazon SimpleDB are just a few examples of popular databases today. Databases are especially needed when data size is large, spread across multiple files, and needs to be organized efficiently. For common data tasks related to SMA of a small and medium-sized organization, spreadsheets may prove sufficient.

Case Study 4.1 Social Media Data Management for Famous Footballer "Max" in the English Premier League on X

Leo serves as a data analyst for Max, a famous English Premier League footballer with a massive following of 1.2 million on X (formerly Twitter. Leo manages and analyzes social media data to optimize Max's engagement, track performance, and further build his personal brand. Max's large following on X provides ample opportunities for fan interaction, endorsement deals, and engagement with the broader football community. However, to effectively leverage his presence, Leo must manage large amounts of social media data to make data-driven decisions. Leo's work is crucial in ensuring that Max's social media activity remains relevant, engaging, and aligned with his professional brand, and that Max's social media strategy is both agile and data-driven.

Accessing Social Media Data

The first task in Leo's data management process is accessing social media data. Since the free X API provides limited access to data, Leo relies on a combination of X Insights (X's native analytics tool) and a paid third-party service that allows access to deeper data points.

- **X Insights**: Max's primary data source is X Insights, X's native analytics tool, which provides key metrics directly from the platform. Leo uses this tool to gather engagement metrics (favorites/likes, retweets, and replies/comments); data about audience demographics (information about Max's followers, such as location, gender, age, and interests); content performance (by tracking the success of different types of content Max posts, such as match highlights, personal life updates, sponsorship promotions, and charitable causes); and follower growth.
- **Paid data service**: To overcome the data limitations of X Insights, Leo uses a paid data service that provides more advanced and comprehensive analytics. This service allows access to additional metrics and deeper insights into Max's social media performance, including historical data: The paid service provides access to long-term data, allowing Leo to track Max's performance over a longer period. This historical view helps Leo identify long-term engagement trends, seasonal fluctuations (e.g., during major football events or the off-season), and content performance changes.

Hence, combining data from X Insights and the paid service gives Leo a rich and multidimensional view of Max's social media activity, making it possible to develop informed strategies to improve engagement.

Data Wrangling: Cleaning and Organizing Data

Once Leo has collected the raw data, the next step is data wrangling—cleaning and organizing the data to make it ready for analysis. This is an essential part of ensuring that the data is accurate, usable, and ready for actionable insights.

- **Data cleaning:** The first phase of data wrangling involves cleaning the collected data to ensure that it is accurate and free of errors. Leo performs several important tasks in this step:
  - Initial data eyeballing: This is done to gain an overview of the data and its context, and identify any noticeable anomalies that could affect subsequent analysis phases. This preliminary scan provides an overarching understanding of the content type and any possible data quality issues requiring attention.
  - Removing irrelevant or spam content: Some of the data gathered may be irrelevant or of low quality, such as spam mentions, bot-generated interactions, or tweets with missing engagement data. Leo sorts and filters out such data to ensure the analysis focuses on authentic fan engagement.
  - Handling missing data: At times, certain data points may be missing—for example, some tweets may not show full engagement metrics, or demographic data for certain followers may be absent. Leo addresses missing data by either excluding incomplete entries or using imputation techniques to fill in the gaps where appropriate.
  - Removing duplicates: When aggregating data from multiple sources (e.g., X Insights and the paid service), duplicates can sometimes occur. Leo ensures that there are no duplicate entries that could skew the analysis, especially when combining engagement data from different platforms.

This cleaned and organized data is stored in spreadsheets, often in tools like Excel or Google Sheets, that allow Leo to perform further analysis, track trends, and generate actionable insights.

Conclusion

By using X Insights and a paid data service, Leo has access to a comprehensive set of data that enables him to manage Max's social media performance effectively. Through meticulous data wrangling, Leo ensures that the raw data is cleaned, organized, and made ready for analysis. By organizing the data into categories such as content type, engagement metrics, and audience segments, Leo is able to draw meaningful insights that inform Max's content strategy. This enables Max's team to continuously adapt, optimize, and maximize the impact of his social media presence in the highly competitive world of football. As Max's digital presence grows, Leo's data management processes will continue to be key in refining the social media strategy, ensuring Max remains connected to his fans while growing his personal brand both on and off the field.

As we conclude this chapter, it is evident that the unstructured nature of social media data presents unique challenges in terms of processing and interpretation (Case 4.1). Social media data are a mosaic of different information types, including text, photos, videos, and audio, with textual data being the predominant form. The process of harnessing social media data for meaningful insights necessitates its transformation from raw, unstructured form to structured format in a spreadsheet. This is a vital transformation step within the Discovery phase of the DAV Framework that is crucial for usability, analysis, and visualization. As we progress to the next chapter, our focus shifts toward the Analysis phases within the DAV Framework. We will specifically delve into text analytics to tackle the intricacies of textual data.

Chapter Summary

- Data accessibility is a fundamental aspect of data analytics.
- Social media data can be classified into several categories, each offering unique perspectives and opportunities for analysis: user engagement or behavior data, demographic data, and network data.
- The choice of where data is obtained is guided by three primary considerations: (1) the analytics goal or the research question, (2) the nature and characteristics of data sought, and (3) the available resources.
- An API is a standard interface that aids data access by providing a clear and ordered structure of an application's data.
- In addition to public APIs, web scraping is an alternative method to collect social media data.
- Ethical and legal concerns often limit the potential of web scraping.
- By exporting data, users can delve deeper into their social media performance.

- Social media listening tools are computer applications that enable organizations and businesses to understand social media activities more effectively across a variety of communication channels.
- Data wrangling is about transforming unstructured data into a more structured and usable format. Organizations and businesses can make informed decisions and stay ahead in the competitive landscape by gathering, cleaning, and organizing this data.

Questions for Review

1. What are the three major categories of social media data? How do they differ?
2. In what way does data collection via API differ from web scraping?
3. Are there any ethical and legal concerns related to social media data?
4. How does exporting data into a spreadsheet offer value?
5. What are the major steps within data wrangling?

5

Textual Data Structuring

Chapter Outline

5.1 What Is Text Analytics?
5.2 Textual Data Structuring
    5.2.1 Text Parsing and Filtering
    5.2.2 Association, Clustering, and Classification
    5.2.3 Text Normalization
    5.2.4 Keyword Identification and Frequency Analysis
    5.2.5 Named Entity Recognition and Relationship Extraction
5.3 Textual Data Structuring Tools

In the first four chapters of this book, we embarked on a journey through the "Discovery" stage of social media analytics, illuminating how data can be gathered and cleaned. The previous chapters provided a foundational comprehension of identifying and collecting relevant social media data. This chapter marks the beginning of our journey into the "Analysis" stage as we transition from Discovery to more in-depth data exploration and structuring. You may recall that Analysis is the second stage of the DAV Framework. This chapter will explore the techniques and tools that transform data into a more refined and structured format.

Social media represents one of the most innovative applications of text analytics (Ittoo et al., 2016). Social media text analytics is about extracting, analyzing, and interpreting the hidden business insights within social media content's linguistic components. Given the importance of text in social media networks, businesses are utilizing text analysis tools more frequently. These tools uncover hidden meanings, patterns, and structures within the enormous ocean of user-generated content, thereby providing invaluable business intelligence.

While images and videos are increasingly taking center stage on social media, the importance of text must not be undervalued. Text captures most of our interactions, thoughts, and opinions in the digital age. Unprecedented volumes of unstructured textual data are continuously generated on online social media.

The Data Analytics Advantage. Laeeq Khan, Oxford University Press. © Oxford University Press (2025).
DOI: 10.1093/oso/9780197814222.003.0005

User-generated textual insights abound in the social digital sphere, from sharing personal experiences about products on forums to expressing emotions on social networks. These insights can be crucial for organizations and businesses to make informed decisions and enhance customer satisfaction. The critical question is, how can we extract meaningful insights from this surge of unstructured text data? How can this textual disarray be transformed into structured, actionable intelligence?

In this chapter, we will explore different procedures for structuring textual data. These procedures and techniques serve as a form of refinement for textual data, enabling us to recognize patterns and meanings. Before we engage in text analytics, which is about interpreting textual data on social media, that data must be structured and transformed. Data structuring can be viewed as an advanced form of data cleaning, processing, and organization that lays the groundwork on which text analytics methods operate. The data structuring process typically involves various steps such as parsing or converting data from one format into another to extract relevant meaning, normalizing it (making it similar or consistent) to ensure consistency, and filtering out irrelevant or redundant elements. In the realm of analysis, we often encounter differing terms that can become a source of confusion. Before we delve into a discussion of text analytics and what it entails, we will unpack some differences between these terms.

Analysis or analytics? Although frequently used interchangeably, "text analysis" and "text analytics" differ in their methodologies for interpreting textual data. In understanding audience interactions and behavior online, social media analytics utilizes methods and techniques in both qualitative and quantitative domains.

Text analysis largely centers on qualitative text analysis, exploring its content, context, and interpretation of themes and patterns. The process involves utilizing content and thematic social data analysis techniques, typically employing a manual or subjective approach. It can be argued that text analysis focuses on comprehending the context within textual data to address the "what" and "why" elements.

On the other hand, text analytics leans toward a quantitative approach that utilizes computing power, including natural language processing (NLP), sentiment analysis, and machine learning algorithms, to handle and examine vast amounts of textual data. Text analytics emphasizes the text's quantitative components, involving the text's frequency and statistical characteristics, to address the "how much" and "how often" questions.

The objective of both text *analysis* and text *analytics* is to measure and derive insights and reveal the hidden meanings in text. Both require converting unstructured or disorganized text into organized, meaningful formats. Through this distinction, we can appreciate the mutually beneficial relationship between both fields, each making specific contributions to comprehending and applying textual information in different areas. Considering the primarily quantitative nature of social media analytics, we only use "text analytics" to refer to a bouquet of techniques and methods to derive meaning from social data.

5.1 What is Text Analytics?

"Text analytics" refers to a collection of techniques and methods to effectively interpret and understand vast amounts of written communication. Text analytics, or mining, has been defined as "the discovery by computer of new, previously unknown information by automatically extracting information from different written resources" (Hearst, 2003, p. 1). Text analytics consists of structuring textual data, extracting patterns, and interpreting data for meaningful insights.

"Text analysis," "text mining," and "text analytics" are sometimes used interchangeably to describe methodologies that help make sense of textual data. This is because text mining and analytics comprise a variety of interdisciplinary techniques and methods that not only structure and organize textual data but also interpret and comprehend its content and context—many of the various methodologies and objectives of text analytics overlap (Hearst, 2003). Data mining or text mining techniques help uncover insights through social media data that would not be visible without analysis (Barbier & Liu, 2011). The diverse interdisciplinary roots of text analytics mean that it draws strength from disciplines such as information and computer science, social science, humanities, data mining, statistics, artificial intelligence, and computational linguistics.

Like social media analytics (SMA), text analytics (a significant part of SMA) is both an art and a science, making it a unique field (Khan, 2017). It is a science because it is a systematic approach that employs empirical methods and quantifiable measures. Social media text analytics is an art because interpretative and presentation skills are combined with understanding the context and nuance of social behaviors and trends. Social media data is mostly unstructured, and dealing with this complexity requires making decisions to clean, organize, and structure the data and then interpret the vast quantity of textual data through various methods. The main challenge lies in processing unstructured data (Ittoo et al., 2016).

Text analytics has applications in numerous fields, including healthcare, finance, marketing, education, telecommunications, and government. Text analytics within social media analytics helps businesses leverage the full potential of user-generated content. For example, textual data in the form of online customer feedback can be transformed into measurable, actionable insights. Such structuring and interpretation of social media data ultimately increase productivity and comprehension for organizations and businesses. Moreover, text analytics can prove beneficial in various domains, such as email filtering, fraud detection, opinion mining, and trend analysis, among others.

As another example, Netflix uses text mining to improve the quality of its content by analyzing the enormous amount of data collected from its members (Khan & Malik, 2022). Through an analysis of text from search queries, it identifies viewer preferences, conducts sentiment analysis of reviews, and analyzes viewing patterns. Through an analysis of text, Netflix also employs text mining to identify genres and thematic elements that help the business optimize content marketing and recommendations.

Within text analytics, data structuring approaches involve preparing and arranging data, while interpretative methods for textual data focus on deriving deeper meaning and insights from structured and organized data. Both textual data structuring and interpretative methods are essential in text analytics, albeit in varying degrees and at different analysis stages. Text analytics begins with curating, preparing, or structuring data and establishing the necessary foundation. Text analytics preparatory measures guarantee the data is trustworthy and ready for nuanced analysis. On the other hand, textual interpretative methods delve deeper, exploring the text's intricate strata, extracting meaning, and deriving insights.

While Chapter 6 delves into text analytics data interpretation methods, this chapter focuses on data structuring. As we progress through this book, the reader will acquire the knowledge and skills to implement these techniques effectively, ensuring optimal outcomes from data analytics initiatives.

5.2 Textual Data Structuring

Textual data structuring or processing techniques emphasize the primary focus of basic arrangement, shaping, organization, and preparation. These data structuring or processing techniques aim to shape and refine data for subsequent advanced analysis. These techniques serve as the foundation in text analytics, preparing the dataset for a more in-depth examination. This is especially relevant when dealing with the multifaceted nature of social media data. Table 5.1 depicts the various textual data structuring techniques vital in preparing the data. The table provides a broad overview of the techniques, descriptions, purposes, and applications.

Table 5.1 Textual data structuring

	Technique	Description	Purpose	Applications
I	**Text parsing and filtering**	The process of breaking down text into manageable chunks and removing irrelevant content. Includes tokenization, eliminating stop words, and addressing textual errors.	To simplify and clean the text, making it easier to analyze.	Preprocessing for advanced analyses, data cleaning, and information extraction.
II	**Association, clustering, and classification**	Identifying relationships between and grouping similar textual elements or categorizing them into predefined groups or clusters.	To discover hidden patterns, grouping similar items, and classifying data for more straightforward analysis.	Topic modeling, customer segmentation, spam detection.
III	**Text normalization**	Standardizing textual data to reduce complexity and variability. Includes lowercasing, stemming, and lemmatization.	To create uniformity in textual data, facilitating more accurate analysis.	Text mining, advanced machine learning models, and data preprocessing for further analysis.
IV	**Keyword identification and frequency analysis**	Determining the most relevant or frequently occurring words or phrases within a text.	To highlight important terms and gauge their significance within the text.	Search engine optimization (SEO), content analysis, and trend analysis.
V	**Entity and relationship extraction**	Identifying specific entities (like names, places, dates) and their relationships or connections within the text.	To extract meaningful information about critical components and their interactions within the text.	Information retrieval, sentiment analysis.

The significance of data structuring increases when social media data is involved. Social data is diverse and can be sourced from disparate social media platforms, user community websites, customer reviews, and so forth. All such textual data is rich but often complex and unorganized. Structuring social data can involve five salient techniques: text parsing and filtering; association, clustering, and classification; text normalization; keyword and frequency identification; and entity and relationship extraction. Let us conduct a comprehensive examination of these fundamental analytic techniques.

5.2.1 Text Parsing and Filtering

Text parsing and filtering are fundamental methodologies for organizing and manipulating textual data. These data preparation techniques ensure that the text is appropriately structured for further comprehensive examination. Text parsing involves systematically deconstructing and examining a text to extract pertinent and crucial observations (Szabo et al., 2018). It entails transforming raw text from a state of disarray to a more ordered one. On the other hand, text filtering is a process that enhances text by eliminating or modifying its content, preserving just the most pertinent information for a specific objective. This procedure can potentially reduce superfluous content, improve clarity, and prepare the text for further analysis phases.

The specific techniques employed in text parsing and filtering are contingent on the nature of the task at hand, the objectives of the analysis, and the inherent attributes of the raw data. The ultimate objective is to convert unprocessed material into a succinct, targeted version appropriate for advanced analysis. Essential elements in this process include the following:

1. **Tokenization**: Tokenization is breaking down long text (such as a sentence or a paragraph) into manageable pieces. This is done so that tokens can be quickly processed for analysis. Tokenization can entail breaking sentences into words, removing punctuations, and handling special characters, symbols, or meaningful elements called tokens (Verma et al., 2014). For example, the sentence "Tokenization is important" would be divided into three tokens: "Tokenization," "is," and "important." Similarly, punctuation may be removed during the tokenization process, depending on the application. Tokenization serves as a prelude to NLP and sentiment analysis. Once you have the text corpus broken down into tokens, you can start doing exciting things like counting how many times each word appears, identifying the topic of the sentence, or even determining the sentiment expressed in the text.

2. **Eliminating stop words**: Removing stop words involves excluding these words from the text to prioritize the more significant terms that truly enhance comprehension of the core idea. Some words such as "the," "and," "is," "at," "which," and "on" do not convey much meaning besides conveying grammar or style. In text structuring and processing, these frequently encountered terms are called "stop words." The presence of stop words introduces "noise" or superfluous clutter. By eliminating stop words, we are left with more refined data with words that add to the meaning of the analysis. For example, in the context of a tweet, common words such as "is," "and," "the," and "of" may not contribute analytical value and can thus be removed from the corpus.

3. **Addressing textual errors**: Given the informal nature of social media, vernacular, abbreviations, and typographical errors are common. You can use tools to change "gr8" to "great" and "u" to "you." Similarly, eliminating irrelevant or illogical comments is essential when dealing with user-generated content. A tweet containing unintelligible text such as "asdfghjkl" or "idk" may be discarded to maintain data integrity. Addressing textual errors may be viewed as a data-cleaning endeavor of a more advanced nature than the one discussed in the previous chapter.

5.2.2 Association, Clustering, and Classification

Within text structuring, *association* enables the examination of the interrelationships between ideas in social media text discussions. *Clustering* offers insights into the dominant topics and public opinions. *Classification* aids in structuring the data into distinct groups for targeted research. Let us unpack the three techniques with the help of examples involving social media data.

Association is a text structuring technique employed to organize and connect ideas within the written text. It is used to discern the correlations among various ideas or concepts expressed in a conversation. Hence, by identifying intricate patterns within datasets (Salloum et al., 2017), one could discover, for instance, a YouTube video about the latest computer tablet users who frequently mention "battery life" in their feedback and also mention "screen brightness." By discovering conceptual linkages within text, such structuring can help brands gain a greater comprehension of user perspectives and preferences. For example, in research investigating tweets related to climate change, we employ association techniques to reveal the frequency of co-occurrence between specific terms such as "emissions" and "policy." Such co-occurrence or associations between terms within a tweet can unveil how specific facets of climate change are interlinked in the public's view and discourse.

Clustering is a text structuring technique for grouping similar entities based on specific characteristics (Fan et al., 2006). By grouping similar text based on content, data can be utilized for various purposes like thematic analysis, sentiment analysis, or simple information retrieval. Clustering, created in the pre-Internet era to group comparable documents, has since evolved and adapted to the complexities of the digital age (Jajuga et al, 2002). Within text analytics of social media data, clustering is employed for aggregating comparable posts, comments, or user profiles. Clustering organizes data dynamically based on its inherent similarities, as opposed to predefined topics. Determining the optimal number of clusters can be challenging. However, recent advancements in machine learning and artificial intelligence (AI) have opened avenues for more advanced text clustering. Clustering is indispensable in the extensive and diverse social media landscape, allowing users to access the most pertinent content efficiently.

For example, in structuring social media data, clustering entails categorizing tweets into different groups or themes based on their similarity in content, without any preexisting labels. For instance, within a given collection of tweets concerning health, clustering could uncover clear categories such as tweets centered around "effects of a healthy diet on weight," "exercise and heart health," or "sleep and health." Clustering offers a comprehensive overview of the discourse, identifying noteworthy public interest and concern areas.

Classification involves assigning entities to categories based on a predetermined set of criteria (Jajuga et al, 2002). Machine learning models are frequently incorporated into the modern analytic landscape to facilitate this process. Classification is similar to clustering but different in how categories, labels, or themes are assigned. The classification technique entails the assignment of tweets to predetermined categories or labels. Hence, the desired categories are already established, and the aim is to assign new data to these preexisting groups. For instance, tweets can be categorized into groups such as "news," "opinions," "questions," or specific sentiment classifications like "positive," "negative," and "neutral." We can safely state that sentiment analysis (discussed in Chapter 6) is a classification method within text analytics.

5.2.3 Text Normalization

When dealing with large volumes of textual data from diverse sources, text normalization is necessary for structuring data for analysis. Text normalization entails transforming text into a standardized and consistent format to enable more straightforward and efficient analysis (Szabo et al., 2018). For instance, date formats may vary within a dataset to include "1st December 2030," "December 1, 2030," and "01/12/2030." Text normalization entails the conversion of all these variants into a uniform standard format, such as MM-DD-YYYY or "12-01-2030." Other forms of text normalization can include lowercasing, removing URLs, stemming, and lemmatization.

1. **Lowercasing, removing numbers, punctuation, URLs, and HTML tags**: Lowercasing all characters in the text is a common practice to achieve consistency and decrease the dimensionality of the data. Moreover, numerical values deemed inconsequential may be excluded from consideration. In other instances, it may be necessary to employ filtering techniques to exclude unnecessary text or symbols (such as URLs and http://) and concentrate on the main content.

2. **Stemming and lemmatization**: These are text normalization techniques. Stemming refers to reducing words to their base or root by removing prefixes and suffixes from words (Szabo et al., 2018). For example, the words "hunting," "hunter," and "hunted" could be reduced to the base form "hunt." Hence, we cut down letters from the end until the stem is reached.

   Lemmatization is an advanced form of text normalization whereby we look beyond chopping off words and consider a language's comprehensive vocabulary, ensuring that the reduced word is valid per language rules (Khyani et al., 2021). Lemmatization considers a given word's part of speech to transform a word to its base form or "lemma." For example, the lemma of "went" is "go."

5.2.4 Keyword Identification and Frequency Analysis

In structuring social media data, it is vital to identify essential keywords to understand the dynamics of word frequency and appearance. The process of identifying and selecting words or phrases that are especially pertinent or significant to a given context or topic is known as keyword identification. These keywords are the primary content indicators or descriptors essential for various tasks, including content categorization, and information retrieval.

In text mining, keywords can assist in identifying the central topics or themes of a larger body of text. It is common for audiences to use these terms when searching for specific information or content. For example, keywords such as "battery life," "camera quality," and "user-friendly" uncovered on social media platforms can immediately cast light on consumer discussions and preferences, such as when analyzing feedback on a newly released smartphone.

Keyword identification relies significantly on the examination of word frequencies within a corpus. Through the analysis of word frequency in a text corpus, it is reasonable to identify the most commonly occurring terms. The rationale behind looking at word counts or frequencies is that phrases with a higher frequency of occurrence in a text are more likely to be meaningful or pertinent to the studied context. For example, suppose the word "comfortable" is frequently included in a set of internet reviews for a specific hotel. In that case, it can be recognized as a keyword indicating a prevailing mood or attribute associated with that hotel. However, further analysis may reveal that customers stated they were "not comfortable." Hence, identifying keywords and the associated frequency count helps us dig deeper into a topic of importance within social media data. As another example, a brand with a social media presence can determine which features or topics receive the most mentions through keyword identification and frequency analysis. Users mention the brand, and by analyzing these mentions, a business can gain insight into what its users value most.

Examining the occurrence rate of particular words, phrases, or hashtags in social media text can be made possible by first having the data in a spreadsheet. Various spreadsheet functions can facilitate the identification and counting of keywords. For such analyses, applications such as Microsoft Excel and Google Sheets are indispensable. To analyze the frequency of words in these spreadsheets, the following are some of the functions that may be employed:

- **Frequency count**: Create a unique inventory of words from your data. The COUNTIF function can be used with each word to determine its frequency within the dataset.
- **Word sorting**: Once the frequency has been determined, terms can be arranged in descending order to highlight the most frequent ones.
- **Pivot tables**: Pivot tables are powerful tools in spreadsheet applications that allow users to summarize and analyze large datasets efficiently. Pivot tables can enhance the analysis by dividing word counts into categories.

A research study by Xiang et al. (2015) illustrates the application of such methods. They utilized data analytics to resolve challenges in the hospitality industry, analyzing a vast corpus of Expedia.com reviews to determine the relationships

Figure 5.1 Sample word cloud

between hotel guest experiences and satisfaction scores. Their methodology included word frequencies such as "hotel" and "room," as well as many other words to provide a comprehensive view of their guest experience.

Numerous modern tools, mainly social media monitoring and other text structuring tools, generate word clouds, which are graphical representations accentuating the frequency of words. Visualization tools such as word clouds can help enhance text analysis by graphically displaying topic prominence based on term frequency, thereby assisting businesses in refining their strategic responses. However, despite the aesthetic appeal of word clouds, critics argue that these visualizations can sometimes obfuscate critical insights.

Word clouds or tag clouds display words proportionally, according to their frequency in the text (see Figure 5.1). The more frequently a word is used, the larger and more prominent it appears, providing a concise summary of the most frequently discussed topics in a text source. This method highlights the most critical aspects of a text and permits comparative analyses between distinct text fragments, thereby disclosing similarities.

5.2.5 Named Entity Recognition and Relationship Extraction

"Named entity recognition" refers to the systematic identification and categorization of critical components in text, such as individuals' names, organizational entities, geographical places, dates, monetary values, and other distinct pieces of information (Nasar et al., 2021). For example, the entities derived from the line "Nelson Mandela was born in South Africa" are "Nelson Mandela" (identified as a Person) and "South Africa" (identified as a Location).

Relationship extraction refers to detecting and extracting connections or associations between the items stated in the text (Nasar et al., 2021). The objective is to comprehend the interconnections between entities. The entities "Nelson Mandela" and "South Africa" can be linked together in a connection of "born in" inside the same sentence.

5.3 Textual Data Structuring Tools

Data cleaning, organization, and structuring are crucial steps in the text analysis process. Various tools provide a means to effectively structure and modify textual data, converting unprocessed, disorganized data into neat, organized information. Structuring textual data is crucial for academic research, business analytics, and SMA, as it forms the basis for exploration.

The data structuring tools below offer a wide range of functionalities, including simple text manipulation and advanced data cleaning and transformation capabilities. They are suitable for both novices and experienced professionals in data analytics.

1. Google Sheets

Google Sheets is a popular cloud-based spreadsheet application that efficiently organizes and manages textual data. The software provides features for manipulating text, such as dividing text into columns, finding and changing text, and doing rudimentary data cleaning, organization, and analysis. The collaborative features and add-ons of the platform, such as the ability to pull data from websites, significantly increase its functionality.

2. Microsoft Excel

Microsoft Excel (MS Excel) is a well-known spreadsheet application. It is included in the Microsoft Office 365 productivity software suite but can also be purchased separately. MS Excel is extensively used for various tasks, from fundamental data entry and accounting to advanced data analysis, charting, and financial modeling (Case Study 5.1). As a spreadsheet program, Excel operates by organizing or structuring data in rows and columns. Excel is mainly intended for numerical data, but it also offers a variety of tools and functions for text analysis. The following MS Excel functions can be used for text analysis:

- **Text functions**: Excel includes a variety of text functions that can be utilized to manage and analyze text data. For example:

- Data import and export: Excel can import text data from various sources, including .txt, .csv, and other file formats. Analysts can also export data or results for other applications or utilities.
- FIND and REPLACE can extract and locate cell-based textual data.
- CONCATENATE/CONCAT can combine two or more text strings into one string.
- TRIM can be used to remove extra spaces from text.
- LOWER, UPPER, PROPER can be employed to change the case of text.
- The COUNTIF function can determine the frequency of specific words or phrases in a range of cells for frequency analysis.
- Text filters: Excel's filter tool filters records based on specific text criteria, allowing analysts to focus on subsets of your text data.

- **Data transformation functions**: Textual data can be transformed or better structured for further analysis using the following functions in Excel:
  - TEXT TO COLUMNS: This Excel functionality separates textual data from a single column into multiple columns based on delimiters such as commas, spaces, or custom characters.
  - PIVOT TABLES: For summarizing, analyzing, exploring, and presenting a data summary. Pivot tables can assist in rapidly summarizing large quantities of textual data by displaying counts of unique text entries and other pertinent summaries.
  - Conditional formatting: This Excel functionality can emphasize cells based on particular textual characteristics or content, making it more straightforward to analyze text data visually.
  - CONCATENATE: This can combine text from multiple cells or append text to existing data.

Hence, MS Excel provides several functionalities for basic text structuring and analysis. However, it is essential to note that it has limitations, mainly when dealing with large datasets or when advanced text analytics capabilities are required. For more complex text analysis, specialized software or programming languages such as Python or R, commonly paired with NLP software, would be preferable. In the near future, the integration of artificial intelligence is set to further facilitate how users are able to engage in text structing an analysis.

3. Visual Basic

Visual Basic is a programming language developed by Microsoft. It is a component of the Microsoft Visual Studio suite. Visual Basic (VB), commonly abbreviated as VB, is designed to have a user-friendly learning curve and be accessible to novices while offering robust capabilities for advanced programmers. Visual

Basic for Programs (VBA) is a variant of the Visual Basic programming language specifically designed for use within Microsoft Office programs such as Excel. Users can generate scripts to automate recurring operations. Visual Basic (VB) has a drag-and-drop interface that simplifies designing user interfaces, allowing for convenient arrangement of application layouts. For a tutorial on textual data structuring using VBA, please see Example 5.1 on the companion website.

4. OpenRefine

OpenRefine (https://openrefine.org) is a powerful, free, open-source software designed to handle textual data. It allows users to clean, convert, and enhance data by utilizing online services and other data sources. OpenRefine is similar to spreadsheet applications in that it has a familiar interface. It is ideal for data transformation, structuring, and normalization.

Case Study 5.1 Leveraging Excel for Textual Data Structuring in an African NGO's YouTube Comments

---

As part of their mission to provide essential social services across Western Africa, a private NGO, the West Africa Social Development Network (WASDN) has embraced social media platforms, including YouTube, to spread awareness about their initiatives. The organization receives hundreds of comments on its engaging videos—mostly feedback that could offer invaluable insights into public mood and the effectiveness of their efforts. However, before any meaningful analysis could occur, the unstructured nature of this data needed to be addressed.

This case study explores how WASDN's social media analyst employed Excel to structure and prepare this textual data, ensuring it was ready for more advanced analysis. This process is critical in transforming raw, chaotic text into organized data that can yield actionable insights.

The Challenge of Unstructured Data

YouTube comments are inherently unstructured. They vary widely in length, language, tone, and relevance, making it difficult to directly analyze them for trends, sentiment, or other useful metrics. For WASDSN, this presented a significant challenge: how to efficiently organize and prepare thousands of diverse comments for further analysis.

The key issues included:

- **Irrelevant and noisy data**: Many comments were either spam or contained noninformative content such as emojis, links, or repeated phrases.
- **Inconsistent language use**: Comments were written in various languages, including slang, abbreviations, and colloquial expressions, making direct analysis challenging.
- **Volume of data**: The sheer number of comments required an approach that could handle large datasets without overwhelming the analyst.

The Role of Data Structuring

Data structuring is the process of organizing raw text into a format that allows for easy analysis. For WASDN, this meant using Excel to clean, normalize, and categorize the data, setting the stage for more advanced techniques like sentiment analysis and thematic identification.

1. **Text Parsing and Filtering**: The first step involved parsing the text to break it down into manageable parts. Using Excel's functions, the analyst could:
   - **Separate useful data**: By filtering out irrelevant content such as spam, hyperlinks, and nontext elements, the dataset became more focused on actual feedback.
   - **Separating data by language**: Although English was the main language being used in the videos, the comments were made in a variety of local languages besides English. Separating comments by language was vital for proper analysis.
   - **Identify relevant comments**: The analyst could focus on comments that directly addressed WASDN's content or services, which were most valuable for analysis.

2. **Text normalization**: Normalization is crucial for dealing with the inconsistencies in language use across comments. In Excel, this involved:
   - **Dealing with abbreviations and slang**: Common abbreviations and slang terms were expanded or standardized, ensuring that variations of the same word were treated as identical.

3. **Keyword identification**: Once the text was cleaned and normalized, the next step was to identify key terms and phrases that appeared

frequently. Using Excel's search and frequency functions, the analyst could:

- **Highlight common themes**: By identifying the most frequently used words or phrases, the analyst could start to see patterns in the data, such as recurring topics or concerns.
- **Prepare for sentiment analysis**: Keywords related to sentiment (e.g., "happy," "frustrated") were identified and categorized, laying the groundwork for later sentiment analysis.

4. **Frequency analysis**: Finally, the structured data was subjected to frequency analysis to determine how often certain words or themes appeared. This helped in:

- **Quantifying engagement**: Understanding which topics were most discussed provided insight into what issues resonated most with WASDN's audience.
- **Prioritizing content**: The frequency of certain terms helped WASDN prioritize areas for further content development or immediate attention.

By the end of this process, the analyst had transformed a chaotic collection of unstructured comments into a well-organized dataset. This structured data was then ready for more sophisticated analyses such as sentiment and thematic analyses.

This case study underscores the critical role of data structuring in the analysis of textual data. For WASDN, using Excel to parse, normalize, and categorize YouTube comments was not just a preparatory step—it was the foundation that made all subsequent analysis possible. By turning raw text into structured data, the NGO was able to extract meaningful insights that directly informed their content strategy and enhanced their ability to serve their community.

In the following chapter, we will delve deeper into the data interpretation part of text analytics.

Chapter Summary

- "Text analysis," "text mining," and "text analytics" are sometimes used interchangeably to describe methodologies that help make sense of textual data.

- Data structuring can be viewed as an advanced form of data cleaning, processing, and organization that lays the groundwork on which text analytics methods operate.
- Tokenization is breaking down long text (such as a sentence or a paragraph) into manageable pieces.
- Association is a text structuring technique used to discern the correlations among various ideas or concepts expressed in a conversation.
- Lemmatization is an advanced form of text normalization whereby we look beyond chopping off words and consider a language's comprehensive vocabulary, ensuring that the reduced word is valid per language rules.

Questions for Review

1. In what way is text analysis different from text analytics?
2. What is the critical difference between textual data structuring techniques and interpretative methods?
3. What are the different ways textual data can be structured?

6

Text Analytics Interpretative Methods and Tools

Chapter Outline

In the previous chapter, we explored textual data structuring techniques, elucidating the complexities of preparing and organizing text for text analytics. In this chapter, we will shift our focus from data structuring to data interpretation. "Text mining," "text analytics," and "data mining" are terms used interchangeably to refer to the deriving or interpreting of deeper insights from textual data. We will explore various methods that extract textual data insights, patterns, and sentiments.

Beginning with fundamental techniques such as frequency analysis and keyword extraction explored in the last chapter, we will now progress to more intricate analytics methods such as topic modeling, content analysis, and sentiment analysis. Each method will be elaborated on according to its underlying principles and potential applications. Moreover, with the help of examples, we will discuss the tools and technologies that support text processing and machine learning.

Readers will gain an understanding of the technological underpinnings that make text analytics feasible. Throughout the chapter, readers will be able to understand the practical applications of methods through case studies. By the

The Data Analytics Advantage. Laeeq Khan, Oxford University Press. © Oxford University Press (2025).
DOI: 10.1093/oso/9780197814222.003.0006

end of this chapter, readers should have a thorough understanding of the various text analytics methods and determine which technique is best suited for a given dataset or research question.

6.1 Textual Data Interpretative Methods

Textual data interpretation methods are diverse methods used to extract meaning and understanding from written text. At the core of these methods is the objective to systematically analyze and derive meaning through patterns, themes, and sentiments. Methods such as topic modeling, thematic analysis, content analysis, and sentiment analysis are essential to understand textual data. These methods are crucial in various fields, including social sciences, business, humanities, linguistics, informatics, and computer science. The applicability and use of textual interpretative methods in diverse fields reflect their interdisciplinary applicability and importance. Some interpretative methods are qualitative, while many are quantitative (see Table 6.1).

Table 6.1 provides a broad overview of all methods discussed in this chapter. Each interpretative method provides distinct insights, yet they frequently overlap and complement one another, resulting in a comprehensive understanding of texts. You will notice that within the realm of social media analytics, most of these methods are quantitative, making what is not measurable, measurable.

As digital technologies advance, the tools and methodologies for textual data interpretation become more sophisticated, opening new opportunities for research and application to decode the vast and diverse terrain of human language and communication. In our investigation of text analytics, we will examine these methods in detail as we proceed further, elucidating their central roles and practical implications.

Adopting a particular method is inherently contingent on the research project's specific objectives and the character of the dataset under consideration. An integrative approach combining these text analytics techniques enables a more nuanced understanding of the content's intrinsic composition and structure. In turn, this enables researchers and practitioners to make educated decisions regarding the utilization and interpretation of the data.

6.1.1 Topic Modeling

Within the broader realm of text analytics, various methodologies and algorithms help extract pertinent insights from vast textual datasets. One notable technique is topic modeling, rooted in computer science, which is recognized for its efficacy in deriving meaning from textual data. In the ever-changing world

Table 6.1 Textual data interpretative methods

Technique	Approach	Methodology	Applications	Output
Topic Modeling	Quantitative, algorithm-driven	Statistical algorithms to identify topics (e.g., LDA)	Large-scale text analysis, digital humanities, social media analytics	Set of topics represented by clusters of words
Thematic Analysis	Qualitative, interpretative	Manual coding and identification of patterns and themes in data	Psychology, sociology, qualitative research involving smaller datasets	Set of themes with narrative explanation
Content Analysis	Mixed (qualitative and quantitative), systematic	Systematic coding and categorizing of text to interpret meaning	Media studies & communication, journalism, business research, sociological studies, social media data	Categories, frequencies, relationships among themes or concepts
Sentiment Analysis	Quantitative, often using machine learning	Analysis of text to determine emotional tone (positive, negative, neutral)	Consumer feedback, social media monitoring, brand analysis	Scores or categories representing emotional tone of text
Engagement Analysis	Quantitative and qualitative	Analysis of user interactions and responses (likes, comments, shares)	Social media marketing, audience research data	Metrics of user engagement, patterns of interaction
Hashtag Analysis	Quantitative, sometimes qualitative	Tracking and analyzing the usage of hashtags in social media posts	Trend analysis, social media marketing, sociopolitical studies of social media text data	Trends, frequency, and context of hashtag usage
Temporal Analysis	Quantitative, time-oriented	Examination of patterns and trends over time in textual data	Historical research, trend analysis, event-based studies of textual datasets with time-stamped entries	Trends, anomalies, and patterns over specified time periods

of text analytics, topic modeling is a robust method for analyzing text, which helps identify key data characteristics and discern the primary concepts discussed within a document (Ramage et al., 2009; Karami et al., 2020; Vayansky & Kumar, 2020). As an advanced unsupervised method within machine learning, topic modeling inductively detects consistent clusters of co-occurring words in the text, proficiently unveiling latent themes and trends (Tornberg & Tornberg, 2016; Barde & Bainwad, 2017).

Topic modeling combines frequently co-occurring terms in documents, thereby revealing underlying thematic structures (Tornberg & Tornberg, 2016). These clusters correlate with distinct topics. The primary objective is to identify a set of topics that capture the essence of the text corpus. This is accomplished by determining the frequency of each word within a document. Documents are then distilled into a predetermined number of topics, ensuring that these topics remain focused without employing an excessively verbose vocabulary. Adhering to this methodology ensures that the derived topics accurately represent the document's central themes and concepts (Ramamonjisoa, 2014).

To further comprehend the utility of topic modeling, consider navigating a massive jigsaw puzzle with countless pieces while attempting to ascertain the overall picture without tedious assembly. In this case, topic modeling functions as a guide, providing intuitive insights and indicating the potential presence of patterns or themes, such as a beach scene or a celebration within the puzzle. When online textual content proliferates exponentially, deciphering overarching themes is analogous to putting together this puzzle. Millions of individuals voice their opinions online daily, making it a daunting task to identify prevalent conversations painstakingly. Here, topic modeling acts as a discerning eye, sifting through the ocean of digital expressions to highlight the central "pictures" or "themes." Similarly, it is essential to understand the central themes to write concise summaries of documents.

The method is especially effective when applied to textual data from social media platforms like X (Hong & Davison, 2010). In big data, manually filtering through such data to identify patterns is nearly impossible due to the data's overwhelming volume and complexity. However, topic modeling makes it possible to quickly identify prevalent conversations, particularly during significant events or trending occurrences.

Topic modeling must be approached with caution. Despite its wide range of applications in disciplines ranging from sociology to linguistics, it presents obstacles. Some models, as indicated by Gerlach et al. (2018), struggle with quantifying the optimal topic count, and occasionally, the statistical properties of particular texts do not align flawlessly with expected models. Nevertheless, the overall effectiveness of topic modeling makes the method well-adapted across varied disciplines.

Various topic modeling methods have been developed to account for diverse relationships and constraints inherent in datasets. One widely used method with topic modeling is LDA or latent Dirichlet analysis (Vayansky & Kumar, 2020). LDA is a prominent technique within the vast discipline of topic modeling (Blei et al., 2003). It is based on the premise that each document within a dataset can be described as a mixture of various topics. A topic in this context is not merely a collection of terms but a probability distribution of vocabulary words. Through its sophisticated mechanism, LDA examines the frequency of words across documents to identify diverse topics, effectively constructing a thematic mosaic representing the entire dataset.

LDA has undergone numerous modifications and expansions over the years. Notable is the fact that its adaptations have played a pivotal role in areas such as social media research. Topic modeling within the domain of social media aids in deducing user interests from their postings, shaping insights into social interactions, tracking news trends, and highlighting emergent discussions (Hong & Davison, 2010). Topic modeling is fundamentally quantitative and computational. It utilizes algorithms rather than human intuition to identify topics in large text corpora. Hence, topic modeling is algorithmic and quantitative.

6.1.2 Thematic Analysis

The purpose of both topic modeling and thematic analysis is to identify patterns and themes within the text (Case Study 6.1). However, their approaches diverge significantly. A significant difference between the two methods is related to scale. Typically, topic modeling is applied to large datasets, whereas thematic analysis is more suited to smaller datasets where the emphasis is on depth of understanding.

Case Study 6.1 Data Analysts in Ohio Decode Climate Change Discussions on YouTube Using Topic Modeling

---

In 2025, a global climate change documentary series was released on YouTube, aiming to educate audiences about the most pressing environmental issues of our time. The series covered critical topics such as glacier melting, deforestation, ocean acidification, urban pollution, and climate justice. The documentary series featured expert interviews, eye-opening visuals of environmental degradation, and a call to action for governments, industries, and individuals to address the climate crisis. The documentary received significant attention across different countries, including Germany, Nigeria, Brazil, Australia, and India. These nations, with diverse environmental challenges, contributed a wide range of comments that provided valuable insight into public discussions regarding climate change.

A group of data analysts in Athens, Ohio, USA, wanted to study the concerns and hopes of the global audiences surrounding issue of climate change. They analysts believed that their endeavor would inform environmental NGOs (such as Greenpeace) and policymakers, aiding their advocacy and public outreach efforts. Hence, they wanted to understand the prevalent themes within the YouTube community regarding a climate change documentary series.

Methodology

Data was collected utilizing YouTube's API to collect comments on multiple videos of the documentary series. The dataset consisted of 100,000+ user comments from viewers located across various countries. The collected data contained a rich diversity of opinions, from concerns about specific environmental issues to requests for immediate action or hopes for technological solutions. In total, over 500,000 words were collected across multiple languages, including English, Portuguese, German, and Hindi.

Comments were processed or structured to standardize text and prepare for analysis. To explore the data in-depth, topic modeling was employed to identify the dominant themes within the viewer comments. This analysis aimed to extract actionable insights about the issues that were most concerning to viewers, as well as the overall tone of the discussions—whether they leaned toward urgency, hope, frustration, or optimism.

RapidMiner, a software application known for its proficiency in managing textual data and extracting topics, was employed to make sense of data. RapidMiner's text analysis functionality is capable of, among other things, tokenizing (splitting it into words), removing overly common words (stop words), locating the roots of words (stemming), and locating phrases in the documents prior to generating the word frequency table that describes the relative importance of words in documents. The analysis revealed the most prevalent topics and the dominant discussions through topic modeling.

Findings

Four dominant topics or themes emerged from the analysis of the comments:

- **Topic A: Disappearing glaciers**. Keywords: "ice," "melting," "polar," and "glaciers."

- **Topic B: Deforestation.** Keywords: "trees," "Amazon," "logging," and "forests."
- **Topic C: Ocean-related concerns**; Keywords: "ocean," "coral," "acid," and "sea life."
- **Topic D: Urban pollution.** Keywords: "smog," "cars," "cities," and "pollution."

These themes align closely with environmental issues faced by countries like Brazil, Nigeria, Australia, India, and Germany. The findings from this analysis are valuable for organizations like Greenpeace, which has long advocated for environmental protection and sustainability. By understanding the concerns expressed by global audiences, NGOs and policymakers can tailor their advocacy efforts to address the most pressing issues raised by the public, driving more focused and impactful climate action campaigns.

Implications and Conclusion

The analysis of viewer comments on the climate change documentary series revealed a number of significant themes that reflect public concern about climate change and its consequences. Findings can prove useful in the following key ways:

- **Content strategy**: Understanding that urban pollution is a pressing concern for the documentary's audience could influence the themes of future episodes or intensify the focus on solutions related to urban pollution.
- **Policy and advocacy**: Policymakers and environmental activists can use these insights to highlight urban pollution in their campaigns or policies, knowing that it is a topic that resonates with a substantial online community.
- **Business choices**: This information can be utilized by businesses, particularly those in the environmental solutions industry, to align their product or service strategies and tailor their offerings to resolve concerns about urban pollution.

The efficacy of topic modeling, particularly when combined with robust tools such as RapidMiner, provides a unique perspective on the collective concerns of an online community. In this instance, by analyzing YouTube comments, analysts were able to extract actionable insights into the public's perspective on climate change. These methodologies can serve as guides for content creators, policymakers, and businesses to remain attuned to the digital audience's pulse.

In social sciences, thematic analysis, which is profoundly entrenched in qualitative research, is frequently the method of choice. It thrives on analyzing data from sources such as interviews, using a systematic categorization procedure to identify patterns. Thematic analysis is thus human-centered and qualitative. Due to its qualitative nature, thematic analysis frequently yields more profound and nuanced data insights. Thematic analysis can be performed manually or with software for qualitative data analysis, such as NVivo or Atlas.ti.

6.1.3 Content Analysis

Content analysis is an increasingly critical element in text analytics, allowing both academic and business sectors to extract profound insights from diverse textual sources. The essence of this method is its systematic, objective, and frequent quantitative analysis of the characteristics of textual, visual, and auditory messages. Extending to news articles, website comments, videos, and social media postings, content analysis meticulously analyzes patterns within these messages to provide a clear comprehension of inherent themes, biases, or intentions.

The origins of content analysis can be traced back to the 17th century, although, in that age, the method was not necessarily systematic in the modern sense. In the 19th century, content analysis of historical documents may have laid the foundation of modern-day content analysis. The advent of newspapers in the 20th century, which coincided with the mass production of printed materials, led to increased demand for quantitative analysis of printed words.

Influential scholars, such as Holsti (1969) and Krippendorff (2004), have emphasized that content analysis goes beyond superficial textual content analysis to discover hidden meanings. Holsti (1969) advocates using latent content analysis, which uses inference and interpretation to go beyond the surface-level meaning and reveal hidden themes, emotions, and cognitive processes. Krippendorff (2004) emphasizes the significance of validity and reliability in content analysis, contending that a thorough study necessitates meticulous consideration of the text's context, purpose, and audience, as well as the researcher's prejudices. Based on the need for reliability and validity, Krippendorff (2004) presents coding strategies and reliability criteria to guarantee the coherence and accuracy of interpretations. Thus, Content analysis is a rigorous method researchers employ to derive meaningful insights from vast amounts of textual data. According to Weber (1990), the crux of content analysis is the categorization and organization of qualitative data to identify distinct themes and comprehend their relationships.

6.1.3.1 Methodological Approaches for Content Analysis

Manual coding: Coding, a crucial aspect of content analysis, facilitates the classification and organization of qualitative data. Here, labels (words, numbers, or phrases) are designated to significant themes within the responses, condensing massive quantities of text into manageable categories. The manual classification procedure involves:

- Choosing an appropriate coding strategy, which can be deductive (applying preestablished codes to the data) or inductive (developing codes based on the data).
- Familiarizing oneself with the dataset to develop an initial set of codes, which involves thoroughly examining and interpreting the data.
- Coding data systematically with continuous refinement of the codes to ensure specificity and relevance.
- Organizing codes coherently by categorizing them hierarchically or thematically.

Given the vast quantity of available textual data, there has been a pressing need for methodological advancements. This is especially pertinent when dealing with large textual datasets where traditional hand-coding methods are impractical (DiMaggio et al., 2013).

Automated content analysis: With the introduction of computer science techniques, computational methods for content analysis have gained significance. Computers automate the categorization of documents, efficiently manage large datasets, and generate descriptive data such as word frequency (Van Der Meer, 2016). Nonetheless, these tools frequently employ the "bag of words" methodology, prioritizing word frequency (Schwartz & Ungar, 2015). Consequently, while they increase reproducibility and decrease bias, they may occasionally compromise the profundity of insights.

6.1.3.2 Content Analysis of Social Media Data

Given the proliferation of social media, specialized techniques like named entity recognition (NER) and text classification have emerged. These aid in extracting specific entities from textual data and classifying content based on predetermined criteria. Such methodologies allow researchers to derive insights from large quantities of data by identifying prevalent themes or frequently discussed entities.

Currently, the overwhelming quantity of textual data has prompted methodological changes. Such changes have been in the form of a shift toward automated content analysis and the rise of machine learning, deep learning, and artificial intelligence (AI). Traditional hand-coding appears impractical when applied to enormous datasets. Both supervised and unsupervised automatic text analysis offer promising avenues, albeit with their own challenges, such as defining categories in advance or determining the number of categories post hoc.

In conclusion, content analysis continues to be an indispensable method for gleaning insights from textual data. Whether performed manually or with the aid of sophisticated computational tools, the true power of content analysis resides in the complex combination of data, methodology, and human comprehension. As technology advances further and more textual data is generated, the methods and techniques of content analysis will continue to evolve, ensuring its continued relevance to the field of research. The essence of content analysis is its systematic, objective, and frequently quantitative analysis of the characteristics of textual, visual, and auditory messages.

6.1.3.3 The Coding Process for Content Analysis

The initial phase is the collection of relevant data. Once obtained, the data should be thoroughly evaluated, cleaned, and related to the research objectives and queries. Next is the development of coding units. A coding unit is the smallest unit that can be analyzed. For example, the number of words of praise within a text would be a coding unit. During this phase, coding units are produced, and textual data are then encoded according to the specified codes.

After coding, instances are quantified to derive statistical insights. Coding is fundamentally concerned with classifying and organizing qualitative insights. By assigning specific labels or identifiers to particular words or phrases within responses, it becomes possible to generate a comprehensive summary of textual results. During this process, identifiers, which may be words, phrases, or numbers, are assigned to prominent themes in each response. As codes, it is best to use single words or short phrases for optimal recall and organization. Table 6.2 depicts a sample coding scheme for content analysis of social media data. The matrix showcases how codes are applied to different segments of the data. These are assigned in a spreadsheet such as Google Sheets or MS Excel. The capabilities of a spreadsheet where data can be further sorted and analyzed increase the utility of social media content analysis as a mixed methods approach.

Table 6.2 Sample coding scheme for tweets

Gender & Organization	Occupation	News link shared	Information seeking	Information sharing	Image shared	Video
1: Male 2: Female 3: Organizations, companies, clubs, groups, services. 0: Not provided or not recognizable	1: Mass media person/figure (journalist, TV anchor, radio presenter, filmmaker) 2: Media organization (TV station, newspaper, media house, production company, magazines, film studios) 3: Lay person (commoners, amateur, just someone who is interested) 4: Politician or political worker (somebody who identifies him/herself as a politician or someone who is holding political office, or a political worker) 5: Government officials, govt. entities, and armed forces (central government)	1: The tweet content a link to a news article (can be video or a text article) 0: No news link shared	1: The tweet content indicates seeking of some form of support. Look for keywords such as donate, give, share, etc. 0: No Mention of support seeking	1: If some form of information is shared about the issue) 0: No Information shared	1: The tweet contains some image or photo (e.g., an image of the product). This includes both system-generated images from the link or separate images. 0: No Photos shared	1: The tweet contains a video. 0: No video shared

6.1.4 Sentiment Analysis

Sentiment analysis, also known as "opinion mining," systematically identifies, extracts, and interprets the emotional nuances embedded in textual content (Pang & Lee, 2008). Sentiment analysis employs natural language processing, text analysis, and computational linguistics to extract, quantify, and interpret nuances within text. The utility of sentiment analysis extends across different fields, such as consumer feedback in business and marketing, patient data in healthcare, audience engagement on online platforms and social media, and so forth.

Sentiment analysis is a branch of text mining that utilizes natural language processing (NLP) to detect and classify opinions conveyed in text (Thelwall, 2016). Its primary objective is to ascertain whether the writer's sentiment toward a specific subject, product, and so on, is positive, negative, or neutral. Accurate sentiment analysis requires a comprehensive evaluation of context and linguistic interaction. Herein resides the value of semantics, a branch of linguistics concerned with meaning within language. Certain grammatical structures, idioms, and expressions highlight the need for deep semantic analysis to capture sentiments that surface-level interpretations might miss.

Understanding audience sentiment is essential for brands. Continuous monitoring through sentiment analysis can reveal evolving consumer preferences, identify emerging trends, and proactively address concerns. This feedback loop enables brands to anticipate concerns, refine messaging, and prevent potential crises.

In an increasingly digital marketplace, the ability to analyze and adapt to public sentiment is a key competitive differentiator. By leveraging these insights, brands can refine their engagement strategies, foster trust, and position themselves for sustained success in dynamic environments.

6.1.4.1 Principal Elements of Sentiment Analysis

a. **Classifying polarity**: Determining the sentiment polarity of a text, whether at the document, sentence, or feature/aspect level, is a fundamental task in sentiment analysis. The purpose is to determine whether the opinion conveyed is positive, negative, or neutral. For instance, consider:
   - Positive words: adore, incredible, finest, ideal
   - Negative words: evil, horrible, dreadful, worst, loathe
b. **Beyond polarity**: Advanced sentiment classification probes deeper into emotional states such as happiness, rage, disgust, dread, and astonishment.
c. **Sentiment scaling**: An alternative method employs a system that assigns numerical values to words (Thelwall, 2016). For example, from −10 (the most negative) to +10 (the most positive). This scale facilitates the

adjustment of the sentiment of a term with its context, typically at the sentence level (Thelwall, 2016). When an unstructured text is analyzed, each concept is scored based on the relationships between sentiment words and their respective scores (Taboada et al., 2011).

6.1.4.2 Sentiment and Social Media

The introduction and subsequent proliferation of social media platforms have increased the value of sentiment analysis. Through evaluations, ratings, and recommendations, online opinions have become a form of virtual currency. Organizations and businesses can use sentiment-based information to strategize their marketing, seize opportunities, and protect their reputations. Sentiment analysis within social media empowers various entities, including government agencies and commercial enterprises, to actively observe and comprehend the public's sentiment in real time. This enables these organizations to assess the effectiveness of marketing campaigns, determine consumer sentiment, detect changes in public opinion, forecast market trends, and even electoral results by analyzing the public's online expressions of sentiment.

As described by Karami et al. (2020), sentiment analysis relies on employing advanced NLP methods to ascertain the emotions expressed in social media content. It goes beyond a basic numerical tally of mentions by striving to uncover the underlying emotions. Despite its revolutionary potential, sentiment analysis faces challenges in the form of contextual and emotional variability, sarcasm, and dialectic variability. Let's explore each of these in further detail.

- **Contextual variability**: The meaning of words can change based on their context (Thelwall et al., 2011). For example, the sentiment conveyed by the statement "my internet service provider excels at taking my money" could be interpreted in various ways.
- **Emotionally charged yet neutral phrases**: Some expressions may not convey a feeling despite containing emotionally charged terms. The phrase "Can you suggest a good tool?" contains the word "good" but lacks emotional connotation.
- **Sarcasm**: In sarcasm, words express an emotion, but the underlying sentiment is contradictory, as in "I love it when my computer crashes during an assignment."
- **Dialectic variations**: Words like "sick" can have varying meanings based on context or region.

When evaluating the effectiveness of sentiment analysis tools, their capacity to precisely detect and categorize the emotional tone of textual information is considered. Achieving an accuracy rate ranging from 70% to 90% is commendable within the present domain of sentiment analysis technologies (Liu, 2022). Human language is intricate, encompassing cultural terms, idiomatic expressions, sarcasm, and subtle, context-specific sentiments. Deciphering these complexities is challenging.

6.1.4.3 Sentiment and Artificial Intelligence

In several industries, AI has emerged as an agent of change, advancing innovation and enhancing overall performance. Among the numerous applications of AI, sentiment analysis stands out as a field that has benefited significantly from these innovations. Historically, traditional sentiment analysis methods focused on identifying specific words labeled as positive or negative. However, such methods could be rudimentary and insufficient, failing to capture the nuances and complexities of human emotions, mainly when context-dependent words convey distinct emotions.

Sentiment analysis has been revolutionized by AI's capacity to learn from immense quantities of data and mimic cognitive functions (Taherdoost & Madanchian, 2023). AI digs deeper than merely identifying whether certain words in a text convey a positive or negative sentiment. It comprehends the entire statement's tone and effectively grasps the underlying sentiment. This is crucial in circumstances where the meaning of individual statements may be misconstrued if taken out of context. For example, the phrase "You are sick!" could be an expression of concern or a vernacular compliment, depending on the tone and context, a distinction that AI is becoming increasingly adept at making.

Incorporating AI into sentiment analysis enables more precise, context-aware, and adaptable analysis (Case Study 6.2). AI systems can refine their understanding of sentiments through iterative learning processes or machine learning, considering sarcasm, cultural nuances, and evolving language trends. The combination of AI and sentiment analysis exemplifies the expanding capacity of technology to comprehend and mimic human cognitive processes. As AI develops, sentiment analysis tools are expected to be even more refined, nuanced, and contextually appropriate, bridging the divide between machine recognition and human emotion.

Case Study 6.2 Leveraging Sentiment Analysis to Improve the Membership Experience at Vitality Peak Fitness

Customer feedback is essential for businesses to adapt and flourish in the digital age. Vitality Peak Fitness, a premier fitness facility in Christchurch,

New Zealand, acknowledges the significance of this feedback. To gain actionable insights, the business utilized the SentiStrength sentiment analysis tool, focusing specifically on Facebook feedback. The business had a large fan following of about 5,000 members who used its facilities in six major locations across the city.

The primary objective was to assess member satisfaction, identify areas for development, and then tailor services to better accommodate member preferences. For this purpose, the SentiStrength sentiment analysis instrument was chosen.

Methodology

Data Collection: Through its social media, namely its Facebook page, Vitality Peak Fitness actively solicited feedback from its members. This feedback covered a wide range of topics, including equipment efficiency, a variety of fitness training, and the overall atmosphere.

Analysis of sentiment utilizing SentiStrength: The collected textual feedback in the form of user comments was analyzed with the SentiStrength tool, which is capable of classifying sentiments from extremely negative to extremely positive.

Strategic management: The management identified prevalent trends and patterns using SentiStrength's insights, allowing them to resolve specific areas of concern.

Key Insights

A significant fraction of members expressed satisfaction with the quality and condition of the equipment, highlighting its modernity and consistent maintenance. However, a few indicated the need for improvement in weight organization. The desire for prolonged operational hours, particularly on weekends, to accommodate a variety of schedules was a recurring theme in customer feedback. While the existing fitness trainings were well-received, there was a demand for a broader range of fitness classes tailored to different age groups.

Members' concerns regarding the facility's hygiene were a significant finding from X feedback collected by SentiStrength. This negative sentiment was an important discovery.

Armed with SentiStrength data, Vitality Peak Fitness implemented the following actions:

- Improving its equipment maintenance protocols.
- Extended business hours, especially on the weekends.

> • Introduced a broader selection of fitness classes to meet the unique needs of its members.
> • Implemented stricter hygiene and sanitation measures in response to the sanitary concerns.
>
> The strategic deployment of the SentiStrength sentiment analysis tool enabled Vitality Peak Fitness to gain a deeper understanding of the preferences and concerns of its members. By proactively resolving these insights, the business not only increased member satisfaction, but also strengthened its reputation as a responsive and member-centric organization that was set to grow further.

6.1.5 Audience Engagement Analytics

Understanding engagement is essential in assessing the effectiveness of social media content (Kietzmann et al., 2011). By analyzing key indicators such as views, likes, comments, shares, and retweets, organizations can determine the level of engagement and interest among their target demographics (Khan, 2017; see Case Study 6.3). High levels of engagement indicate a higher level of content resonance with the audience, whereas low levels of engagement may necessitate a reevaluation of the content or messaging strategy.

Audience engagement varies across social platforms. Not all engagement types hold the same value. For example, while a like may indicate casual or conversely a deeper endorsement, a high share count suggests resonance and insightful comments may indicate even deeper engagement. Consider how LinkedIn's professional networking environment and thoughtful writing process make comments more valuable than simple "likes." Conversely, on TikTok, views and likes are more significant indicators of audience involvement due to shorter attention spans and the inherently visual nature of the platform focused on short-form videos.

A study by Rietveld et al. (2020) highlights the significance of content design in fostering customer interaction on visually driven social media platforms. They discovered that emotional content elicits a more engaging response from viewers in comparison to purely informational content. Many medium to large businesses are allocating significant sections of their marketing efforts to platforms like Instagram, Facebook, Pinterest, and LinkedIn, acknowledging the importance of social media engagement as a crucial marketing indicator. This investment aims to create content that effectively utilizes these emotional motivators to enhance customer engagement and, eventually, to attain marketing triumph.

It is known that platform algorithms also influence the value of different interactions. A strategic approach to understanding these subtleties can stimulate significant engagement and foster a dynamic community. Hence, it is crucial to understand the context of engagement, the platform, and audience traits before measuring audience engagement.

6.1.5.1 Analyzing Data on Audience Engagement

Examining data on audience engagement requires a systematic approach to comprehending the interactions between audiences and content on different social media platforms. Quantifying the success of social media campaigns and optimizing engagement approaches is essential for organizations, businesses, or anyone interested in analyzing their social media presence.

Audience engagement analytics starts by gathering engagement indicators, including likes, comments, shares, view length, and click-through rates. Analysts utilize various techniques and methods to analyze and examine these indicators or engagement metrics. The knowledge acquired from these assessments may guide the formulation of content production strategies, modifications to marketing campaigns, and even the enhancement of product development. The goal is to analyze engagement metrics and convert these numbers into practical insights that drive an organization's social media influence forward.

The relevant social media metrics may vary depending on a company's goals and the platforms on which it engages. If the objective is to determine how an audience reacts to a brand's content, the most important engagement metrics to track are likes, comments, direct messages, shares, and saves. Using metrics such as user count, page views, session durations, and conversions, Google Analytics can be utilized to evaluate website engagement. Platforms like YouTube offer extensive engagement analytics, displaying metrics such as when users stop viewing a video.

Before we discuss the methods for audience engagement, let us shed light on the salient engagement metrics, which can be categorized as follows:

- **Applause rate**: Likes, reactions, and favorites, which indicate favorable user feedback.
- **Comment rate**: Comment and reply rate, which measures user responses. Such data is textual.
- **Amplification rate**: Shares and retweets, which indicate the content's virality potential.

Overall engagement provides a comprehensive view of user interactions throughout the report, taking into account factors such as likes and shares. Overall engagement is often offered as a combined and already calculated metric on native analytics tools such as Facebook Insights.

There are other metrics that can be calculated based on the available data.

- **Follower growth**: The number of net new followers during a given time period. Along with the growth rate, this metric provides insight into the efficacy of content strategies and campaigns. Rapid expansion can indicate a high ROI for specific content varieties and initiatives.
- **Awareness metrics**: These metrics connect your social media marketing strategy to the brand awareness it generates. Impressions (how often a post is displayed), reach (potentially unique viewers), video views, and brand mentions are notable metrics for brand awareness.

Now that we have established the different types of engagement metrics, let us delve into the various methods employed to assess audience engagement on social media. Most of the analyses for audience engagement are descriptive. However, it is also possible to conduct a more advanced form of analysis which is predictive or prescriptive.

1. **Descriptive analysis**: As evident from the name, a descriptive analysis describes and summarizes the main characteristics of data. This entails computing the total number of likes, comments, and shares for social media engagement data. Descriptive analysis can also include computing means, frequencies, and other descriptive measures for various forms of engagement.
2. **Correlational analysis**: A correlational analysis investigates the relationship between two or more variables. For social media engagement metrics, correlational analysis is employed to evaluate the connections between various forms of interaction. This entails employing statistical techniques to ascertain the presence and nature of relationships between various engagement measures.
3. **Predictive modeling**: This involves the application of statistical models and machine learning algorithms to forecast engagement levels or identify the elements that have the greatest impact on engagement, such as post timing, content type, or platform characteristics.
4. **A/B testing**: This is a method used to perform controlled trials by manipulating individual variables (such as post time, hashtags, or content kind) to methodically ascertain their impact on engagement.

6.1.5.2 Measuring Audience Engagement in a Spreadsheet

Measuring audience engagement metrics in a spreadsheet can be informative and efficient, especially when the size of data is manageable. The procedure entails recording specific data points and then using the spreadsheet's built-in functions to calculate the desired metrics. Here are a few steps:

1. Create a new spreadsheet (using Excel or Google Sheets).
2. Label columns with the data elements you wish to monitor, such as "Date," "Post Title," "Likes," "Comments," "Shares," "Clicks," "Views," and any other pertinent metrics. You can freeze the header row (the row on top).
3. Logging data and Collection: Analysts can input data regularly for each post or piece of content. Data entry can be performed on a daily, weekly, or monthly basis. Alternatively, collected social media data can be analyzed for engagement if any of the engagement metrics are included in the dataset.
4. Calculate engagement rates: To compute the engagement rate for a single metric, use the following formula to determine the engagement rate for likes:

   (Number of Likes/Total Reach or Views) * 100.

   For instance, if a post has 100 likes and was viewed 1,000 times, the engagement rate would be 10%.
5. Calculate overall engagement rate: To get a holistic view, an analyst may want to consider multiple metrics. For example:

$$(Likes + Comments + Shares) / (Total\ Reach\ or\ Views)^* 100$$

However, as discussed above, engagement metrics are not equal, therefore, we can assign weightages to each and then compute an overall engagement rate. For example, if we consider that comments and shares indicate a deeper level of engagement than likes, we might weight them more heavily. Here is a suggested formula for calculating a combined engagement score with higher weightage for comments and shares:

Overall Engagement Rate (OER) with weightages:

$$(OER) = (L \times W_L) + (C \times W_C) + (S \times W_S)$$

Where:

L is the number of likes and W_L is the weightage assigned to the like (e.g., 1)

C is the number of comments and W_C is the weightage assigned to the comments (e.g., 3)

S is the number of shares and W_S is the weightage assigned to the shares (e.g., 5)

Assigning weights is important because it can help ascertain the dollar value that can be hypothetically assigned to each like.

6. Compute growth rate: Formula for calculating the *growth rate* of specific metrics (e.g., followers, subscribers):

$$\frac{(\text{Previous Month's Metric} - \text{Current Month's Metric})}{\text{Current Month's Metric}^* 100}$$

Further analyses can also be conducted. The spreadsheet's *conditional formatting* feature can be used to highlight posts with above-average engagement rates. This can help quickly identify high-performing content. Using pivot tables in Excel can help break down engagement rates by categories, such as type of post (video, image, text), author, or any other segmentation relevant to the strategy.

Case Study 6.3 Enhancing Customer Engagement and Visibility for a Family-Owned Pakistani Restaurant in Ottawa Through Instagram

---

Introduction

This case study showcases a family-owned authentic Pakistani restaurant in Ottawa, Canada. The restaurant aims to improve its customer engagement and visibility by utilizing the social media platform Instagram. The restaurant owner's daughter, Sarah, was a data enthusiast, passionate about utilizing social media data to bolster the restaurant business. As an undergraduate student, Sarah had honed her analytics skills in a social media analytics course at her university. Her expertise in tracking and analyzing social media data has helped elevate the restaurant's online presence and foster a deeper connection with its audience.

Data Management Process

Sarah utilizes Instagram's native insights tool to monitor and analyze the performance of the restaurant's posts and Instagram Stories. Each week, she reviews metrics such as impressions, reach, engagement rate, and the overall performance of both photos and videos (Reels). She pays close attention to how food photography, in particular, drives engagement. The engagement rate provides her with an idea of the top-performing image posts. She keeps track of this data in a spreadsheet, which helps her take a deeper dive into the analysis. She measures engagements with tweets that feature hashtags. The restaurant's food-centric content, especially images and videos with related hashtags featuring signature dishes like Sindhi Biryani, Kabuli Pulao, Chapli Kebab, Beef Nihari, and Karachi Bun Kebab, consistently performs well.

Social Data Evaluation

Sarah dives into the data by evaluating the following Instagram metrics:

- **Engagement metrics**: She tracks likes, comments, shares, and saves, paying special attention to which posts generate the highest engagement. Reels featuring mouthwatering food photography tend to attract the most attention, with users often tagging friends or commenting on the vibrant colors and details of the dishes.
- **Reach and impressions**: Sarah monitors the reach (the number of unique accounts that have seen a post) and impressions (total number of times posts have been displayed) to determine how well content is spreading. High-performing posts often correlate with specific hashtags related to the restaurant's signature dishes, such as #SindhiBiryani, #KarachiBunKabab, and #OttawaFoodies.
- **Audience demographics**: Using Instagram's insights, Sarah examines the demographic data of users engaging with the restaurant's posts. This includes age, gender, location, and other interests. The data helps her tailor content to appeal to specific audiences, such as food enthusiasts in Ottawa or Pakistani cuisine lovers.
- **Content analysis**: Sarah also closely analyzes the visual elements of successful posts. High-quality food photography, often showcasing vibrant, well-lit images of the restaurant's dishes, consistently yields strong engagement. Additionally, Reels that show behind-the-scenes cooking processes or highlight customer experiences have garnered positive feedback and boosted interaction.
- **Best time to post**: By analyzing the time of day and day of the week when posts receive the most engagement, Sarah optimizes the restaurant's posting schedule to maximize visibility. For instance, posts about lunch specials tend to perform better when shared mid-morning, while evening posts about dinner options get more engagement around dinnertime.

Refining Strategy with Insights

By carefully analyzing Instagram data, Sarah has been able to fine-tune the restaurant's social media strategy. For instance, she discovered that posts showcasing traditional Pakistani dishes with bold, colorful photography generate more engagement compared to generic images of food. This insight led her to prioritize the use of vibrant, close-up food shots that highlight textures and ingredients.

In addition to static images, Instagram Reels have become a key part of the restaurant's content strategy. Sarah found that Reels showcasing the preparation of dishes or customer reactions to their meals perform especially well, further boosting the restaurant's visibility.

> The use of location tags and popular local hashtags has also helped expand the restaurant's reach within Ottawa's food community. Partnering with local food influencers and getting featured in Instagram Stories has driven additional foot traffic and raised awareness.
>
> Conclusion
> Through a data-driven approach to Instagram, Sarah has helped the family restaurant refine its online presence, improve customer engagement, and increase visibility in Ottawa's competitive food scene. By analyzing food photography performance, audience behavior, and engagement metrics, the restaurant can continuously optimize its content strategy. The combination of Sarah's data insights, the restaurant's culinary expertise, and high-quality content has created a strong synergy that drives the restaurant's continued success. Instagram's analytics tools have proven to be invaluable in navigating customer preferences, optimizing posting schedules, and refining marketing strategies. This approach ensures the restaurant stays relevant in the ever-changing social media landscape, fostering deeper connections with both existing and potential customers.

6.1.6 Hashtag Analytics

Hashtags, denoted by "#," have become essential for categorizing and linking content across the extensive social media landscape. It is believed that the concept was introduced by Chris Messina on Twitter on August 23, 2007, to streamline topic discussions (Cooper, 2013). This elementary innovation revolutionized user engagement with content by simplifying the categorization and monitoring of keywords. Hashtags can also be considered an engagement metric, but because they are so important they are discussed separately.

Over time, hashtags have expanded beyond their initial confines on Twitter (now X), establishing a presence on multiple social media platforms. Hashtags are hyperlinked, and clicking on a hashtag directs users to a curated collection of public posts tagged with that hashtag, nurturing a streamlined browsing experience and community engagement on topics or interests in common. Hashtags in the digital landscape provide multiple benefits. They increase a post's reach and engagement by connecting users with similar interests. In addition, they have become an essential element of a successful organic social media strategy. As described by Bruns and Moe (2014), Twitter hashtags serve as a "macro" layer of communication that streamlines conversations around specific topics and themes (p. 16). Due to the numerous channels of information dissemination, however, not everyone has the same experience with hashtags.

The true potency of a hashtag rests not only in its application but also in its influence. Intensive monitoring and analysis of a hashtag can provide in-depth insights into its effectiveness, enabling strategic adjustments. This process has been expedited by tools such as Hashtagify and Keyhole, which provide insights into hashtag application, context, and user dynamics.

In the modern digital landscape, content categorization is crucial for optimizing visibility and engagement. In other words, there are various types of hashtags. Categorizing hashtags is an effective strategy for understanding audience interactions on social media (Nam et al., 2017). Some of the hashtag categories are as follows:

- **General hashtags**: These are general terms that can be incorporated into posts in order to increase their visibility.
- **Brand-centric hashtags**: For example, terms such as #JustDoIt by @Nike highlight and advocate for the brand's identity and guiding principles.
- **Trending terms**: These terms reflect ongoing events or extensive discussions in real time.
- **Event-related hashtags**: Specifically formulated for specific occasions, they enhance the discourse surrounding them.
- **Campaign hashtags**: These terms are customized for specific marketing campaigns, generating intrigue for distinct brand initiatives.

To analyze these categories, we can follow an approach similar to that used for engagement metrics, discussed above. Spreadsheet applications such as Microsoft Excel and Google Sheets can be very helpful in extracting and analyzing hashtags in terms of their frequency, types, associations, and so forth.

6.1.7 Temporal Analysis

Temporal analysis is the methodical examination of data across time. The word "temporal" is derived from the Latin word for "time," and temporal analysis seeks to identify patterns, trends, or anomalies as they develop over specified time periods. Insights derived from temporal analysis are vital due to their application in a wide range of fields.

Time-stamped data, the foundation of temporal analysis, is ubiquitous in a variety of industries. As technological instruments evolve, sensors provide time-stamped or time-series data routinely. Examples include meteorological pattern surveillance and real-time medical monitoring. Similarly, platforms such as X time-stamp each tweet, allowing for the categorization and analysis of responses to ongoing events. This type of analysis could depict the volume of tweets over time, thereby shedding light on collective user behaviors as opposed to isolated actions.

In the broader realm of data analysis, temporal examination serves several crucial purposes, including identifying trends, seasonal analysis, event detection, and forecasting. Temporal analysis, when applied to social media, examines the patterns of post timings and frequencies across platforms during a specified period. It can help gauge trends on social media. Temporal insights can also reveal recurring patterns associated with specific periods, such as an increase in ice cream sales during summer. Moreover, temporal analysis facilitates the identification of sudden data anomalies, which may be indicative of significant events. An example would be an increase in brand mentions on social media following a significant brand-related event. It also seeks to identify user behavior patterns, optimal content release schedules, and overall engagement metrics, among other objectives. Finally, using historical data trends as a basis, it becomes possible to project potential future trends or data points. Social listening and managing tools such as Hootsuite, Sprout Social, and Google Analytics play a crucial role in facilitating temporal analysis by providing in-depth insights into user behavior, post timing, and engagement rates.

Temporal analysis provides a dynamic lens to comprehend, foresee, and respond to the data's ever-changing patterns. For example, Moghadas et al. (2023) analyzed real-time Twitter data regarding the German floods of 2021 in an effort to enhance disaster resilience. Their methodology consisted of a combination of textual analyses and an examination of spatiotemporal patterns in online disaster communication. The researchers conducted temporal clustering of tweets across distinct phases of the crisis, providing a granular view of the temporal characteristics of tweets related to the disaster.

Figure 6.1 depicts the tweet frequency over time as a temporal representation of Twitter data about the Wall of Kindness initiative, which spread across various countries through social media (Khan et al., 2018). Employing a text analytics framework, the study highlighted the vital role of social media for charity.

Please refer to Tutorial 06.01 for a walkthrough on temporal analysis.

6.2 Text Analytics Tools

- This section provides an overview of widely used text analytics tools, detailing their key features and functionalities in extracting meaningful insights from textual data.
- **Mallet**: Mallet (https://mimno.github.io/Mallet/index) is an acronym for "The Machine Learning for Language Toolkit," a Java-powered tool

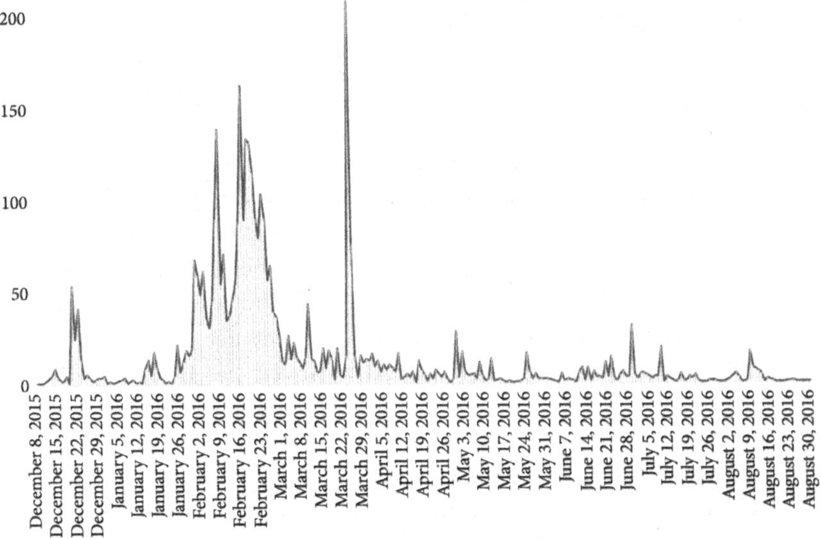

Figure 6.1 Temporal distribution of tweets (Khan et al., 2018). Reproduced with permission from Khan, et al. (2018). Communicating on Twitter for charity: Understanding the wall of kindness initiative in Afghanistan, Iran, and Pakistan. International Journal of Communication, 12, 25. https://ijoc.org/index.php/ijoc/article/viewFile/7726/2267

designed for statistical NLP, document classification, clustering, topic modeling, and information retrieval (Barde & Bainwad, 2017). Developed by researchers at the University of Massachusetts, Amherst, this toolkit serves as a multipurpose tool for various NLP and text mining tasks.

- **RapidMiner**: RapidMiner (rapidminer.com) is a data science software platform with strong text analytics capabilities. The tool offers various data mining, machine learning, and advanced analytics functionalities. It is designed to facilitate the creation, delivery, and maintenance of predictive analytics and other data-driven solutions. Among the most prominent features and aspects of RapidMiner are its graphical user interface (GUI), a drag-and-drop system that allows users to design and implement analytical workflows without having to write code. It also provides functionalities for data transformation, cleaning, and enrichment. Using Rapid Miner, users can construct, validate, and deploy machine learning models, and process text for analysis. Rapid Miner offers a basic free version of the tool, in addition to commercial versions that include additional features and support. It is extensively utilized in a range of industries for predictive modeling, fraud detection, risk analysis, and a variety of other applications that require data analytics and machine learning.

- **WordStat** (Provalis Research): WordStat (https://provalisresearch.com/products/content-analysis-software/) is software designed for data extraction from unstructured data, including open-ended responses, interviews, news articles, and written content. It is used for qualitative research in social sciences and business domains. WordStat analyzes textual data to identify patterns, trends, and insights, facilitating the extraction of themes, sentiments, and keywords. It also allows topic modeling, sentiment analysis, keyword extraction, dictionary-based content analysis, and visualization of data. Users can use WordStat independently or integrate it with QDA Miner, another Provalis Research software program for qualitative data analysis. The software also provides geospatial text analysis tools for location-based analysis and visualization. WordStat is used by researchers and professionals in various fields, including market research and political science, to analyze, visualize, and extract insights from textual data.

- **SentiStrength**: SentiStrength (http://sentistrength.wlv.ac.uk/) is a software application designed to extract sentiment strength from short texts, such as social media comments. Created by Professor Mike Thelwall, from the University of Wolverhampton, UK, it provides scores for positive and negative sentiments, employs linguistic principles and sentiment terms, and evaluates emoticons. Users can customize SentiStrength to specific contexts or domains by adding their own sentiment terms to its dictionary. Ideally suited for analyzing sentiment in social media platforms like X and YouTube comments, SentiStrength is widely used in academic research for sentiment analysis tasks, particularly those involving social media. The application has demonstrated competitive performance in its intended context.

Please refer to Tutorial 06.02 for a walkthrough on sentiment analysis.

- **Communalytic**: Communitylytic (https://communalytic.org/) is a computational social science research tool that analyzes data from social media platforms like Reddit, X, Facebook/Instagram, YouTube, and Telegram. It uses advanced text and social network analysis techniques to identify interactions, bots, influencers, and misinformation spread. The tool has two versions: Communitylytic Edu for educators and students, and Communitylytic Pro for academic research communities and large-scale projects.

Both versions provide resources and infrastructure for independent investigations in the public interest.

- **MonkeyLearn**: MonkeyLearn (https://monkeylearn.com/) is a text analytics platform offering an easy-to-use interface and prebuilt models for analyzing and extracting insights from textual data. It offers pretrained models for common tasks like sentiment analysis, topic classification, entity extraction, and language detection, and allows users to train their own custom models with specific labels and datasets. The platform allows easy import and export of data, automation of workflows, and connection with other applications. MonkeyLearn offers scalability, flexibility, and cost-effective pricing plans. However, it is limited to text analysis, requires more technical expertise for custom models, and is less customizable than advanced tools. MonkeyLearn is suitable for those starting with text analysis or looking for a quick and easy way to get started.

- **Leximancer**: Leximancer is a text analysis software application that helps discover and visualize concepts and themes within large amounts of text data. It can analyze text data from articles, surveys, reviews, and social media texts and automatically group related words into meaningful concepts. The identified concepts are then presented in a visual map, showing their connections and relative importance. The tool is used by researchers, businesses, educators, and government agencies for analyzing textual data from various sources. In addition to the paid version, a trial version of the tool is also available.

- **Voyant-Tools**: Voyant Tools (https://voyant-tools.org), whose slogan is "see through your text," stands out as a cloud-based, user-friendly text analysis solution. Voyant can be considered a text analytics or interpreting tool that offers various functionalities in interpreting text data. The Cirrus tool provides a recognizable word cloud visualization in which the frequency of individual words is readily discernible by hovering over them. In contrast, the Reader tool displays the entire corpus. The Trends tool displays the relative frequency of words across a corpus. The Summary tool provides an overview of the textual data, providing information about its duration, vocabulary density, and even unique words. With Voyant-tools, users can identify textual patterns, quickly highlight notable words or phrases within vast corpora, and even gain insights into broader word usage trends.

Please refer to Tutorial 06.03 for a walkthrough on text interpretation with Voyant-tools.

In summary, these text analytics tools offer a diverse range of capabilities, from topic modeling and sentiment analysis to network visualization and automated text classification. Each tool is designed to address specific analytical needs, making them valuable for researchers, businesses, and analysts seeking to extract insights from textual data. The choice of tool depends on factors such as data complexity, desired outputs, and technical expertise. As text analytics continues to evolve, leveraging these tools can enhance decision-making, improve audience understanding, and drive more effective communication strategies.

With the rapid advancement of AI, future text analytics tools will become even more sophisticated, offering greater automation, deeper contextual understanding, and enhanced predictive capabilities, further transforming the way textual data is analyzed and utilized. AI-driven automation will also streamline workflows, allowing these tools to scale effortlessly across vast datasets and multilingual contexts. However, as AI adoption grows, ethical considerations—such as algorithmic bias mitigation and transparency in automated sentiment judgments—will become critical to maintaining trust. Ultimately, the synergy between these tools and AI will empower organizations to not only interpret public sentiment with unprecedented granularity but also anticipate trends and adapt dynamically in an era where language remains a cornerstone of human-digital interaction.

Chapter Summary

- Topic modeling, a primarily automated quantitative approach to text analytics, identifies the key topics discussed in large volumes of text.
- Thematic analysis, a primarily qualitative method, explores underlying themes and patterns.
- Sentiment analysis measures the emotive tone underlying a series of words.
- Content analysis is the systematic categorization of text content that facilitates comprehension and interpretation.
- Hashtags on social media are usually hyperlinked, and clicking on a hashtag directs users to a curated collection of public posts tagged with that hashtag, nurturing a streamlined browsing experience and community engagement on topics or interests in common.
- Temporal analysis is the methodical examination of data over time.

Questions for Review

1. What are the different ways textual data can be interpreted?
2. In what way is topic modeling different from thematic analysis?
3. What is sentiment analysis? What tools can facilitate sentiment analysis?
4. What are the different audience engagement metrics and how are they measured?

7

Social Network Analysis

Chapter Outline

In the previous chapter, we ventured into the multifaceted world of text analytics, which illuminates the nuanced topics, recurring patterns, and underlying themes and sentiments in vast textual datasets. This investigation gave us a comprehensive understanding of how audience engagement can be measured and how textual data can provide deeper insights. As we advance in our investigation of social media analytics, particularly during the Analysis phase, our perspective further expands.

This chapter signals a turning point, leading us to another dimension of digital interactions. Beyond the meaning of words and emotions, we now explore who the people are within those online social networks and how they relate to each other. We explore how social media users establish connections, build

The Data Analytics Advantage. Laeeq Khan, Oxford University Press. © Oxford University Press (2025).
DOI: 10.1093/oso/9780197814222.003.0007

communities, and influence one another through interconnected networks. This chapter will direct our focus toward an in-depth analysis of the strength, direction, and patterns of digital connections in online social networks. This comprehensive examination will enable us to gain a better understanding of the underlying dynamics of these linkages and will serve to enhance our overall proficiency in understanding networks.

7.1 Understanding Social Networks: How We Connect

Human connections are complex. Every human interaction conveys the significance and weight of deeply ingrained connections. Consider your most recent family reunion, coffee breaks with colleagues, or countless conversations with close friends. Each moment, each shared story, and even a simple acknowledgment creates a unique connection. Consider a large garden celebration or gathering. Each guest, from your cousin recounting their travels to a colleague discussing the most recent project to an old acquaintance reminiscing, represents a node in your vast network of interactions. Every time we shake hands, embrace each other, or gaze into each other's eyes, we establish a connection, a bond, and a tie that binds us together.

In this sizeable online gathering known as "social networks," each participant occupies a unique position, whether a close relative, a distant relative, a friend, or a coworker from a different department. The complex social fabric that forms our lives is intricately woven through the shared experiences, stories, and interests we possess. It is through these shared connections that we build and maintain meaningful relationships with those around us. The marvel of this is that no one is solely a bystander, regardless of their position or relationship. We all actively contribute to the story, leaving an online imprint or a trace of our presence and actions.

Herein resides the brilliance of network science. On online social media platforms, each connection within the network represents a digital interaction. A key aspect of its brilliance is that it illuminates complex interconnections and relationships that might otherwise be invisible or difficult to discern. Through the study of networks, we can gain insights into phenomena ranging from the spread of diseases to the behavior of social groups. Network science serves as our lens, illuminating and contextualizing these intricate interactions. This powerful field of network science holds great promise for advancing our understanding of our online world. It helps us visualize and decipher the intricate web of our digital interactions by employing mathematical tools and cutting-edge network techniques (Jamali & Abolhassani, 2006).

The known foundations of network science can be traced to the graph theory introduced by Leonhard Euler in 1736, which formalized the study of relationships between discrete objects through his resolution of the Seven Bridges of Königsberg problem which is an old riddle involving a city with a split river around an island (Biggs et al., 1986). There were seven bridges connecting different parts of the city, and the challenge was to walk through the city in a way that crosses each bridge exactly once without repeating any. Leonhard Euler worked on this problem and proved that such a path cannot exist. This puzzle inspired graph theory, which is utilized in computer networks, mapping, and logistics.

For nearly two centuries, graph theory remained abstract with occasional progress. In the 1930s, Jacob Moreno and Helen Jennings revolutionized it by introducing sociometry, using graph-based visualizations to study social interactions. Their work laid the foundation for modern social network analysis, turning graph theory into a practical tool for real-world applications. (Grandjean, 2015). The advent of the digital age, characterized by inexpensive computation and the emergence of social networking platforms such as LinkedIn, Facebook, and X, heightened interest in SNA. Today, the abundant data some of these platforms provide fuels advanced analysis, revealing a deeper understanding of online social relationships and trends.

7.2 Social Network Analysis

At the core of the appeal surrounding social networks is the concept of "six degrees of separation," which posits that any two people on the planet can be connected through no more than six intermediary connections (Watts, 2004). Originating in 1929 with the Hungarian author Frigyes Karinthy, this concept emphasizes the complexity of human relationships (Watts, 2004). Despite criticisms that it oversimplifies complex social dynamics, the concept remains compelling, as evidenced by the observation that the average path length in actual social networks is frequently even shorter than six degrees.

Social structures can be analyzed through SNA, a methodology that examines the connections between various individuals, groups, and institutions (Borgatti et al., 2018). SNA is the examination of social structures using networks and graph theory (Otte & Rousseau, 2002; Scott, 2011). In practical terms, it is the visualization of these networks that enables us to observe behaviors, identify influence, and predict the actions of individuals or groups. SNA provides a comprehensive framework to understand and evaluate social structures, including the identification of key players and communication patterns. It is a powerful tool for researchers, managers, and policymakers to gain a better understanding of complex social systems. Hence, SNA stands out as a crucial instrument for comprehending the complex web of relationships that bind us (Butts, 2008).

The primary objective of traditional SNA is to investigate the structural characteristics of a network. A node (or vertex), which stands for persons, and edges, which express the connections that exist between nodes, are the two components that make up a representation of a social network. Once all of the nodes and edges of the network have been identified, a variety of statistical analyses can provide significant insights into the structure of the network. SNA visualizes complex connections to provide actionable insights for better decision-making and strategy.

SNA has revolutionized our ability to comprehend and interpret relationships and interactions across a variety of disciplines. It has applications in law enforcement, commerce, and even cybersecurity. Researchers in sociology, psychology, communication, and economics can discover patterns relating to information flows, influence dynamics, and resource distribution through the application of mathematical and statistical methods.

SNA is employed in sociology and anthropology to investigate community social structures and interactions. It facilitates comprehension of social cohesion, roles, and positions within groups, the dissemination of information, and the influence of social capital. Through the analysis of relationship patterns, researchers can reveal the fundamental social mechanisms that govern behaviors and impact the structure of communities. These insights are essential for comprehending a vast array of phenomena, from the intricate patterns of disease transmission and innovation diffusion to the emergence and spread of social movements.

In the field of government and law enforcement, SNA plays a crucial role in predicting potential criminal activities. Authorities can effectively monitor and analyze suspect relationships, providing a clearer picture of potentially complex criminal networks. In addition, SNA enables agencies to discover novel investigative avenues by mapping known connections between events, timelines, and locations. While SNA can identify associations, it cannot determine causation, making it difficult to definitively predict individual criminal behavior.

SNA has emerged as a transformative instrument in the realms of marketing and business. Its ability to reveal insights and patterns in social networks has made it an invaluable tool for companies to better understand their markets, customers, and competitors (Sharma et al., 2018). The application of SNA enables businesses to identify key influencers, detect emerging trends, and optimize their marketing strategies. Professionals utilize its capability to identify and communicate with influential figures, including industry-specific decision-makers and thought leaders. Businesses can proactively anticipate consumer needs, adjust their product positioning, and augment their services based on the complex web of relationships and preferences revealed by SNA.

SNA plays a crucial role in the field of public health, specifically in examining the transmission of contagious diseases and the execution of health interventions (Valente & Pitts, 2017). By mapping individuals' social networks, health officials can identify key groups that contribute to the spread of diseases. This allows them to focus on treatments more efficiently. SNA also aids in comprehending the social factors that determine health and the impact of social support networks on health outcomes. The widespread use of SNA in numerous disciplines showcases its adaptability and the significance it holds in revealing intricate relationship patterns that form the foundation of diverse social, economic, political, and technological events.

7.3 Theoretical Foundations of SNA

SNA is supported by a variety of theories that seek to explain how particular network properties influence diverse outcomes. The investigation of these theories provides context and depth to the study of networks. Here are some of the most influential SNA-related theories:

1. **Diffusion of innovations**: Diffusion of innovations is a classic theory developed in 1962 to describe how new ideas, behaviors, or products spread through a network (Rogers et al., 2014). The influence of key individuals, or "hubs," in a network can significantly speed up or slow down this diffusion process. The structure and dynamics of social networks are intrinsic to the essence of the diffusion process. The structure of a network, including who is connected to whom and how, plays a significant role in the rate and scope of an innovation's diffusion. Densely connected networks, for instance, may facilitate speedier diffusion than sparsely connected networks. According to the theory of the diffusion of innovations, early adopters or opinion leaders play a crucial role in the process of adoption. SNA offers instruments for identifying these prominent characters in a network, typically through metrics such as degree centrality, betweenness centrality, and eigenvector centrality. SNA can be crucial for targeted interventions or marketing campaigns to identify these influencers. If a certain innovation spreads within one group but not another, it can provide insight into cultural, behavioral, and other obstacles to diffusion.

2. **Strength of weak ties** (Granovetter, 1973): In SNA, weak ties frequently serve as connections between distinct communities or clusters. These connections are essential for the dissemination of innovations across diverse populations. It may seem counterintuitive, but tenuous links or weak connections within a network frequently serve as conduits for new information and resources. This suggests that the commonly held notion that strong ties are more valuable for disseminating information and facilitating resource flow may not necessarily hold true. Instead, it is often the weak links that provide new and novel information, resources, and opportunities, thereby playing a critical role in the functioning and growth of networks. Thus, it is important to recognize and leverage the potential of weak ties in network analysis. Weak connections, which may be disregarded at first glimpse, serve as vital links between disparate communities, facilitating the flow of new ideas and information.

3. **Homophily**: In SNA, homophily refers to the principle that individuals with similar characteristics prefer to connect (Tsvetovat & Kouznetsov, 2011). Homophily can be observed in various social settings, such as workplaces, schools, and online communities. This phenomenon has been studied extensively by researchers, who have found that individuals tend to seek out and interact with others who share similar traits, such as age, gender, race, religion, and interests. Understanding homophily can be useful in a variety of contexts, such as marketing, politics, and social policy, as it can help explain why certain groups of people are more likely to form connections than others. By studying homophily, researchers can gain insights into the dynamics of social networks and develop strategies for promoting diversity, inclusion, and social change. Homophily has a substantial influence on social media.

4. **Social influence theory**: Social influence theory (Kelman, 1958) refers to the study of how network members influence each other's beliefs, attitudes, behaviors, and opinions. Individuals are not isolated actors; rather, their decisions and actions are frequently influenced by those with whom they are connected in a network. Social influence theory enables researchers to comprehend the mechanism of social influence on social media platforms and investigate the factors that determine users' imitational behaviors. By examining the ways in which users interact with one another on social media, researchers can gain a more nuanced understanding of how online communities function and how they can be influenced. This knowledge can prove invaluable to businesses and other organizations looking to leverage social media as a means of achieving their goals. Overall, social influence theory represents a powerful framework for understanding the complex dynamics of social media and for developing effective

strategies for engaging with online audiences. Social influence causes similarity among connected elements. This is comparable to the concept of homophily, which refers to the tendency of similar social groupings to form bonds.

5. **Structural hole theory**: Burt's (1992) structural holes theory offers insight into competitive advantages derived from openings or "holes" in social networks. In social structures, individuals who lack connections form gaps, also known as structural holes. To overcome this, intermediaries act as bridges between disconnected individuals, thereby filling the structural holes. The theory focuses not on the intensity of ties between entities (as Granovetter's "weak ties as bridges" from 1973 did), but rather on the absence of connections or ties between them. Within dense networks, redundant information circulates, making it difficult to discover new insights. Those positioned near or bridging these structural gaps, however, have a distinct advantage. They are more likely to access diverse, nonredundant data from multiple networks (Burt, 2004; Cowan & Jonard, 2007). This positioning increases their capacity to generate innovative ideas and successfully translate and transmit them across networks (Burt, 2004).

   The theory has implications for numerous organizational activities. Among other things, it can amplify creativity and innovation (Burt, 2004; Cowan & Jonard, 2007) and foster the growth of new ventures (Adams et al., 2014).

To fully utilize the potential of SNA, it is essential to comprehend both its theoretical foundations and practical applications.

7.4 Network Structures and Properties

The output of network analysis is both graphical and numerical. Network graphs are frequently referred to as "maps" because they depict how network participants are interconnected. Understanding how numbers influence visualizations helps comprehend network activity.

SNA provides a quantifiable method for analyzing social relationships and interaction patterns among actors in a social network. This includes the key people in the network, their roles, which groups they reside in, and how they connect (Golbeck, 2013). A social network is defined by the underlying data that defines its numerous characteristics. To visualize a social network succinctly, several measures or metrics are employed to define these characteristics and

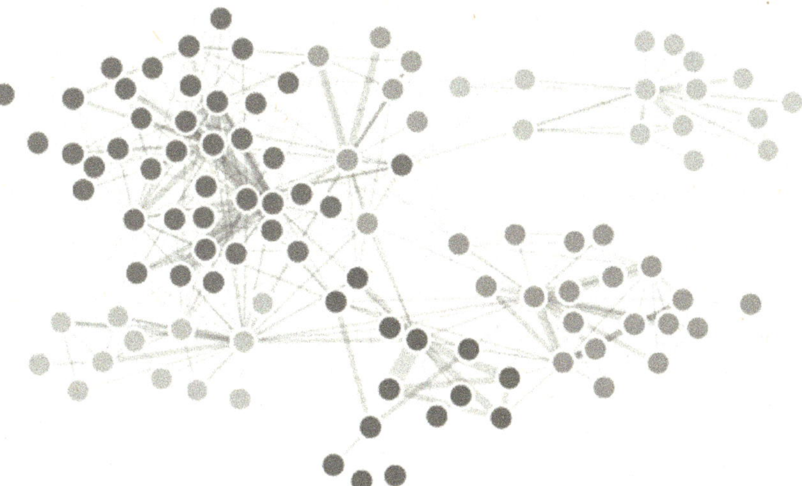

Figure 7.1 Social Network Graph depicting Nodes and Edges

other influential nodes quantitatively. Let's look at the most frequently employed metrics for analyzing social networks and their respective meanings.

In a network map, an individual, group, or organization is referred to as a node. The lines that connect one node to another are called edges or connections (see Figure 7.1). Relationships are illustrated using graphs, and the structure of a social network can be distilled to its fundamental nodes and edges.

- **Nodes** (or vertex, vertices): representing entities—be they individuals, organizations, or digital constructs.
- **Edges** (or ties/links): representing the connections or relationships between entities or nodes. These relationships can be directed (unidirectional or bidirectional) or undirected (mutual).

In addition to nodes and edges, there are additional fundamental structures that must be understood to describe and comprehend networks adequately (Wasserman and Faust, 1994). They contain descriptions of the nodes as well as their relationships and functions within the network.

When examining social networks, it is essential to comprehend the differentiation between directed and undirected networks. Both types of networks depict associations between individuals or entities, but their representation of these associations varies considerably. When connections in a network graph are directional (shown by an arrow on the line linking two nodes), it implies that node A may be connected to node B, but B may not be connected back to A. Directed relationships refer to interactions or connections between nodes, such as individuals or organizations, that have a definite direction. This indicates that the relationship is not reciprocal or symmetrical. Consider the process of "following" someone on social media—it involves focusing your attention on them, but there is no guarantee that they would reciprocate by following you in return. This is in contrast to "undirected" interactions, which are characterized by mutual connection without any specific directionality. Analyzing influence and information flow involves utilizing metrics such as in-degree (the count of incoming connections) and out-degree (the count of outgoing connections).

In undirected networks, connections may exhibit bidirectionality. Both nodes are interconnected. Envision having a mutual friendship with someone on Facebook, where the relationship is reciprocal. Examples include several types of networks, such as friendship networks, collaboration networks (depicting working relationships on projects), co-occurrence networks (illustrating terms that frequently appear together in papers), and transportation networks (representing the roadways that connect cities).

In addition to the basic properties of networks, such as the number of nodes and edges, and various centrality measures, several other important characteristics can be used to describe network structure and function. These include network density, network diameter, modularity, clustering, and network weightage (see Table 7.1). We will discuss each of these in furtherdetail.

Table 7.1 Key network terms and metrics

Term	Definition
In-degree	For directed networks, it represents the incoming edges to the node.
Out-degree	For directed networks, it represents the outgoing edges from the node.
Network Density	Density is calculated as the total number of existing edges divided by the number of all possible edges. Value range: 0–1.
Network Diameter	The size of the network is defined as the number of nodes or edges.
Modularity	Groups of nodes that are more densely connected than the remainder of the network, form clusters. Modularity is a metric that measures clusters or communities.
Network Weightage	Weight represents the strength, intensity, frequency, or another characteristic of the relationship between connections or edges.
Degree of a node	Represents the number of edges connected to that node.

7.4.1 Network Density

In SNA, network density is a fundamental concept that provides insight into the connectedness or cohesion of a network (Golbeck, 2013). Essentially, it assesses the proportion of prospective to actual connections within a network. Calculating network density involves dividing the number of actual connections (or ties) in a network by the maximal number of prospective connections between nodes. A network density value close to 1 (or 100%) indicates that nearly all conceivable connections between nodes in the network exist, indicating that the network is highly interconnected or cohesive. In contrast, a density value close to 0 indicates sparsity, which means that very few of the conceivable connections between the nodes exist.

A higher population density may indicate a close-knit community or group in which information or behaviors may disseminate quickly. Multiple paths between nodes may transport similar information, so a high density may also imply redundant information flow. While high-density networks may be resistant to individual node failures (due to the presence of multiple alternate paths), they may be more susceptible to outside threats, which can propagate rapidly through the interconnected nodes. Insights into the underlying social structures can be gleaned from network density. For example, a corporate communication network with low density could indicate departmental silos.

Network density is a key metric in SNA that provides a bird's-eye view of the overall interconnectedness of a network, which can provide vital insights into the network's dynamics, information flow, and structural nuances.

In SNA, a "clique" is a subset of network nodes in which each node is directly connected to every other node in that subset (Jamali & Abolhassani, 2006). In other words, a clique represents a subgraph that is maximally complete. A clique has a density of 1, meaning every possible pair of nodes within the clique is connected. Typically, cliques refer to organizations where every member knows every other member. In a school context, a clique may refer to a small group of close acquaintances. In corporate or organizational networks, cliques can represent teams or departments in which each member interacts with each other.

7.4.2 Network Diameter

Network diameter illuminates the "spread" or "reach" of a network. Specifically, it assists in comprehending the distance between the network's most distant nodes. The network's diameter is the longest path of all the shortest paths between any two nodes (Tsvetovat & Kouznetsov, 2011). In simplified terms, it is the maximum number of steps required to travel from one node to another while always taking the shortest route. Even in large networks, a small diameter suggests that any two individuals are only separated by a few intermediaries. This is frequently associated with the "six degrees of separation" phenomenon, which states that on average, any two individuals on Earth are separated by only six acquaintances. A large diameter, on the other hand, indicates that the network is more dispersed, and that information or resources may take longer to transit between the most distant nodes.

A network with a smaller diameter can disseminate information more effectively due to the shorter distance between its most distant nodes. A smaller diameter may imply a more cohesive network, whereas a larger diameter may indicate the possibility of fragmentation or the existence of discrete subgroups. In social networks such as Facebook, for instance, the diameter is typically small, indicating that members are closely connected.

7.4.3 Modularity and Clustering

Clusters are useful for investigating the underlying structures within social networks, uncovering important details on how individuals establish connections and engage with one another. Groups of nodes that are more densely connected than the remainder of the network, form clusters. In other words, clusters in a social network refer to groupings of nodes, or persons, that have stronger connections with each other compared to nodes outside the group. Clusters are also referred to as "communities" in SNA. For example, individuals with similar interests, hobbies, or occupations could be better connected and thus have stronger bonds.

The identification of such clusters can disclose subgroups, hierarchies, or communities within a larger network and provide valuable insights into the network's structure. Clusters also offer insight into localized patterns and behaviors, whereas the larger network provides a macro view. Moreover, clusters can help identify groups of people who share similar interests, behaviors, or responsibilities. Additionally, in business contexts, clusters can refer to teams, departments, or organizations that collaborate closely.

Several metrics help identify and measure clusters in social networks. Modularity is one of the most employed metrics that function as a measurement for clusters or communities. Modularity refers to the quality or state of being modular, which means being composed of separate, independent parts. Modularity quantifies the extent to which nodes may be partitioned into clusters characterized by robust internal connections and relatively weaker inter-cluster links. A larger modularity number indicates a more distinct cluster structure. Identifying and analyzing these clusters is essential for a variety of applications, including those in the social sciences, business, and beyond.

In addition to modularity, the clustering coefficient quantifies the propensity of acquaintances to form connections with one another. Elevated values indicate that a network has a substantial number of densely interconnected clusters.

7.4.4 Network Weightage

A weighted network is one in which the connections or edges between nodes (individuals, entities, etc.) are assigned a weight to represent strength, intensity, frequency, or another characteristic of the relationship. In contrast to binary networks, in which connections are either present or absent, weighted networks provide more information about the relationship by designating a numerical value to each edge. The weight designated to an edge can represent the intensity or strength of a connection. In a communication network, for instance, the weight could symbolize the number of messages exchanged between two individuals. Weighted networks allow for more nuanced analysis. In a social media network, for instance, the weight between two individuals may indicate the number of interactions, shared postings, or message exchanges. Consequently, weighted networks in SNA provide a more accurate representation of relationships, enabling researchers and analysts to capture and examine the nuances of connections in various contexts. In a network graph, a weighted network is represented by the thickness of lines or edges between nodes.

SNA explores the fundamental structure of a network by utilizing centrality measures. These measures address the fundamental inquiry: What constitutes a significant node? (Bonacich, 1987). Numerical ratings are assigned to each node, based on different parameters, to determine their "importance" inside the network (Borgatti, 2005). Examining these centrality scores provides access to valuable information about the network's comprehensive configuration and operation, including its level of interconnectedness, dynamics of information dissemination, and the comparative significance of individuals or groups. Although there are numerous centrality measures available, each with its advantages and disadvantages, it is important to recognize that they only provide a single aspect of the overall picture. By integrating them with additional methodologies and qualitative analyses, a more comprehensive depiction of the intricate dynamics inside social networks can be achieved.

7.5 Centrality Measures

Centrality measures serve as the foundation of SNA, shedding light on how networks operate. Centrality offers an estimate of a node's importance in the network (Tsvetovat & Kouznetsov, 2011). These metrics go beyond merely acknowledging the existence of nodes and connections; they provide insight into the relative importance and influence of nodes within the vast network fabric. What constitutes "central" can vary based on the application and perspective.

The majority of network analysis software programs compute various centrality measures. Grasping the fundamental principles underlying each measure is necessary for determining when to use it for analysis. There are various types of centrality measures, including degree centrality, betweenness centrality, and closeness centrality (Case Study 7.1).

7.5.1 Degree Centrality

Degree centrality is the most straightforward indicator of node connectivity. Degree centrality quantifies a node's significance based on the number of connections, links, or edges held by each node (see Figure 7.2). Consider Sarah's profile on Facebook. If she has one thousand acquaintances, her

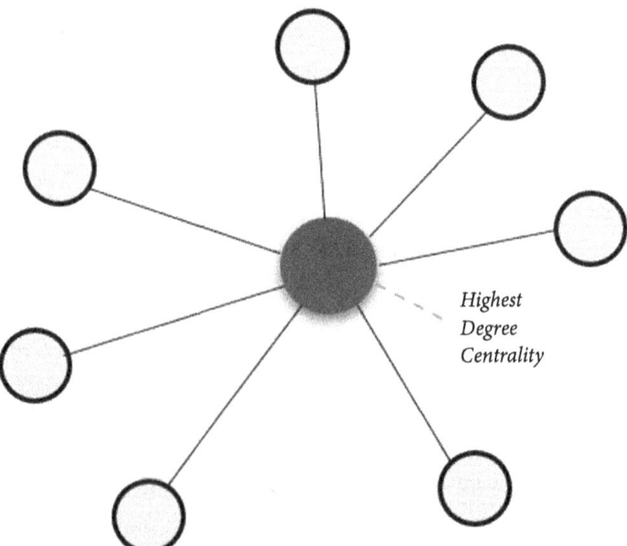

Figure 7.2 Degree Centrality

degree centrality would be one thousand. Therefore, the higher the degree, the more centralized the actor/node/person within the network (Golbeck, 2013). Degree centrality reveals the immediate relationships a user has within the network. This is useful for identifying influential individuals with extensive networks.

Network data that is directed offers richer information than undirected data (Prell, 2011). There are two measures of degree in directed graphs: in-degree and out-degree. The in-degree is determined by the number of incoming edges at a node. It can be useful to consider in-degree (the number of inbound connections) and out-degree (the number of outbound connections) as separate measures to identify interconnected individuals, individuals with the most information, or individuals who can quickly connect to the larger network. For example, on platforms such as X, we can differentiate between a user's followers (in-degree) and those they follow (out-degree). In network diagrams, in-degrees are represented by edges with arrows that point to the node. The out-degree centrality is the number of edges that originate from a node and connect to other nodes. These are represented by arrows that point away from the node. The total degree of a node is the sum of its in-degree and out-degree centrality scores.

7.5.2 Betweenness Centrality

Betweenness centrality is one of the most used measures of centrality. It assesses the degree to which a node is located on the path that is physically the shortest between two other nodes (see Figure 7.3). It is a representation of the node's capacity to connect separate areas of the network (Liu & Liu, 2011). This metric calculates the frequency with which a node appears on the shortest path between two other nodes. For example, if Ahmed is the mutual connection between many professionals on LinkedIn, he has a high betweenness centrality.

Nodes with a high betweenness centrality are crucial to the network's information flow and cohesion; they are considered central to the network due to their important function in the information flow. Betweenness is a valuable concept for analyzing communication dynamics and hence identifying those who control or influence information flow. A high betweenness count may indicate that an individual has authority over disparate clusters in a network, or that they are merely located on the periphery of both clusters (Golbeck, 2013). A person with a high betweenness may either dominate multiple network clusters or exist on the periphery of multiple groups. A high betweenness count may also indicate that an individual has authority over disparate clusters in a network.

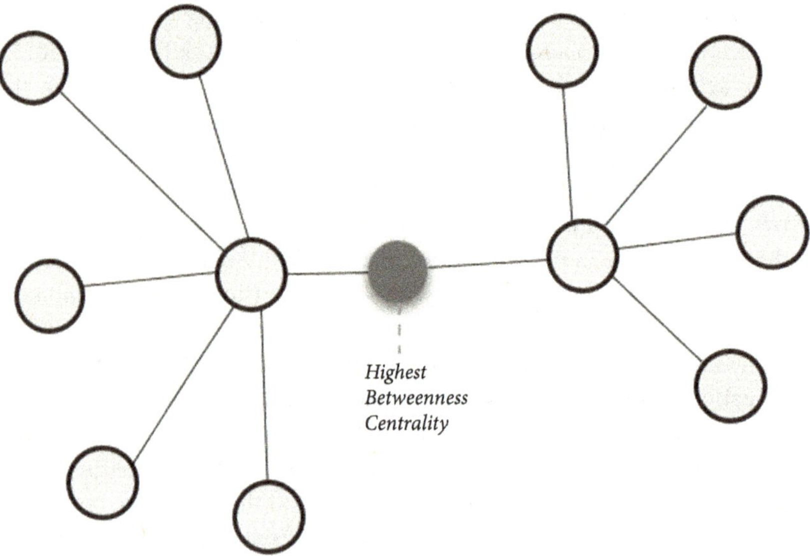

Figure 7.3 Betweenness Centrality

7.5.3 Closeness Centrality

Closeness centrality is a metric used for ranking nodes in a network based on their proximity to all other nodes (Liu & Liu, 2011). This metric allows for the identification of nodes that are central to the network and thus have a significant impact on communication and flow of information across the network (see Figure 7.4). In other words, the closeness centrality measure helps find nodes or people best positioned to influence the entire network most rapidly.

Closeness centrality is a measure that assesses the effectiveness of a node in accessing information or resources that are spread out throughout the network (Liu & Liu, 2011). Closeness centrality quantifies the average minimum distance from a certain node to all other nodes in the network, indicating the node's accessibility within the network's structure. In the context of academic partnerships, a researcher with high closeness centrality is someone who works with a wide range of other academics from different fields or disciplines. This individual does not need to be the most published or cited, but they should be prominently positioned within the collaborative network, allowing for quick and direct connection with peers. This measure is particularly valuable for identifying crucial connectors and facilitators within multidisciplinary research networks. These individuals play a vital role in bridging diverse scientific communities and accelerating the exchange of knowledge across disciplinary borders.

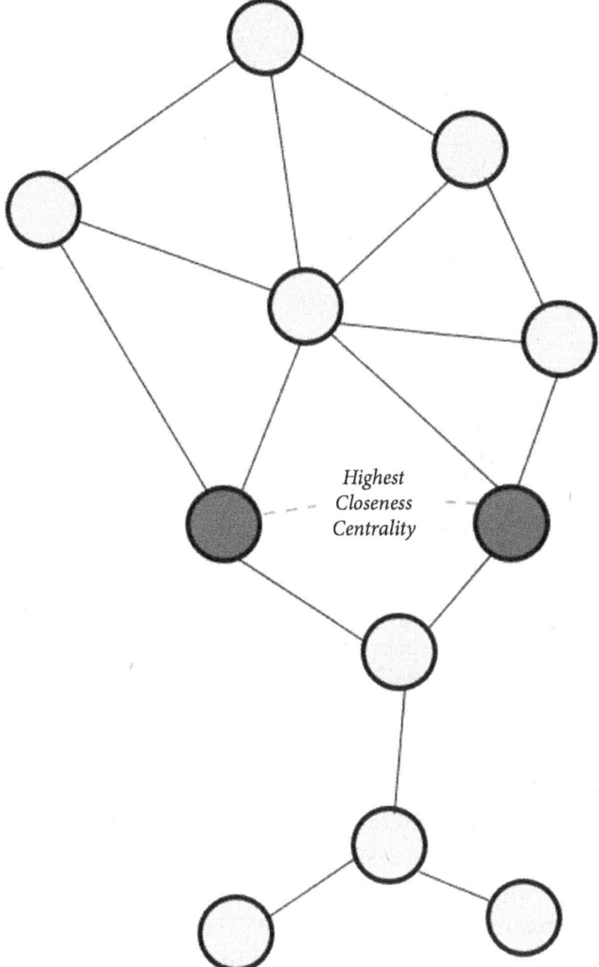

Figure 7.4 Closeness Centrality

7.5.4 Eigenvector Centrality

Unlike degree centrality, eigenvector centrality evaluates the connectivity of a node's neighbors and their subsequent connections (see Figure 7.5). A node with 300 relatively unpopular Facebook friends, for instance, would have a lower eigenvector centrality than a node with 300 extremely popular Facebook friends. In the case of an X (Twitter) scenario, a high score would be awarded to a user who not only has a large number of followers but also has followers with substantial followings. Thus, eigenvector centrality identifies influential entities whose

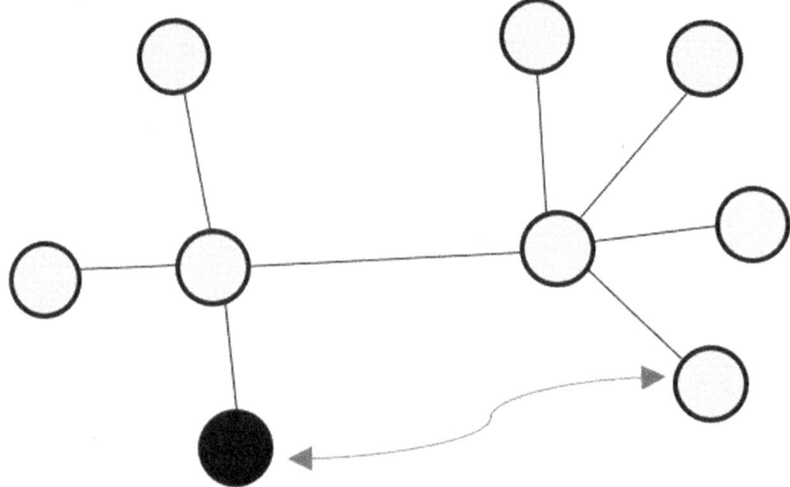

Figure 7.5 Eigenvector Centrality

effects extend beyond their immediate vicinity. This can be particularly useful for comprehending complex networks, from social media communities to malware dissemination mechanisms.

Links from significant nodes or important individuals (as measured by degree centrality) are more valuable than links from insignificant nodes. While degree centrality, a relatively simple measure, provides a count of the number of connections (edges), or *the popularity* a node has, eigenvector centrality considers the importance of connected nodes in addition to their numbers. Initially, all nodes are treated equally, but as the computation progresses, nodes with more edges acquire importance (Golbeck, 2013). Their significance spreads to the nodes with which they are connected. After multiple iterations of recomputing, the values stabilize, resulting in the final eigenvector centrality values.

7.5.5 Page Rank

Page Rank is an extension of eigenvector centrality that evaluates nodes based on the direction and weight of their connections (Liu & Liu, 2011) (see Figure 7.6). For example, academic citations on Google Scholar can serve as an excellent example. If a research paper is frequently cited by influential papers, its page rank would be high. Page rank thus identifies nodes whose influence extends beyond their direct connections. Due to its emphasis on link direction and weight, it is well-suited for evaluating academic citations and authority. As a variant of eigenvector centrality, page rank is at the heart of Google's algorithm that ranks web pages.

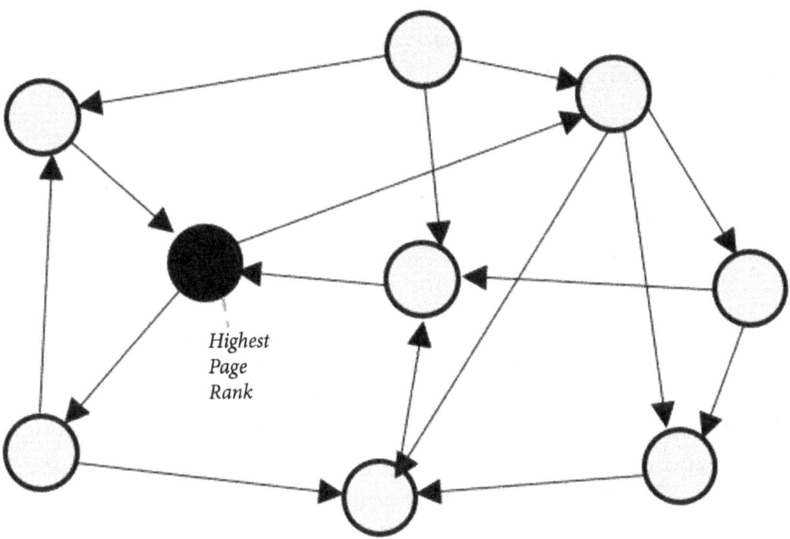

Figure 7.6 Page Rank

Case Study 7.1 Social Network Analysis of X/Twitter Data on US Ambassador to Ireland

Overview

This case study examines the implementation of SNA on X (formerly Twitter) data concerning US ambassadors' official social media handle in Ireland. Our analysis of the social network helps understand network structure, its key actors, and engagement of ambassadors' account with publics. The X platform can serve as potent tool for digital diplomacy. The utilization of the NodeXL tool helps understand various network metrics and visually see the network connections and online communities on X. We delve into SNA concepts such as betweenness centrality and eigenvector centrality, showcasing the influence of engagement techniques on community development and public diplomacy.

Context

The US ambassadors to Ireland have been utilizing X as a means of engaging in diplomatic activities. Their distinct approaches offer an opportune environment for examining the impact of social media engagement on networking and diplomacy. This investigation utilized the NodeXL tool, which is well-known for its capacity to gather and examine network data from social media networks.

Approach

The extensive features of NodeXL, an add-on for Microsoft Excel, were utilized for network data collecting, analysis, and visualization. The following actions were executed:

1. **Data collection**: NodeXL's interface with the X/Twitter API facilitated the retrieval of tweets, retweets, mentions, and responses associated with the verified account of the US ambassador during a designated six-month time frame.
2. **Network construction**: The data underwent processing to generate a directed graph: depicting the network surrounding the US envoy. The graph depicts X/Twitter users as nodes, with directed edges indicating the flow of conversation.
3. **Centrality measures**: NodeXL enabled the computation of different centrality measures, such as betweenness centrality and eigenvector centrality, to evaluate the roles and influence of the ambassador in their individual network.

Examination and Conclusions

- **Betweenness centrality**: This measure highlighted the important function of the US ambassador as a mediator in the X/Twitter network, enabling communication between various user groups. Since the US ambassador was very active on social media and tweeted frequently, he had a high betweenness centrality, which suggested that his account had more control over the network. In comparison with other related accounts from other embassies, the US ambassador had higher betweenness, suggesting considerable influence within the network.
- **Eigenvector centrality**: As demonstrated by the high score, the US ambassador's successful approach of interacting with significant Twitter users (including Irish celebrities, media personalities, and prominent influencers), not only led to greater goodwill and a positive image among X followers but also demonstrated effective integration within the community. Comparatively, ambassadors from other countries having a social media presence had a diminished score reflecting their lesser engagement with significant individuals, which impeded the formation of a unified community network.

The NodeXL-supported SNA clearly demonstrated the distinct effect of the ambassadors' engagement techniques on the structures and influence of their social networks. The dynamic and mutually beneficial communication by the US ambassador contributed to the development of a lively and integrated community, as evidenced by the high centrality scores.

Utilizing NodeXL to conduct a SNA on X/Twitter data related to US ambassador to Ireland yielded valuable metrics regarding their strategy for social media diplomacy. The analysis emphasized the significance of active participation and mutual exchange in constructing influential and unified social networks. The approach of the US ambassador served as a prime example of effective digital diplomacy, promoting positive relations and active participation within the network.

7.6 SNA Data Collection and Analysis

We have already shed light on social media data collection in Chapter 4. Network data includes information about nodes, which represent the distinct entities within the network, and edges, which represent the relationships or connections between these entities. Network data from social media is organized in tabular form, organized into rows and columns. Such network data can contain information about nodes in the form of ID, name, and node attributes, and edges in the form of source, target, weight, and timestamp.

Effective analysis requires proper data formatting, particularly when dealing with large and complex datasets. This data is typically organized as adjacency matrices or edge-lists. The complexity of this procedure depends on the size and complexity of the network. For example, to do SNA on Reddit data, it can be advantageous to begin the process by organizing data in tabular formats. Consider the matrix below (Table 7.2), which outlines relational data among Reddit users within a particular subreddit community, as an example. The first column depicts the original commenter (User 1), the second column displays the users

Table 7.2 Sample network relationships

User 1	User 1	Upvotes (1-4)	Nature of Interaction
REDDITORA	RedditorB	3	Direct Reply
REDDITORC	RedditorD	4	Mention
REDDITORA	RedditorE	2	Shared Link

with whom they have interacted (User 2), the third column quantifies the trust or upvotes, and the fourth column describes the character of their interaction—whether it was a direct reply, a mention, or a shared link. Notably, this is only one of numerous methods to structure and classify Reddit-based network data.

The selection of analytical tools will determine the level of data preparation and cleaning required. Generally, readily accessible tools require greater manual intervention, whereas premium subscription-based software automates a significant portion of this preparatory work. For example, data collected through NodeXL already includes network information that is organized in a tabular format thus making SNA easier.

When collecting data, it is essential to protect privacy, obtain required permissions, and anonymize data as needed. Respecting these ethical boundaries is essential for preserving the trustworthiness and integrity of work. It is also important to consider how SNA results will be implemented. For instance, network analysis can be used to assess an individual's degree of isolation to target them with interventions.

7.7 Visualizing Networks

In the contemporary digital landscape, modern cameras empower us to capture images of crowds gathering for events such as elections, concerts, and public demonstrations. These images or visual records provide insights into numerous aspects of the gathering, including the number of participants, the proximity of individuals to one another, and the overall density of the crowd.

Translating this capability to the digital realm, where interactions and assemblies often transpire virtually, can prove challenging. How might we visualize and understand the collective presence and interactions of individuals in the online world? This is where SNA offers a solution, functioning as the lens through which we can observe and analyze these digital congregations. SNA visually portrays the various entities (nodes) and the relationships between them (edges), thereby bringing into focus the otherwise invisible network of online interactions.

Visualizing networks in SNA is a powerful technique that enhances our comprehension of complex relationships (Butts, 2008). These network visualizations provide researchers and critical decision-makers with an in-depth lens for dissecting the network's complexity, revealing both macro and micro insights. In the context of interconnected organizational networks, network visualization reveals several crucial characteristics and inherent benefits:

- **Structural clarity and community detection**: Network visualization helps illuminate nodes (representing organizations or individuals) and edges (depicting their interconnections) to provide a panoramic view of the entire ecosystem. The graphical depiction overcomes the constraints of unprocessed data, enabling a more immediate and lucid comprehension of the network's depth, interconnectedness, and scope. Visualization can also effectively separate distinct communities or subgroups from the overall network (Scott, 2011). SNA can visually reveal clusters and communities with metrics such as modularity numbers. These communities have the potential to naturally come together due to common objectives, congruent interests, or frequent interactions. Through the identification and comprehension of these clusters, stakeholders can customize their strategies to guarantee the fulfillment of the distinct dynamics and needs of each subgroup.
- **Visualizing centrality**: An effective way to emphasize centrality is by employing visual indicators. The graphical differentiation of nodes and clusters facilitates the swift detection of network players that hold significant importance. Irrespective of their classification as high-connectivity hubs, critical intermediaries, or strategic connectors, the visibility of these nodes aids in the recognition of influential actors and the potential impact they may have within the network An effective way to emphasize centrality is by employing visual indicators; this improves the visibility of centrality metrics. The graphical differentiation facilitates the swift detection of network nodes that hold significant importance. Irrespective of their classification as high-connectivity hubs, critical intermediaries, or strategic connectors, the visibility of these elements aids in the recognition of influential individuals and the potential consequences they may have.
- **Identifying outliers and opportunities**: Network visualizations act as a radar for outliers, which are nodes that may be tenuously connected or less integrated. Although seemingly inconsequential, these anomalies could potentially serve as unexplored sources of value or weak points in the network's unity.
- **Capturing network evolution**: Visualizations have the ability to dynamically represent the changes in a network over time, beyond the limitations of static snapshots. An examination of time can uncover patterns such as changing connections, rising individuals with influence, and shifting dynamics of importance. These insights are crucial for forecasting patterns, understanding past shifts, and strategizing future actions.
- **Increasing stakeholder engagement**: Visualizations are highly effective instruments for communication. Showing complex connections in a readily understandable style makes it feasible to involve a broader audience,

ranging from high-level decision-makers to grassroots participants, and guarantees that all stakeholders have a consistent understanding of the network's structure.

SNA visualization transforms into an essential tool by merging data with visual clarity, facilitating well-informed decision-making, strategic network planning, and optimized network dynamics.

7.8 SNA Tools and Software

SNA software is designed to assist in the collection, refinement, analysis, and visualization of network data. It simplifies the process of data analysis, eliminating the need for manual data entry and thus reducing the potential for human error. Additionally, SNA software provides an array of tools for visualizing network data and computing network metrics, making it easier to identify patterns and trends within the data. Based on this knowledge about the network structure, businesses and organizations can make informed decisions and develop more effective strategies.

While there are free tools that provide basic functionality and limited support, premium subscription-based platforms typically offer a more user-friendly interface and wide-ranging support. Specific user needs often dictate which SNA tool is employed. It is wise to adopt an SNA tool that has an intuitive interface while also providing most of the needed SNA metrics. More advanced tools have a learning curve; however, these tools can offer better quality visualizations. NodeXL and Gephi are two well-known SNA software applications that can be used for a variety of purposes.

- **NodeXL**: A project of the Social Media Research Foundation, NodeXL is a comprehensive network analysis and visualization tool. Available as an add-in for Microsoft Excel 2007, 2010, and later versions, it is predominantly designed for Windows platforms. The basic version of this open-source software is available for free distribution, which is advantageous for both researchers and professionals. NodeXL facilitates the complex process of SNA for individuals with minimal or no programming experience. Employing NodeXL, users can gather relational information in terms of its structure, and obtain network metrics such as centrality, degree, and clustering. NodeXL Pro offers advanced capabilities by importing data from various social media platforms. Furthermore, NodeXL is user-friendly because it can work as an Excel extension, thus providing a familiar workbook interface (see Figure 7.7).

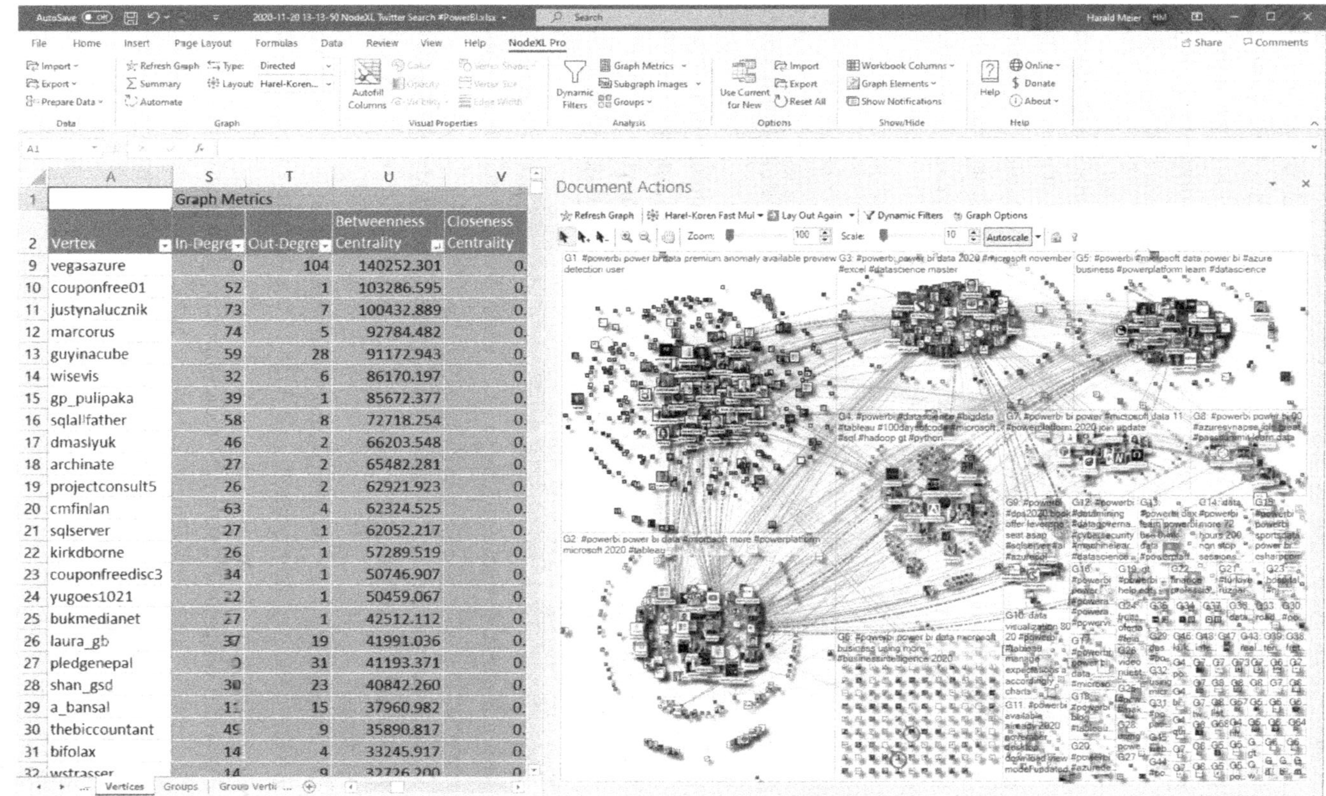

Figure 7.7 NodeXl Interface

- **Gephi**: Gephi is a well-known Java-based, open-source, network analysis and visualization software. The software is compatible with Windows, Mac OS X, and Linux systems. Gephi has received significant acclaim for its ability to render a wide variety of network visualizations, from intricate technical network graphs to visually breathtaking network art. In comparison to NodeXL, Gephi can generate more appealing network visualizations and is stronger in terms of flexibility in the types of visualizations (see Figure 7.8).

  This software specializes in both visualization and the analysis of numerous metrics, including centrality, clustering, and network diameter, among others. Gephi's intuitive point-and-click interface is suitable for network analysis novices and experts alike. In addition, Gephi's design capabilities support a wide range of networks, including static and dynamic networks, geolocated data, and multimode/multiplex networks.

Chapter Summary

- Every human interaction conveys the significance and weight of deeply ingrained connections.
- Social structures can be analyzed through SNA, a methodology that examines the connections between various individuals, groups, and institutions.
- SNA offers instruments for identifying these prominent characters in a network, typically through metrics such as degree centrality, betweenness centrality, and eigenvector centrality.
- It may seem counterintuitive, but tenuous links or weak connections within a network frequently serve as conduits for new information and resources.
- Social influence theory (Kelman, 1958) refers to the study of how network members influence one another's beliefs, attitudes, behaviors, and opinions.
- In a network map, an individual, group, or organization is referred to as a node. The lines that connect one node to another are called edges or connections.
- Centrality offers an estimate of a node's importance in a network.
- Nodes with a high betweenness centrality are crucial to the network's information flow and cohesion; they are considered central to the network due to their function in the information flow.
- Modularity quantifies the extent to which nodes may be partitioned into clusters characterized by robust internal connections and relatively weaker inter-cluster links.

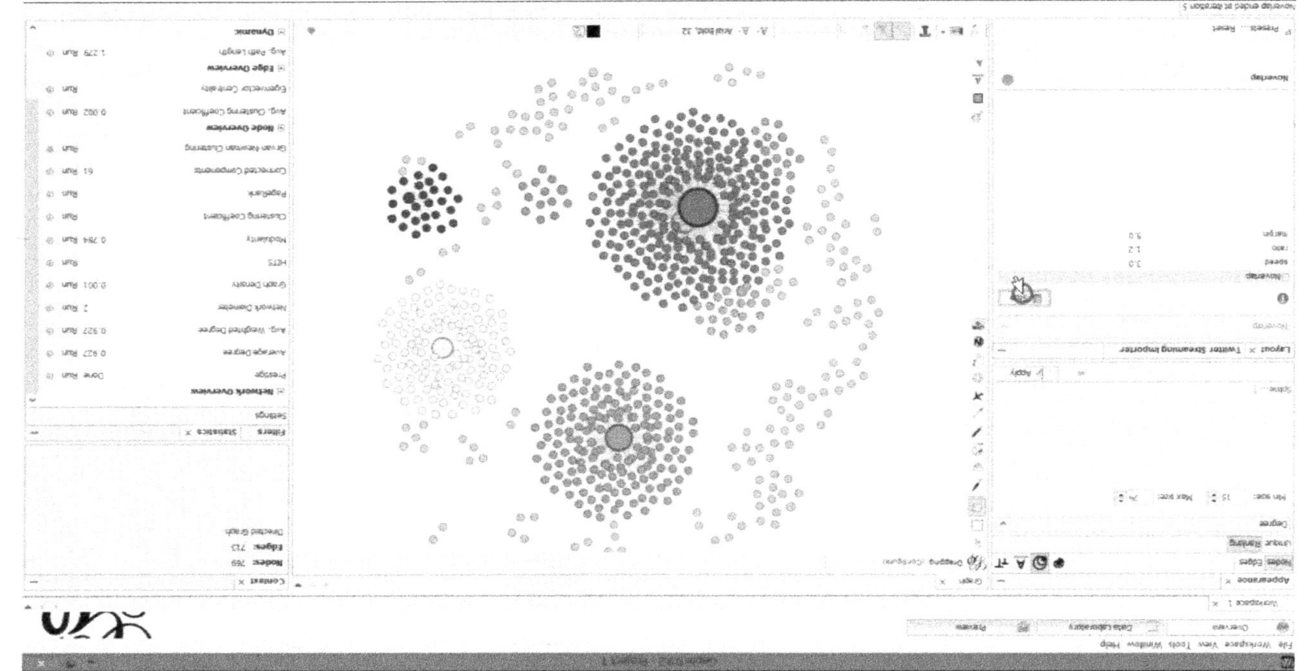

Figure 7.8 Gephi Interface

Questions for Review

1. What is SNA and how can it prove beneficial in different disciplines?
2. What is the strength of weak ties? How does it relate to our understanding of social networks?
3. How does the concept of homophily relate to clustering and modularity?
4. What is degree centrality? In what way does it differ from eigenvector centrality?
5. What are the different benefits of visualizing social networks?

8

Image and Video Analytics

Chapter Learning Objectives

The age-old adage, "A picture speaks a thousand words," holds truer than ever. In the digital age, we are experiencing an unambiguous tilt toward visual storytelling. The image as a vivid capture of a person or a thing. A video offers a wealth of unfolding narratives that include moving images and sound. Both videos and images demonstrate the dynamic range of visual content currently available. Smartphones and social media platforms enable images and videos to circulate globally in real time, revolutionizing how visual content is shared. As inherently dynamic mediums, images and videos not only capture audience attention but also enhance content memorability, shareability, and engagement potential (Goh et al., 2009).

Traditional social media analytics were founded on text analysis, but the new frontier is undeniably image and video analytics. For example, instead of merely identifying posts that contain the term "computer," modern image analytics can highlight posts that contain visual representations of computers and also any other words within the image. This progression enables nuanced insights, from assessing emotion through facial expressions to depicting complex scenarios replete with brand logos and particular settings (Colombo et al., 2023). However, this shift toward the visual does not diminish the significance of text.

The Data Analytics Advantage. Laeeq Khan, Oxford University Press. © Oxford University Press (2025).
DOI: 10.1093/oso/9780197814222.003.0008

To holistically understand the nuances of social media conversations, an integrated approach of textual and visual analysis is essential. Consider this: while textual discourse might suggest adults actively discussing Disney's *Frozen*, a visual analysis could reveal that the predominant audience engaging with the film's imagery is, in fact, children.

This visually stimulating era necessitates a thorough comprehension and analysis of the image and video content to navigate it successfully. This undertaking, although daunting, presents an opportunity for academicians and digital enthusiasts to make sense of vast amounts of image and video data. In this chapter, we will shed light on image and video analytics, elucidating its methods, advancements, and challenges.

8.1 The Power of Images

Within the digital communication landscape, visual content stands out, exhibiting advantages unmatched by textual content. Images and videos excel at conveying nuanced narratives evoking deep emotional connections. This superior impact is attributable to the inherent ability of visual content to instantly engage audiences, maintain their attention consistently, and leave lasting impressions. The sophisticated human sensory system is the source of this ability. Visual communication is fundamentally dependent on our eyesight and the brain's ability to transmit, process, and interpret the vast amount of sensory data it receives (Eisenberg, 2014). Visual communication encompasses a wide array of elements, including but not limited to signs, maps, diagrams, drawings, infographics, illustrations, animations, color schemes, sketches, charts, photographs, videos, models, and a variety of electronic resources (Wilmot Li & Berthouzoz, 2011).

Even a cursory examination of human cognitive systems reveals the natural human inclination for visual information. Visual data elicit strong emotional responses and occupy a lasting position in memory (Marotta, 2024). It is notable that the human brain identifies, stores, and retrieves images and infographics with remarkable fluidity and frequently on a subconscious level, encoding ideas securely in our long-term memory banks (Lankow et al., 2012).

A seminal study conducted by the University of Minnesota's Management Information Systems Research Center in collaboration with 3M Corporation confirmed the importance of visual aids in enhancing presentations (Vogel et al., 1986). Their research aimed to determine the effect of visual aids on the persuasiveness of presenters. Unsurprisingly, the findings revealed an increase in the presenter's perceived credibility, audience engagement, comprehension, and receptivity, culminating in concrete actions when visual supports were included, in striking contrast to when they were not (Vogel et al., 1986).

The evolution of technology especially in the form of smartphone cameras and social media advancements has facilitated the production and distribution of images. However, the increasing prevalence of visual content is not solely attributable to the simplicity of sharing. Visual media—with their inherent memorability, engaging nature, and shareability—consistently surpass textual content in impact (Nelson et al., 1976). Empirical evidence supports this change. With the proliferation of camera-equipped devices and the development of photographic technologies, there has been a meteoric increase in the number of images populating the internet. According to current data, over 95 million photos are uploaded daily (Tsvetkova, 2023). This visual proliferation is bolstered by improvements in wireless networks, camera accessibility, and photographic quality. Platforms such as Snapchat, Instagram, Pinterest, and Tumblr prioritize images, relegating text to a secondary position. Even pioneers such as Facebook and X (formerly Twitter) have shifted their strategies to be more visual. Today, Facebook is the preeminent platform for image sharing, and Twitter prioritizes visual-rich postings. This development does not signal the end of the text but rather illustrates its synthesis with the persuasive power of images.

Malik et al. (2016) dug deeper to investigate the factors that motivate individuals to distribute digital photographs on platforms such as Facebook. Their research illuminated six compelling gratifications: affection, attention-seeking, personal disclosure, habitual sharing, information dissemination, and wielding social influence. The increased engagement metrics associated with images demonstrate their allure. For example, the Content Marketing Institute discovered that content with relevant visuals receives 94% more views (Valyaeva, 2021). Similarly, BuzzSumo's analysis indicates that Facebook posts and tweets on Twitter (now X) with visual enhancements receive 2.3 times and 150% more engagement, respectively (Valyaeva, 2021).

Moreover, the increasing preference for visual communication, as exemplified by the rapid transmission of emotions via visual tools such as emoticons, transcends ordinary technological advancements. This paradigm shift toward visual communication is not only reshaping interpersonal interactions but also the complex relationship between brands and consumers. Recognizing the significant impact of visuals in the digital realm, it is necessary to investigate the strategies and tools used to decode and utilize this vast visual information.

8.2 Introduction to Image Analytics

Image analytics, also known as "computer vision," "image analysis," and "image recognition," is a subfield of artificial intelligence and computer science (Asif et al., 2021; Barnes & Rutter, 2019; Zhan et al., 2024). It focuses on extracting meaningful information from images, emoticons, parodies, and other rich media formats. This advanced technology enables computers to recognize specific characteristics within an image, similar to Google Photos and Apple's Photos, which classify images based on identified subjects or themes.

Object detection, facial recognition, and scene comprehension are the fundamental capabilities of image analytics. Its adaptability is evident in the varied fields of big data analytics and social media analytics. Numerous applications exist, ranging from identifying and tracking objects and people for surveillance, traffic management, and criminal identification to assessing facial expressions to gauge consumer sentiment or detect deceit. In addition, image analytics enhances image categorization and searchability through precise classification and can create hyperrealistic images. The ability to discern objects even when partially obscured or distorted is a distinctive characteristic.

The exponential development of image analytics has resulted in its implementation in numerous industries. Retailers, for example, utilize it to monitor in-store dynamics, highlight attention-grabbing products, and customize recommendations (Marder et al., 2015). Advertisers use their insights to customize advertisements for specific demographics, evaluate campaign results, and identify anomalies. Moreover, it assists law enforcement with suspect identification, threat tracking, and crowd monitoring. Healthcare professionals are already utilizing medical imaging technologies to diagnose issues, identify abnormalities, and monitor patient progress (Li et al., 2018; Zhang & Metaxas, 2016). Likewise, image analytics is beneficial for transportation agencies seeking to enhance traffic control, accident detection, and safety protocols. To fully comprehend visual nuances, image recognition, and artificial intelligence–powered tools are essential. They aid in clarifying aspects such as logo visual perceptions, product placement, and their practical applications.

When utilized appropriately, image analysis can provide profound insights through the lens of descriptive, predictive, and prescriptive analytics. We have discussed the application of this lens for the analysis of text in the previous chapters. The following section presents the relationship of descriptive, predictive, and prescriptive analytics for images:

- **Descriptive analytics for images**: The purpose of descriptive image analytics is to interpret the content embedded within images. Utilizing advanced technologies, it is possible to identify an array of components in photographs, from logos and features to activities, objects, and contextual settings. These technologies can also generate applicable captions, such as "Elderly man fishing by the lake wearing a Columbia hat."
- **Predictive analytics for images**: Utilizing visual data, predictive analytics can help forecast potential future events. In the healthcare industry, for example, these analytics can determine which patients may be

more susceptible to certain diseases, such as diabetes or heart disease. An important study by Reece and Danforth (2017) utilized computational machine-learning techniques to screen Instagram photographs for depression indicators.

- **Prescriptive analytics for images**: Prescriptive analytics goes beyond solely predicting outcomes by providing actionable recommendations based on image data. This type of analytics can guide optimal decisions to accomplish desired outcomes or avoid undesirable ones. For instance, in the fashion industry, by analyzing images of current fashion trends, prescriptive analytics might propose certain design modifications or introduce new color palettes to meet impending seasonal demands. Prescriptive analytics is a forward-thinking method for interpreting image data because it not only identifies trends but also recommends actionable insights.

After laying the groundwork for understanding image analytics and its critical significance across a variety of industries, it is necessary to investigate the nuances and specific methodologies inherent to this field. Whether the challenge involves distinguishing facial characteristics or detecting objects in complex environments, the techniques utilized are sophisticated and varied. As we progress in the field of image analytics, it is essential to classify and comprehend its numerous subtypes. This classification not only facilitates comprehension but also highlights the multifaceted nature of this field. With this context as a foundation, we will now discuss the various categories of image analytics and its application.

8.3 Application of Image Analytics

In the ever-changing social media landscape, where content reigns supreme, image analytics provides the means to comprehend this content in depth. As consumers continue to communicate with images rather than words, the demand for sophisticated image analytics will continue to increase. The technological advancements in image analysis now enable brands to access context, environment, and emotions that are inaccessible via textual information alone. Hence, image analytics can prove beneficial in a range of disciplines such as marketing (Dzyabura et al., 2021), retailing (Marder et al., 2015), medical imaging (Li et al., 2018; Zhang & Metaxas, 2016), tourism and hospitality (Marine-Roig, 2019; Zhan et al., 2024), and brand image tracking (Sabuncu & Atmis, 2020). When discussing image analytics within the context of social media analytics, several significant types emerge:

1. **Object detection and classification**: In the context of social media, object detection and classification can be extremely advantageous (Asif et al., 2021; Knura et al., 2021). For example, a brand could use this method to determine the frequency with which their product appears in user-generated content. By analyzing millions of photographs, brands can determine whether their product is typically associated with beach excursions, urban environments, or family gatherings. This type of knowledge can inform marketing campaigns and branding choices. In addition, applying image analytics to social media posts and utilizing deep learning algorithms for picture categorization and object identification helps automate emergency response decision-making in disaster management (Asif et al., 2021).

2. **Facial recognition and emotion analysis**: While facial recognition identifies individuals in an image, emotion analysis goes one step further by determining the affective state of the detected face(s). Understanding the emotional responses of users to specific content can be invaluable for brands and advertisers. For example, a study by Mazhar et al. (2022) used facial recognition and emotion analysis, using machine learning algorithms to evaluate viewer reactions to movie reviews, aiming to determine how people are affected by reviewers' writing. Additionally, emotion analysis can be used to monitor real-time reactions during live events or product launches on platforms such as Instagram Live and Facebook Live.

3. **Scene recognition**: Scene recognition identifies a photograph's context or location. Understanding whether a photograph was shot in a mountainous terrain, beach location, or urban landscape can be crucial for a travel company. This information aids in customizing advertisements and content suggestions for users based on their preferred travel experiences or destinations, as evidenced by the scenes that frequently appear in their uploads and shares (Lin et al., 2021).

4. **Pattern analysis**: Social media platforms are replete with trends that frequently center on specific patterns or textures. Whether it is a specific type of apparel print or a wallpaper texture that is popular in interior design circles, pattern analysis can help businesses remain ahead of the curve. By analyzing patterns frequently displayed in influencer posts or popular images on Pinterest, fashion brands, for example, can use this to anticipate fashion trends (Gu et al., 2017).

5. **Semantic segmentation**: This is the process of comprehending each pixel in an image and identifying the object or entity to which it pertains. This could be notably beneficial for augmented reality (AR) features in social media. Snapchat and Instagram, which allow users to superimpose digital information on real-world images, significantly rely on this type

of analysis. By comprehending the content at the pixel level, these platforms can integrate AR elements into user content more seamlessly (Ko & Lee, 2020).

6. **Machine learning**: Machine learning employs statistical techniques to recognize patterns in data and is a crucial component of advanced image analytics. Previously discussed essential domains such as object detection, facial recognition, and scene identification are trained by these techniques. The selection of image analysis instruments is heavily reliant on the particular application. For simpler duties, straightforward instruments may suffice. However, for complex duties such as object recognition in images, machine learning becomes indispensable. By comprehending the various types of available image analyses, marketers, brand managers, and social media strategists can make more informed decisions and design more engaging campaigns for their target audiences.

8.4 Image Analytics and Social Media Analytics

In an era characterized by a shift toward visual content, image analytics has transitioned from a luxury to a necessity for brands seeking to comprehend and effectively engage their target audiences. This specialized discipline, which is a subset of computer vision, expands the scope of social media analytics by enabling companies to extricate actionable insights from images across multiple platforms. These insights can range from recognizing objects and individuals to analyzing emotions and sentiments.

Consider a brand assessing the effectiveness of a recent marketing campaign. With image analytics, it becomes possible to quantify the frequency and context in which a logo appears within user-generated content. These real-time insights are crucial for optimizing advertising strategies, identifying key influencers, and comprehending actual consumer engagement with a product. Let's delve into the practical applications of image analytics in the realm of social media.

1. **Measure ROI with logo recognition**: Utilizing image analytics, brands can evaluate the ROI of offline advertising campaigns, such as stadium sponsorships, using logo recognition. By quantifying the number of visual impressions, businesses can at last answer age-old queries regarding the efficacy of such endeavors.

2. **Track visual mentions, or "share of eye"**: Traditional metrics, such as "share of voice," measure text-based brand conversations. Image analytics introduces the concept of "share of eye," which focuses on the visual elements, such as logos and product placements, that are frequently untagged

in social media postings. A brand such as Nike, for instance, may dominate text-based dialogues but overlook crucial visual mentions of their products.

3. **Identify moments of consumption**: Image analytics reveals actual product usage, which text-only analysis often overlooks. For instance, a social media photo may depict a person donning a specific brand of shirt or sipping a particular brand of beverage—data elements that are rarely mentioned explicitly in the text but are invaluable for brands. Moreover, a study by Marres et al. (2023) utilized image analytics and "interpretative querying" within a situational analysis framework to examine how COVID-19 testing was visually represented on Twitter. By categorizing and analyzing images, the study explored how visuals depicted testing locations, relationships, and issues. The findings highlight the role of infographics and other visuals in shaping public discourse, revealing patterns in how images communicated disparities in testing accessibility, societal challenges, and collective anxieties (Marres et al., 2023).

4. **Decode audience demographics**: Facial recognition technologies can provide additional information about the age, gender, and affective states of people depicted in images, resulting in a deeper comprehension of the audience.

5. **Enhanced image captioning**: Modern systems are now able to generate detailed image descriptions, such as "a man and a woman wearing Patagonia shirts in front of majestic mountains," thereby providing deeper contextual insights.

6. **Temporal image analysis**: In rapidly evolving industries such as fashion, businesses can monitor trends over time to gain insight into seasonal shifts in consumer preferences through the use of temporal image analysis.

Platforms such as Instagram, with more than 1.38 billion daily users (Newberry, 2023), demonstrate the importance of visual content in contemporary communication. Many images lack accompanying text, indicating that their emotional or contextual substance is wholly visual. If brands restrict their analytics to text, they run the risk of missing a bounty of consumer feedback embedded in images.

Ignoring this sophisticated layer of analytics could result in lost opportunities for brand engagement and expansion. On the other hand, adopting image analytics provides brands with a more comprehensive understanding of consumer behavior, preferences, and attitudes. Image analytics is not solely a theoretical concept; it is a practical instrument for gaining actionable insights about audiences and industries. It provides a comprehensive view of immense image collections, making it simpler for brands to recognize trends, identify emerging influencers, and even detect fraudulent social media activity (Awan et al., 2022).

8.5 Tools for Image Analytics

Image analytics involves the extraction of meaningful information from images to generate insights and assist in decision-making. As the demand for visual content processing has increased, particularly in the age of social media and digital advertising, a variety of sophisticated tools and techniques have emerged to facilitate image analytics. These range from open-source software to commercial platforms and from basic techniques to advanced machine-learning algorithms.

Image analytics, particularly in the social sciences, is still developing due to the skills required in visualization and machine learning (Barnes & Rutter, 2019). The first step in doing fruitful research in image analytics is articulating the nature of the problem, the importance of the issue, and the specific questions you hope to answer. After the problem definition, the first stage is to collect images that need to be analyzed. Using programs like R, Python, MATLAB, and so forth, image data can be obtained publicly, purchased, or scraped off the web. A simple way to gather images is through image URLs in a dataset. Levi and Hassner (2015) proposed "convolutional neural networks" (CNNs) for accurate facial categorization across gender, age, and mood.

8.5.1 Open-Source Tools

Open-source software is vital to the democratization of technology, especially in the field of image analytics. These developer-created and maintained tools offer comprehensive functionality comparable to that of their commercial counterparts. Anyone, from enthusiasts to devoted researchers, can use, modify, and even contribute to the development of these tools due to their open nature. Open-source software not only encourages innovation by removing cost barriers but also promotes transparency, as anyone can inspect and modify the source code. This philosophy has led to the development of a vast array of image processing and analytics applications:

- ImageJ is a robust, open-source software primarily utilized for scientific image processing. The software is flexible and supported by a large community of plugin developers, making it useful for a variety of image analysis tasks.
- GIMP (GNU Image Manipulation Program) is primarily known as an image manipulation program, but it also offers analytical capabilities, especially when combined with extensions.
- OpenCV (Open Source Computer Vision Library) is one of the best-known open-source tools in this field. It offers a comprehensive collection

of both traditional and cutting-edge computer vision and machine learning algorithms. Developers can perform image processing, object detection, and facial recognition using OpenCV.

8.5.2 Commercial Tools

On the commercial front, platforms such as Google Cloud Vision, Brandwatch, and Amazon Rekognition are available. Using machine learning, these cloud-based services provide compelling image analysis capabilities. They can detect objects, read printed and handwritten text, and even identify specific features within enormous image datasets, all without requiring the end-user to have an in-depth understanding of machine learning or computer vision.

Marketers and brand managers may benefit greatly from Brandwatch because of its useful picture recognition capabilities. Users may use this technology to collect and analyze brand-related logos and photos, learn more about their target audience, and spot trends in the making before they achieve broad momentum. The Brandwatch Image Insights platform stands out as a well-known social media analytics listening platform that also provides a suite of educational tools designed expressly with teachers and researchers in mind, including Brandwatch for Classrooms (McGuirk, 2021).

8.6 Challenges and Limitations of Image Analytics

While image analytics offers several opportunities for extracting insights from visual data, it is not devoid of challenges (Ezhilraman & Srinivasan, 2018). Understanding these challenges can assist stakeholders in deploying image analytics more efficiently and in managing their expectations from such tools. Here are some of the most important obstacles and constraints:

1. **Image data quality**: The precision of image analytics is largely dependent on the image data quality. Image analysis may be inaccurate if the inputted images are blurred, low-resolution, or inadequately illuminated.
2. **Diverse data sources**: Images originate from a multitude of devices and sources, each with its own resolutions, file formats, and qualities. It is often challenging to standardize these disparate data formats for consistent analysis.
3. **Privacy concerns**: Particularly in the case of facial recognition, there are significant privacy concerns among users. Unauthorized use of images can result in legal and ethical complications.

4. **Bias and fairness**: Machine learning models, including image analytics models, are trained on datasets. If these datasets are biased, so too may be the output. This is especially concerning in facial recognition applications, where biases can lead to incorrect identifications, especially for minorities and people of color.
5. **Overreliance on automation**: While automation can process immense quantities of image data quickly, a reliance on automation without human oversight can lead to errors or misinterpretations.
6. **Interpretability**: Deep learning models are frequently perceived as "black boxes." While they may provide correct results, it is difficult to comprehend why a particular decision or classification was made.

In light of these obstacles, organizations must approach image analytics with a balanced perspective, recognizing both its immense potential and its limitations. Training, regular model evaluations, and human oversight can go a long way toward ensuring that image analytics achieves its intended purpose.

8.7 An Overview of Video Analytics

Video data is a growing component of the global data sphere, influencing multiple industries. In fact, video constitutes the bulk of consumer Internet traffic. Given the proliferation of video data sources, such as the extensive installation of security cameras around the world, it is obvious that robust, dependable tools are required to analyze this vast data set.

The volume of video data necessitates scalable and effective analytical solutions. Consider optical character recognition (OCR) as an example. This time-tested method converts images comprising typed or handwritten text into a machine-readable format. In principle, one might presume that OCR could easily extract a number from a license plate image; however, real-world applications frequently require more complex solutions.

This does not imply that video analytics is devoid of areas of obvious automation. As evidence of the efficacy of automated video analysis, researchers have cited applications such as license plate recognition in traffic management (Balia et al., 2021) and detecting scene transitions in movies (Islam et al., 2023). Similar to image analytics, video analytics employs computer vision algorithms to deconstruct video content and generate actionable insights. In addition to optimizing the utility of video resources, this data provides invaluable operational information. Innovations in deep learning are largely responsible for the burgeoning academic and industrial interest in video analytics. Such developments have paved the way for automation in traditionally human-supervised fields.

The current landscape of video analytics is rife with innovation. The scope ranges from counting event attendees to implementing intelligent parking solutions. Particularly prominent are characteristics like facial recognition and automatic license plate recognition. Companies that adopted video surveillance infrastructures before the AI surge are now in the vanguard, employing cutting-edge AI solutions to address persistent problems.

Video analytics provides transformative advantages for the retail industry (Marder et al., 2015). It improves queuing management in retail, for instance, by providing granular insights into checkout dynamics. This helps to improve self-checkout procedures and honor-code systems while reducing theft-related hazards. Effective queuing management becomes crucial during health crises such as pandemics to regulate customer movement and reduce the risk of contagion spread. In addition, video analytics assists retailers in consumer counting by revealing the dynamics of foot traffic. This allows for the evaluation of the effectiveness of marketing campaigns and product displays. Observing patterns, such as customer dwell time close to specific product displays, can significantly influence branding and operational strategies (Marder et al., 2015). Such intelligence is essential for enhancing the consumer experience and maximizing business performance as a whole.

Deep learning and machine learning play a crucial role in this development. These pillars of artificial intelligence have accelerated the development of video analytics by introducing automated alternatives to previously human-intensive tasks. An illustrative example is security. Modern video analytics provides sophisticated object detection in video streams, tracing entities, locating unauthorized access, and notifying users of suspicious activities. Techniques such as real-time facial recognition and license plate decoding enable immediate responses to threats and facilitate access management for authorized personnel in restricted areas.

Case Study 8.1 Understanding Image and Video Recognition with Amazon Rekognition

In the digital technology landscape, the capacity to interpret and comprehend the content of an image or video has become indispensable. Image and video recognition, in which computers can identify various elements within visual content, has altered how we interact with digital media. To comprehend the complexities of this domain, the Amazon Rekognition platform provides an in-depth exploration of visual comprehension.

Background

Amazon Rekognition, introduced in 2016, is an innovative service from Amazon Web Services (AWS) that uses machine learning and computer vision to analyze visual content. Imagine giving machines the ability to "see" and "understand" images and videos, precisely processing enormous quantities of data.

Important Attributes and Their Implications

- **Celebrity recognition**: Amazon Rekognition can identify well-known figures across multiple media formats. An advertising agency, for instance, can rapidly sift through hours of footage to discover instances in which a celebrity made an appearance while adhering to usage rights.
- **Labels**: Amazon Rekognition identifies objects, locations, activities, landmarks, and dominant colors in images and videos. Consider a tourism agency that wishes to promote beaches; the system can filter through thousands of images and highlight only those that prominently feature beach landscapes.
- **Object recognition**: The service can be taught to recognize particular objects, such as company logos and brand symbols. A brand can monitor its presence in event footage by identifying instances in which its logo appears, thereby measuring its visibility during the event.
- **Text recognition**: Amazon Rekognition captures and interprets written content within visual data, regardless of how skewed or distorted the text may be. For example, detecting street signs from city footage can provide urban planners with information about locations in need of improved signage.
- **Face search and comparison**: Amazon Rekognition is capable of comparing facial features against a database to identify potential connections. For example, during a large-scale event, administrators can compare faces captured on video with a list of VIP attendees to ensure that special visitors receive the proper privileges. Moreover, the tool can recognize multiple facial characteristics within visual content. A fashion eyewear brand, for instance, can analyze popular designs and preferences by scanning content for images of people wearing spectacles.

Real-World Application: Challenges in the Media Industry

The proliferation of VOD (Video-On-Demand) platforms has given consumers access to an abundance of content options. This has posed difficulties for media companies in terms of categorizing, managing, and monetizing content. Previously, large human teams manually processed content; now, with Amazon Rekognition Video, they can analyze vast volumes of content, expedite tasks, and derive crucial insights, thereby optimizing time and resources. Hence, Amazon Rekognition is a prime example of the advancements in machine learning and computer vision. It demonstrates the transformative potential of such technologies across industries.

8.8 Video Analytics in Social Media

Video content is abundant on social media, and understanding such content is crucial. Video analytics provides a more in-depth understanding of user engagement, preferences, and behavior, making it an increasingly essential component of social media analytics. It facilitates not only improved content strategies but also a more individualized and engaging user experience.

Video analytics provides a granular comprehension of viewer engagement. Analysis of videos helps monitor metrics such as average viewing duration, re-watches, and drop-off points. For example, if a large percentage of viewers cease watching a promotional video within the first 10 seconds, it may indicate that the content failed to attract their interest immediately. Similarly, high re-watch rates may indicate portions of the video that particularly resonated with viewers or were unclear on the initial viewing. Video analytics can be useful in finding these points within a video. YouTube analytics is a prime example of video analytics, whereby YouTube channel owners can understand the granular details about user behavior surrounding their videos.

From Instagram to TikTok, social media managers use video analytics to improve their content delivery. Social media platforms also use video analytics to tweak their algorithms for maximum engagement. By analyzing how users interact with videos—whether they view them in their totality, skip portions, or interact with interactive elements—social media managers can better tailor content feeds to the preferences of each user. This personalized approach not only enhances the user experience but also the efficacy of targeted advertisements.

Emotional analysis using facial recognition is another promising area within video analytics. When incorporated with live video features on platforms such as Facebook Live or Instagram Stories, it can measure responses to content in real time. This provides brands and content creators with instantaneous feedback on the impact of their videos, ranging from happiness and astonishment to bewilderment and disinterest. Additionally, video analytics facilitates trend forecasting. By analyzing the aesthetic styles, themes, and specific content elements of viral videos, brands and influencers can anticipate emerging trends and develop content strategies accordingly.

Chapter Summary

- In the digital age, we are experiencing an unambiguous tilt toward visual storytelling.
- This visually stimulating era necessitates a thorough comprehension and analysis of the image and video content to navigate it successfully.
- Images and videos excel at conveying nuanced narratives and evoking deep emotional connections.
- Image analytics, also known as "computer vision," "image analysis," and "image recognition," is a subfield of artificial intelligence and computer science.
- Object detection, facial recognition, and scene comprehension are the fundamental capabilities of image analytics tools.
- The purpose of descriptive image analytics is to interpret the content embedded within images.
- Utilizing visual data, predictive analytics can help forecast potential future events.
- Utilizing image analytics, brands can evaluate the ROI of offline advertising campaigns.
- Amazon Rekognition identifies objects, locations, activities, landmarks, and dominant colors in images and videos.

Questions for Review

1. What makes images very powerful?
2. What is image analytics and what are its different applications in various fields?
3. How do image and video analytics relate to social media analytics?
4. What are the different challenges and limitations of image analytics?

9

Data Visualization

Chapter Outline

Having navigated through the Discovery and Analysis phases of the DAV framework, where we learned to leverage and interpret social media data, we now arrive at the third and final stage, Visualization. Here, we shift our attention to a fundamental and culminating aspect of social media analytics: data visualization and storytelling. In this chapter, we will examine how to effectively present analyzed data in a way that communicates a compelling narrative, thereby assisting in making intelligent decisions.

The implementation of data visualization techniques can greatly enhance the understanding of social media data. The objective since the beginning has been to transform unprocessed data into practical insights that are visually engaging and readily understandable. A well-designed visualization not only reveals underlying patterns but also stimulates empathy, encourages active involvement, and motivates action, thus becoming a crucial tool in the field of social media analytics.

The Data Analytics Advantage. Laeeq Khan, Oxford University Press. © Oxford University Press (2025).
DOI: 10.1093/oso/9780197814222.003.0009

Data visualization emphasizes the vital importance of design aesthetics and cognitive psychology in understanding and analyzing intricate datasets. Through the utilization of effective visualization principles, analysts can harness and translate complex datasets into meaningful charts and graphs that support strategic decision-making. These visualizations help save valuable time by transforming raw numbers into meaningful information that is visual and quickly understandable. Hence, the skillful use of data visualization in social media analytics not only improves the clarity of data but also deepens its influence, leading to more knowledgeable and strategic decisions in the digital realm.

In this chapter, we delve into data visualization and understand its significance, trace the historical context of data visualization, understand the different types of charts and graphs, and acquaint ourselves with the various challenges within visualizing social media data. We illuminate why data visualization is essential in the realm of social media analytics. We discuss the fundamental components of creating compelling visualizations and how to adapt them to different categories of social media data. We will conclude by discussing the major principles of effective data visualization, its ethical considerations, and its application. It is vital to understand and appreciate the design principles that lead to compelling, accurate, and interactive visual narratives.

9.1 Introduction: Data Visualization and its Significance

It is said that "Seeing is believing." This age-old adage highlights a profound truth about human cognition: our innate tendency to believe and comprehend what we can see. Our ancestors have relied on visual aids to convey stories, make sense of their surroundings, and record knowledge since the beginning. From the intricate narratives depicted in cave paintings to the detailed information engraved into clay tablets, visualization has been a time-tested method of capturing complexity and fostering comprehension.

Today, data visualization stands at the intersection of analysis and art. Converting abstract datasets into tangible visual formats in the form of charts, graphs, and maps, simplifies intricate information structures. The science of visualization, firmly rooted in analytical rigor and design aesthetics, seeks to make complex data understandable, enhancing our ability to gain insights quickly and make confident decisions.

Big data's exponential growth has increased the importance of visualization tools in the contemporary analytics landscape. These tools, designed to depict patterns, trends, and outliers, are indispensable for maximizing the immense potential inherent in data. The development of interactive visualization technologies further enriches this environment and enables users to actively interact with visualizations and modify them, allowing for unprecedented depth and customization.

Due to the extraordinary capacity of humans to rapidly interpret visual stimuli, data visualization is both functional and aesthetically appealing. Our brain can recognize an image in just 13 milliseconds (Trafton, 2014). Exceptional human visual skills, which are guided by color, patterns, and gradients, are evidence of the harmony between vision and cognition.

It is evident from tracing the course of history that as human societies evolved, so did their visual communication methods. Every era has produced novel ways to visualize the world, from Ptolemy's pioneering cartographic endeavors to the Islamic Golden Age's celestial depictions. The computer revolution of the 20th century amplified this phenomenon by enabling real-time, dynamic visualizations of vast datasets.

In our current era of abundant information, data visualization provides much-needed context by transforming numbers into narratives and making sense of the immense amount of data. It is pivotal for brands and businesses to convert raw data into compelling stories that resonate with their audiences. Businesses across industries use data visualization to:

- **Clarify information**: Visual aids provide immediate clarity. There is some evidence to suggest that humans can process visuals much faster than text (Adaval et al., 2019). Instead of cumbersome tables, an airline, for instance, could use a color-coded map to distinguish flight traffic across various centers instantaneously.
- **Determine relationships and patterns**: Using visuals, latent correlations become apparent. Using a matrix, an e-commerce platform may identify a correlation between user-perusing patterns and purchase behaviors and adjust their recommendation algorithms accordingly.
- **Identify emerging trends**: Businesses can anticipate market shifts by mapping data over time. A coffee chain that observes an increase in sales of cold brew via a histogram may decide to introduce new variants or promotions.
- **Communicate insights**: Once discovered, insights require expression. A health organization could use interactive dashboards and reports to highlight global health trends, ensuring stakeholders can comprehend and interact with the data to draw strategic conclusions.

Data visualization combines empirical data with experiential elements, facilitating a more comprehensive understanding of the environment through visual representation. At its foundation, data visualization aims to disclose the invisible, simplify the complex, and visually communicate concepts. Indeed, the origins of visualization date back to ancient civilizations, evolving along-side human progress and technological development. Examining the historical development of data visualization is essential, as it offers a valuable understanding of the progression of visualizing information to enhance comprehension and decision-making abilities throughout the years. Furthermore, it allows us to recognize the evolution of optimal strategies and approaches in efficiently communicating intricate information. As we delve deeper into its historical trajectory, we will discover the numerous ways that visualization has influenced and been influenced by the zeitgeist of each era.

9.2 History and Evolution of Data Visualization

In the modern era of interactive charts, real-time graphs, and complex infographics, it is easy to neglect the origins of data visualization. Recent technological advancements and an explosion of available data have boosted its significance, but its origins date back centuries. The evolution from primitive drawings to today's dynamic digital graphics exemplifies humanity's enduring quest to display information, comprehend complexity, communicate, and simply tell a story.

In the following section, we will navigate chronologically through the evolution of data visualization, emphasizing how the needs of various eras have influenced the refinement of information presentation techniques. Our investigation will commence with primordial cave paintings and continue through the art of cartography (creation of maps), encompassing increasingly complex mathematical and trigonometric representations. We will investigate the evolution of information organization through tables, timekeeping charts, and enhanced geographical maps. Our investigation will culminate in the modern era, characterized by the introduction of advanced statistics, computational technology, and the revolutionary influences of big data and artificial intelligence.

Understanding this trajectory is indispensable because it illuminates the human pursuit of progress and illustrates the interconnected nature of human knowledge. The evolution of data visualization is a testament to humankind's interdependence, learning, sharing, and collaborative wisdom spanning millennia. This shared intellectual heritage comprises ancient civilizations, including the Greeks, Egyptians, and Babylonians, and has witnessed significant transformations and enhancements, particularly during the Islamic Golden Age leading up to the European Renaissance. Understanding the historical context provides a profound appreciation for the incremental developments that have led us to today's data-centric world. This accumulated knowledge builds upon past accomplishments and provides the groundwork for future innovations that promise to benefit all of humanity.

1. The Beginnings of Data Representation: Prehistoric to Ancient Civilizations

Ancient African rock art and visual inscriptions demonstrated humanity's propensity for visual documentation long before the formal development of cartography. Murals from as early as the 7th century BCE were known to depict diverse subjects varying from fauna to intricate urban blueprints. It is argued that the earliest forms of cartography emerged during the Mesopotamian period (Clarke, 2013). Due to the varying definitions of the term, determining the earliest example of a map is difficult. The Babylonian "Imago Mundi" clay tablet, believed to be from the 7th or 8th century BCE and now housed in the British Museum, is a prominent artifact from that era. The cities of the Indus Valley, which flourished between 3300 BCE and 1100 BCE, became well-known for their intricate seal engravings, innovative urban planning, and adequate water management systems (Kenoyer, 1998). In addition, the proto-cuneiform inscriptions in the Sumerian language, which date back to around 3100 BCE, represent an important step forward in representing ancient data (Monaco, 2017). The Turin Papyrus Map, which depicts roads, quarries, and gold mines in Wadi Hammamat (Egypt), dates to approximately 1150 BCE and is presently held in the Egyptian Museum in Turin, Italy (Harrell & Brown, 1992). It is a testament to ancient Egyptian cartographic prowess. In the 5th century BCE ancient India's most notable contribution to mathematics includes the development of the number zero.

While the Greeks excelled at conceptual advancements in geography and cartography, the Romans excelled at creating pragmatic tools and maps to administer their vast territories. The Romans drew ornate road maps, known as "itineraria," that detailed the distances between essential transit points, thereby facilitating the administration of their extensive road networks (Britannica, 2023a). In 150 CE, a Greek scholar, Claudius Ptolemy, wrote a geography book (no surviving copy of his original work is available), presenting a list of several thousand locations around the Mediterranean (Stoner et al., 2023). It can be argued that the ancient cultures forged a legacy that paved the way for future data visualization and mapmaking developments.

2. Scientific Advancement During the Islamic Golden Age (8th to 14th Century)

Contemporary Western literature often overlooks the significant contributions in science and visualization made during the golden age of Islamic civilization.

Also referred to as the "Islamic Golden Age," it refers to a period of significant cultural, scientific, and philosophical advancement in the Islamic world, influenced by Islamic principles and values. Building on the foundational knowledge of earlier civilizations, including Greek, Egyptian, and others, Muslim scholars made significant advancements in geometry and cartography during the 8th to 14th centuries CE (Britannica, 2023b). They translated numerous academic works into Arabic, preserving and enhancing this knowledge. These translations unified disparate knowledge sources under a single language, Arabic, thus facilitating the fusion of Greco-Roman and Indo-Iranian scientific insights within the Arab-Islamic academic community (Pastuch, 2022). During the Islamic Golden Age, advancements in cartography, textual data, numeracy, astronomy, spatial visualization, and chronometry facilitated Islamic religious practices and scientific investigations. Other developments such as anatomy and medical sciences by Avicenna (Ibn Sina) also had a substantial effect on how data/information was structured and displayed. Many of these innovations provided the basis for the evolution of visualization techniques, signaling a turning point in the progression of knowledge. Many of these developments were groundbreaking in those times and are related to timekeeping, mapping the skies, and measuring and mapping the Earth. We will discuss some of these developments in further detail.

- **Timekeeping**: During the Islamic golden era, precise timekeeping was of paramount importance, primarily driven by the need for accurate Muslim five daily prayer times. This necessity spurred advancements in astronomical observations and mathematical calculations. During the Umayyad era (661–750 CE) in Damascus, timekeeping houses started to emerge, where early astronomical instruments were developed to refine prayer schedules (Brentjes, 2008). This practice expanded beyond the Levant, to places like al-Andalus (Muslim Spain) and Cairo (in Egypt), with specialized astronomers, or "muwaqqits," ensuring time precision (King, 1998). Among the most notable muwaqqits (timekeeper and astronomer) was Ibn al-Shatir (1304–1375 C.E.) who served in Damascus's Ummayad mosque. Similarly, the Great Mosque of Granada in al-Andalus boasted advanced timekeeping in the 14th century, driven by top astronomers and mathematicians. Such practices created a demand for astronomical and timekeeping practices across the Islamic world. As a result, scholars developed structured tabular formats (Jadwal in Arabic) to systematically organize numerical data, paving the way for more sophisticated mathematical models and astronomical predictions.
- **Mapping the Skies**: Charting the skies was of great significance for Muslims due to its practical and intellectual implications. Essentially, the

astrolabe (Arabic: al-Asturlab), a sophisticated astronomical device that played a crucial role in determining the qibla—the direction of the Kaaba in Makkah, toward which Muslims must face during their five daily prayers. Regardless of location, accurate qibla determination was a religious obligation, making astronomical precision a vital aspect of Islamic scholarship.

Mariam Al-Asturlabi, was a 10th-century Muslim women astronomer and instrument maker from Aleppo, renowned for her mastery in crafting astrolabes (Gaida, 2016). Beyond religious applications, the astrolabe was also indispensable for navigation and trade, facilitating travel across the vast Islamic world, which stretched from the Iberian Peninsula in Europe to as far as the Straits of Malacca in East Asia. Traders, explorers, and scholars relied on celestial navigation to traverse deserts, seas, and foreign lands, reinforcing the connection between astronomy and economic prosperity. The intellectual pursuit was also fueled by a deep fascination with astronomy, inspired by the Quran's encouragement to explore the natural world and creation. *Suwar al-kawākib*, a book written around 964 CE by Al-Sufi Abd al-Rahman ibn Umar, is the benchmark for depictions of stars (and their names) and constellations (Islam, 2011). Once translated, his works garnered extensive recognition throughout Europe.

- **Measuring the Earth**: Al-Biruni, born in Central Asia (in modern-day Uzbekistan) in 973 CE, became a prominent personality during the Islamic Golden Age due to his extensive knowledge of astronomy, mathematics, geography, and anthropology (Ahn & Juraev, 2024). Al-Biruni was deeply committed to interdisciplinary studies (Malagaris, 2020). Considered one of the "intellectual giants of humankind" (Sparavigna, 2014), Al-Biruni created comprehensive diagrams and charts relating to astronomical phenomena in the 11th century, pioneering early conceptions of information or data representation. In 1036, he completed his magnum opus, "Kitab al-Qanun al-Mas'udi" (Canon Mas'udicus), demonstrating his innovative approach to astronomy and geography. In addition to intricate astronomical observations, this work contains an extensive table of the geographical coordinates of more than 600 significant global locations. He presented the earliest text of the polar azimuthal equidistant projection, a map projection still in use today (King, 1996). While serving as court astrologer in Ghazni (the Ghaznavids' capital in present-day eastern Afghanistan), his seminal astronomical work was concluded in the Jhelum region of the Ghaznavid empire (modern-day Pakistan), signaling a significant milestone in the foundational cartographic efforts. Using his refined trigonometric methods, he estimated the radius of the Earth to be approximately 6335.72 kilometers, a figure that differs from the modern estimate by less than 1% (Earth's modern-day calculated equatorial radius is 6,378 km).

- **Mapping the Earth with Al-Idrisi**: Muhammad ibn Muhammad al-Idrisi (lived between the years 1100 and 1165 CE), a geographer from North Africa in the 12th century, amassed invaluable geographical knowledge through extensive global travel. His travels and extensive knowledge attracted the attention of Sicily's Norman king Roger II. King Roger, recognizing al-Idrisi's expertise, commissioned him to create the Nuzhat al-mushtaq fi ikhtiraq al-afaq (Tabula Rogeriana), a comprehensive geography of the world's main population centers (Stoner et al., 2023). Al-Idrisi collaborated with the Sicilian court for 15 years to compile an amalgam of the socioeconomic, physical, cultural, and political conditions of the time, including 70 maps of population centers, which later culminated in an extraordinary six-foot silver disc (Pastuch, 2022). This compendium (the oldest known copy of al-Idrisi's original geographical work), a testament to his exhaustive research and archived in the National Library of France, was hailed as the apogee of cartography and had a significant impact on both Islamic and European mapping traditions (Hiatt, 2021). Al-Idrisi's pioneering use of the cylindrical projection technique, which Gerard Mercator would later adopt in 1569, further magnifies his significant contributions to the field (Al-Hassani, 2012).

According to Brown-Hejazi and Larsen (2021), when constructing celestial maps, early modern European astronomers frequently consulted translations of books written in the Muslim world from libraries in Andalucía and Baghdad.

3. Transformations of the Renaissance and Early Modern Periods (16th to 19th Centuries)

Around 1440, Johannes Gutenberg, a goldsmith, invented the movable-type printing press in Germany. This invention prompted a revolution in printing, as it involved the use of reusable metal letters which improved efficiency and reduced costs, hence, having far-reaching implications in various fields (Flake, 1994). The European Renaissance ushered in a period of pervasive dissemination of visual data, spurred on by printing innovations. Analytical geometry and statistics developments laid the groundwork for modern data visualization in the 17th century. Here are a few notable people in the history of data visualization between the 16th and 19th centuries, primarily in Europe.

The 17th century witnessed the development of analytic geometry, metrics, and concepts used to quantify time, distance, and space. The era also saw the establishment of statistical methods such as estimation, probability, and demography, which significantly improved problem-solving and paved the way for visual thinking. The following are a few notable developments in this age:

- **The 1507 world map by Martin Waldseemüller**: This map was a product of an ambitious endeavor undertaken in St. Dié, France, whereby a group of scholars and cartographers compiled a comprehensive map that included the Americas from their recent voyages of discovery (Stoner et al., 2023). With its accurate depiction of newly discovered lands and innovative approach to cartography, Waldseemüller's map exemplifies the convergence of exploration, scholarship, and art during the early Renaissance.

- **Gerardus Mercator world map of 1569**: Born in Belgium, Mercator introduced a revolutionary map projection method that became the standard for centuries despite his limited travel. Due to the linear scale of nautical cartography, his method of presenting the globe on a level surface was crucial in advancing the science of cartography (Stoner et al., 2023).

- **The 1631 map by Joan and Cornelius Blaeu**: Joan and Cornelius Blaeu were leading Dutch printers and mapmakers around 1631. Three generations of cartographers ran their Amsterdam business from 1605 until 1696. Joan Blaeu's finest work was in the form of an atlas that included several maps of the earth, oceans, and heavens. "*Nova et accuratissima totius terrarum orbis tabula*": "New and Very Accurate Map of the Whole World"—was the first map in this atlas. Instead of Mercator's projection, Joan and Blaeu represented the earth as a twin hemispherical representation (Stoner et al., 2023).

- **Modern Graphs and Charts in the 18th and 19th Centuries**: The 18th and 19th centuries witnessed the proliferation of graphical methods, such as line graphs, histograms, and scatter plots, contributing to the expansion of data visualization. Many influential explorers and scientists from France and England made substantial contributions to the progress of cartographic and demographic understanding. During this period, economic statistics, including social, moral, medical, and other datasets, influenced government policies and planning.

- **Joseph Priestley** (lived between 1733 – 1804 C.E.) was an eminent personality of 18th century England, a clergyman in the English church, and a scientist. Although Priestley is widely known for discovering oxygen, he contributed significantly to modern-day data visualization. In 1769, he introduced "A New Chart of History," an evolved rendition of demographic charting (Bourne & Weaver, 2018). This groundbreaking work illustrated the tenure of prominent global powers, including the Russian Empire, the Saracens, the Turks, the English, and the Persian Empire.

4. Computers and the Digital Renaissance in the 20th Century

- **Introduction to exploratory data analysis:** John Tukey's 1977 exploratory data analysis (EDA) used visual data analysis to find patterns and outliers, thus revolutionizing data interpretation (Tukey, 1977). Graphical depiction improved the understanding of data under Tukey (Ware, 2019). This visual method improved data comprehension and shaped current data visualization technologies, demonstrating the power of analysis and visualization.

- **Modern data visualization:** Edward Tufte's 1983 book *The Visual Display of Quantitative Information* is a data visualization classic (Tufte, 1983). In his "data-ink ratio" philosophy, Tufte emphasizes visual simplicity and clarity by minimizing nonessential ink (or pixels in a digital format) that does not represent data. He highlighted data misrepresentation in graphics using the "Lie Factor" to emphasize the ethical imperative of correct portrayal (Healy, 2018). Tufte's theoretical and practical insights are vital for data visualization designers and enthusiasts.

- **Computer revolution:** The second half of the 20th century heralded a transformational era for data visualizations as computers revolutionized every field. Prior to this, visualizations were static and manual. Computers quickly processed massive amounts of data, creating heat maps, 3D plots, and real-time animated charts. These innovations improved interaction and personalization. Computer graphics improved visualizations for academic, corporate, and policy communication by making them more comprehensive and attractive.

5. Navigating Big Data and AI Landscapes in the 21st Century

Innovative data visualization techniques have become essential in today's big data–dominated environment. Advanced visualization tools supported by machine learning and artificial intelligence are interactive, intuitive, and multilayered. Moving beyond static graphs and charts, these tools facilitate interactivity, allowing users to zoom in on certain elements and examine the data from various perspectives. Interactive visualizations ensure that users can investigate data at their own pace. Such user-friendliness of tools makes complex data available to a wider user base, democratizing data-driven literacy.

Furthermore, AI technologies combined with historical data help predict future outcomes, empowering organizations to foresee changes and take proactive actions. As a further benefit of AI in data visualization, data can be processed and visualized in real-time, critical for monitoring live data streams, such as financial markets and social media sentiment, where such timely information can provide a competitive edge (Endert et al., 2017). Hence, the synergy of AI and data visualization allows for the creation of more nuanced and responsive visual tools. This is essential for businesses that intend to display complex datasets.

Figure 9.1 sums up the historical progression of data visualization. Visualization has a long-standing connection with humanity's drive for invention and the desire for convenience, just like every other form of communication or tool advancement. The pursuit of greater comprehension and effective transmission of information can be traced back to the primitive yet highly meaningful cave paintings, progressing through the complexities of Indus Valley seal engravings, the meticulousness of Sumerian cuneiforms, and the usefulness of Roman road maps. These historical endeavors in visualization were not solely artistic representations, but rather essential instruments for documenting, comprehending, and disseminating knowledge across different time periods and regions. Historical records show that advancements in human civilization

Figure 9.1 Contributions towards visualization over the ages

have consistently led to the development of new and innovative methods for organizing information. The advancements during the golden Islamic age from the 8th to the 14th centuries included timekeeping methods, celestial maps, meticulous cartography, and navigational aids. Those advancements provided a foundation for even greater advancements.

The progress made in the 16th to 19th centuries, including the invention of the movable-type printing press, the creation of Mercator's projection maps, and the construction of Priestley's Chart of History, were important achievements in the growth of visualization methods. The evolution of visualization, from Tukey's exploratory data analysis to contemporary visual display technologies, demonstrates an enhanced comprehension of data's possibilities and the increasing ability to utilize it effectively. The evolution of society has experienced an unparalleled acceleration in the 20th and 21st centuries, chiefly due to remarkable progress in computing, artificial intelligence, and machine learning.

The advancement of human creativity, namely in the field of visualization, highlights the collaborative effort of civilizations throughout history. The advancements of each period are based on the knowledge and experience gained from previous ones, demonstrating that human creativity is not limited by geography or culture. In a way, our world has always been a global world. Before, the pace of change was relatively slow. Advanced means of transport and communication further propelled globalization and faster exchange of ideas among the human family. The European Renaissance, ignited by the rediscovery of classical philosophies and further enhanced by the knowledge gained from the prosperous Islamic civilization, stands as evidence of the interrelated progress of humanity. Likewise, the Islamic civilization reached its highest point by adopting and expanding on the intellectual heritage of the Greeks, Romans, the inhabitants of the Indus Valley, Sumerians, Mesopotamians, and the ancient Indians. Essentially, the history of visualization is a dynamic collage of human creativity, serving as evidence of our inherent desire to gain a deeper understanding of our reality and convey our discoveries more efficiently. It is influenced by and also contributes to the collective human pursuit.

9.3 Types of Charts

Data visualization is a vast discipline that encompasses numerous techniques designed to present, analyze, and clarify data. Each visualization type appeals to particular data configurations, objectives, and narratives. While quality data is a prerequisite for a compelling data-driven narrative, it is not sufficient on its own. Effective data-driven storytelling occurs only when it conveys novel insights, provides new perspectives, or elicits actionable responses. We will now delve into prominent visualization methodologies and discuss their respective applications.

9.3.1 Bar Charts

Bar charts are one of the most fundamental forms of data visualization, effectively depicting categorical data with rectangular bars. The length of each bar directly corresponds to the magnitude or frequency of the data point it represents. Bar charts are available in both horizontal and vertical orientations and are ideal for comparing distinct categories. For example, a bar chart can be created to compare the engagement metrics of various social media posts over a month.

Bar charts are widely utilized because they facilitate immediate recognition of data patterns, strengths, and anomalies. By categorizing numerical data, these graphics reveal any hidden tendencies. Whether the orientation is horizontal or vertical, representational clarity remains consistent.

Bar charts are ideal for comparing data across various categories (see Figure 9.2). For example, bar charts can bring to life data depicting the prevalence of various hashtags across social media platforms or comparing the number of followers gained by a brand's X, Instagram, and Facebook accounts over a specified period. Here are a few tips and examples for the effective utilization of bar charts:

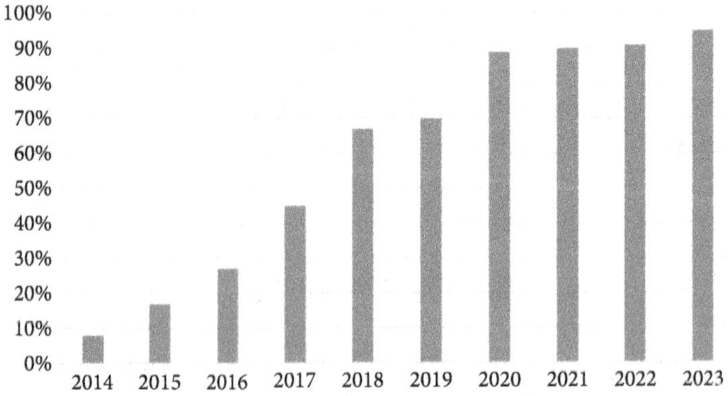

Figure 9.2 Bar Chart

- **Color variation**: Bar charts can be even more effective when differences are shown by adding distinct colors to improve visual clarity. For instance, the length of a bar could reflect the number of social media mentions, while its color could represent the social platforms associated with those mentions. Hence color variations can add another layer of information to a bar chart.
- **Stacked or side-by-side bars**: Stacked or adjacent bars offer additional information within the same chart and thus facilitate a multidimensional analysis. Stacked charts permit the concurrent representation of related metrics. For example, a bar chart could compare the number of likes, shares, and comments on multiple Facebook posts, depicted as a stacked chart in the same visualization.

Maximizing the potential of bar charts and making intelligent design decisions makes it possible to create a compelling visual narrative, particularly in social media analytics.

9.3.2 Histograms

Histograms, which look much like bar plots, are the best way to show the frequency ranges in continuous datasets. Each successive bar or cell in a histogram quantifies the frequency of data points within specified intervals. These graphical representations are particularly useful in illuminating data distribution patterns (see Figure 9.3).

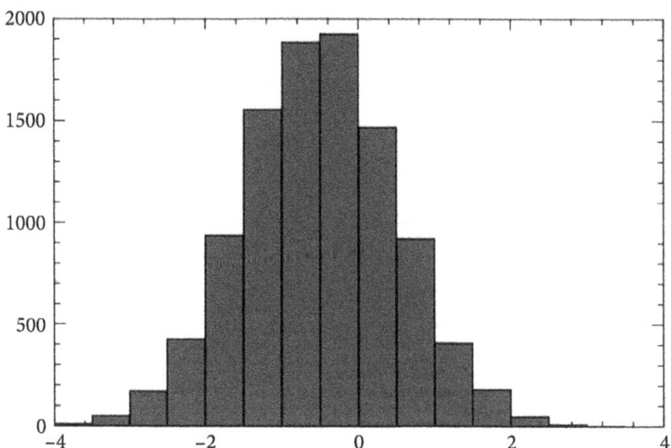

Figure 9.3 Histogram

Consider, for example, a dataset detailing the engagement durations of social media video viewers. It is simple to classify and depict these engagement periods using a histogram, thereby disclosing patterns, such as prevalent engagement timeframes. A histogram can adeptly visualize the distribution of likes on posts, signifying the number of posts that received, for instance, 0–50 likes, 51–100 likes, and 101–150 likes.

It is essential to recognize a significant distinction between histograms and bar charts: histograms feature continuous bars representing their representation of continuous data in which numerical data is depicted in fixed intervals, thereby sustaining a consistent sequence. In contrast, bar graphs typically represent categorical data and can present bars in descending or ascending order of magnitude.

9.3.3 Line Charts

Especially when the focus is on a continuous domain such as time, line charts excel at displaying data trends. Connecting individual data points with lines effectively illustrates the trajectory of values over a given time period. For example, line charts can be used to track the growth of a social media influencer's number of followers over a month or a year. Due to their straightforward depiction of sequential data, line charts are among the most popular visualization tools. Their strength lies in capturing and elucidating temporal patterns with clarity.

As depicted in Figure 9.4, line charts visually record and depict the fluctuations and patterns of data over time. Line charts also emphasize temporal trends

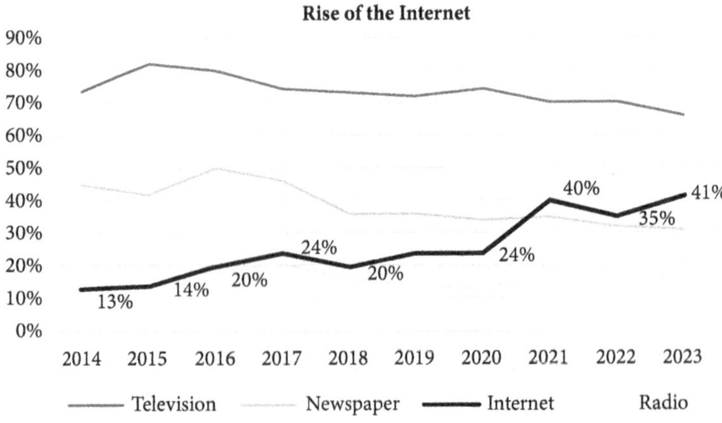

Figure 9.4 Line Chart

and patterns, such as the rise and decline of a brand's tweet mentions over several months or the seasonal fluctuations of a company's Instagram engagement metrics. Using the linear narrative capacity of line charts, professionals can construct a compelling story, which is beneficial for deciphering temporal patterns within social media data.

9.3.4 Pie Charts

By slicing a circle into segments, pie charts illustrate data about subsets of the whole.

Each segment corresponds to the data value it represents. The primary purpose of pie charts is to illustrate relative proportions or percentages within a dataset. When comparison is the objective, bar charts or layered bars provide a more precise visual representation, relieving the observer of the burden of deciphering overlapping or closely spaced pie slices.

Although frequently employed, they are best fitted for datasets with few categories, and should ideally be avoided. Although they are simple to understand and effectively communicate the three to four categories within a whole, they are often overloaded with more than needed categories thus eroding their usefulness in understanding data. This misuse can result in ambiguous presentations, leaving the audience with difficulty deciphering the data. For example, in Figure 9.5, the pie chart depicts the distribution of different media sources used for information

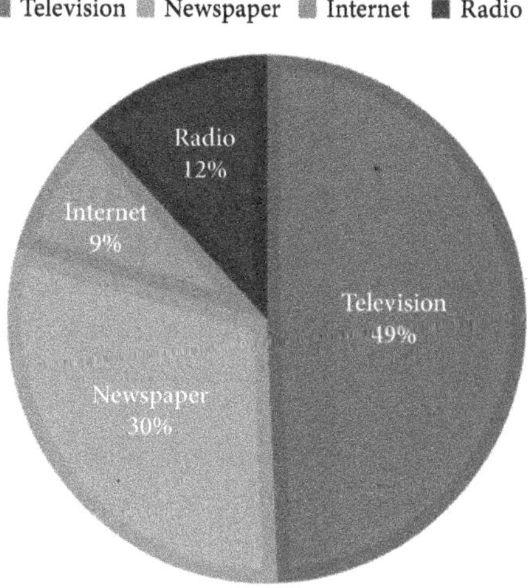

Figure 9.5 Pie Chart

or communication. The four categories shown are Television, Newspaper, Internet, and Radio, with their respective percentages indicating how much each medium contributes. However, if the pie chart were to show 7 or 10 categories, it would become difficult to make sense of the pie chart and visually differentiate between the slices of pie within the chart. Nevertheless, in depicting social data, pie charts can help illustrate the proportion of comments, favorites, and shares a particular post received, providing a snapshot of audience engagement. Here are a few points to consider for effective utilization of pie charts:

- **Slice limitation**: Limiting pie portions to no more than four or five segments is prudent. Conveying more than five ratios might dilute the clarity and purpose of the chart. Consider utilizing bar charts if a dataset contains numerous categories, as they can represent numerous data points without sacrificing readability. Overcrowded pie charts with numerous narrow segments can be challenging to comprehend. The essence of a pie chart is its simplicity; adding too many segments diminishes its usefulness.
- **Readability**: While pie charts can effectively illustrate relative proportions, their usefulness diminishes with increasing complexity. Their application should be judicious, bearing in mind the lucidity and comprehension of the audience, particularly in the context of social media data, where rapid comprehension is frequently of the utmost importance. For example, 3D pie charts and pie charts with lots of textual information should be avoided and they should be kept simple and clear.

9.3.5 Scatter Plots

Scatter graphs visually represent the relationship between two variables on a two-dimensional plane (see Figure 9.6). For example, a scatter diagram can graphically reveal patterns such as the correlation between post frequency and follower engagement or the relationship between video duration and viewer retention rates. These plots are convenient for emphasizing trends, concentrations, and outliers.

To make scatter plots even more effective, including a trend line can highlight the underlying correlation between data elements, providing a clearer understanding of the trajectory or direction of the data. For instance, by overlaying a trend line on a scatter diagram comparing the number of daily posts to daily engagement rates, one can discern whether increased posting frequency

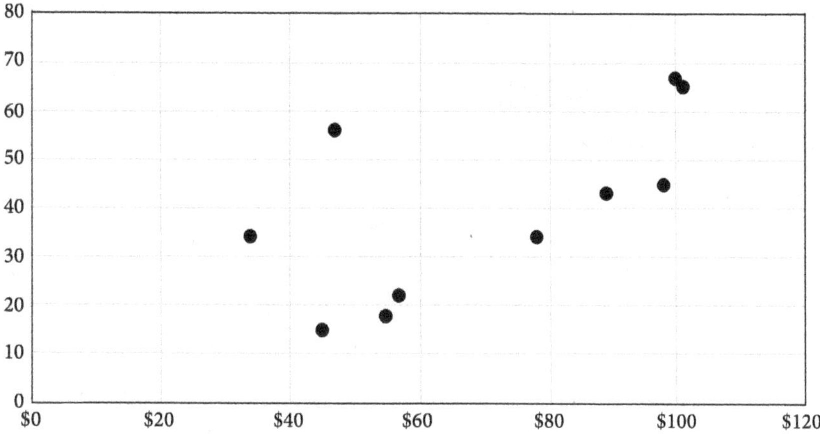

Figure 9.6 Scatter Plot

tends to enhance engagement on a particular platform. Hence, scatter plots are indispensable for discerning the relationships between variables, particularly when supplemented with elements such as trend lines to improve clarity and insight.

9.3.6 Box Plots

Box plots are also known as box-and-whisker plots (see Figure 9.7). These were introduced by John Tukey to depict quartile data distributions concisely. These diagrams illuminate the dataset's median, identify outliers, and provide insight into distributional skewness. For instance, box diagrams can compare engagement durations across campaigns or platforms in a social media context.

This type of visualization could disclose the median engagement time, prospective outliers (e.g., posts that are notably viral or underperforming), and the overall distribution of engagement times for each campaign or platform.

9.3.7 Heat Map Tables

Heat map tables are essentially tables that offer richer information by using color gradients to depict data values across two categorical dimensions. Heat maps are useful for highlighting variances effectively. These visualizations enable quick identification of high and low concentrations at the intersections of two categories.

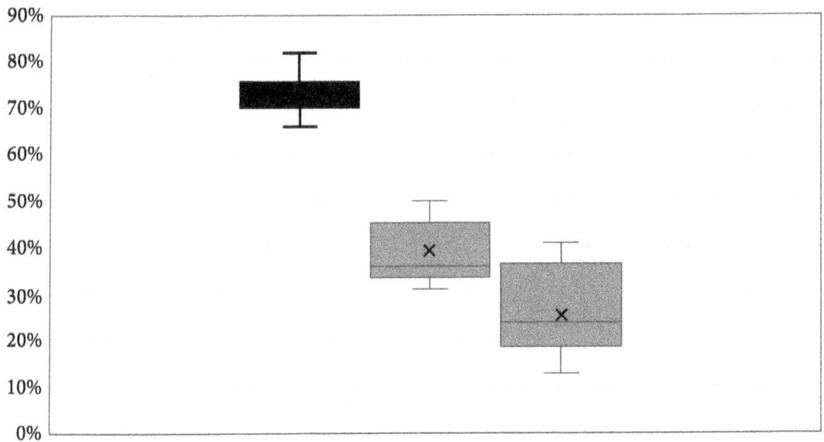

Figure 9.7 Box Plot

Year	Television	Newspaper	Internet	Radio	YouTube
2014	74%	45%	13%	18%	8%
2015	82%	42%	14%	21%	17%
2016	80%	50%	20%	18%	27%
2017	74%	46%	24%	21%	45%
2018	73%	36%	20%	16%	67%
2019	72%	36%	24%	14%	70%
2020	74%	34%	24%	13%	89%
2021	70%	35%	40%	18%	90%
2022	70%	32%	35%	17%	91%
2023	66%	31%	41%	16%	95%

Figure 9.8 Heat Map

For example, as shown in Figure 9.8, the heat map in tabular format depicts media types and their user base across the years. Darker hues denote heightened interest and adoption of different mediums, whereas lighter hues suggest decreased adoption. By modifying the size of individual squares, heat maps can convey an additional dimension. This nuanced illustration offers deeper insight.

9.3.8 Tree Maps

Tree maps depict hierarchical data efficiently by nesting rectangles. By its size and hue, each rectangle can represent a variety of data dimensions. A rectangle is assigned to each branch of the tree, and this rectangle is subsequently filled with smaller rectangles that represent the sub-branches. For example, Figure 9.9

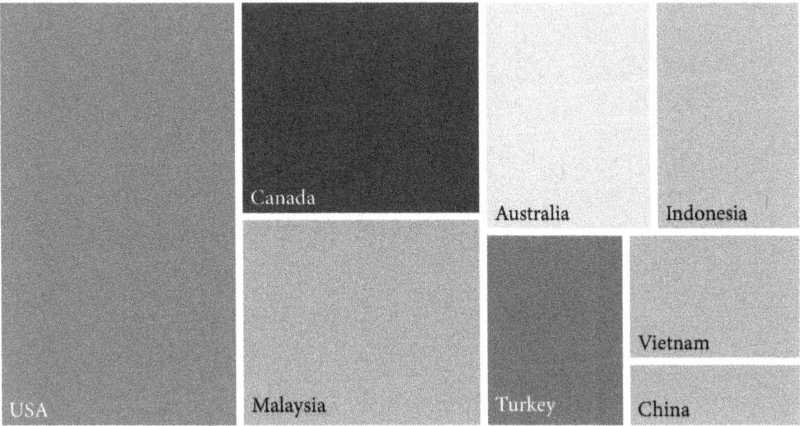

Figure 9.9 Tree Map

shows how the audience location numbers the determine size of each box or the rectangle.

The tree map data visualization approach offers a concise and effective manner of presenting information that is inherently organized in a hierarchical structure. It enables users to observe patterns and connections within the data at various levels of granularity. In addition, the advancement of interactive tree maps enables users to navigate to lower levels of the hierarchy. Functionalities related to color, interactivity, and size within a tree map aim to improve the usefulness and flexibility of these visualizations for exploring complex datasets.

Tree maps also have limitations, such as the possibility of clutter and overplotting in heavily populated sections of the visualization, the challenge of comparing the sizes of nonadjacent rectangles, and the requirement for effective color-coding schemes to distinguish between categories or levels of hierarchy.

9.3.9 Word Clouds

A word cloud is a graphical depiction of textual information, where the magnitude of each word signifies its frequency or significance within the original text. In some word clouds, color may also convey additional data dimensions or nuances. Although word clouds may not possess the same level of accuracy as other visualization methods, they do offer a quick and intuitive summary of the most prominent topics or keywords in a text corpus. For example, word clouds help identify the most frequently mentioned topics or themes in user comments

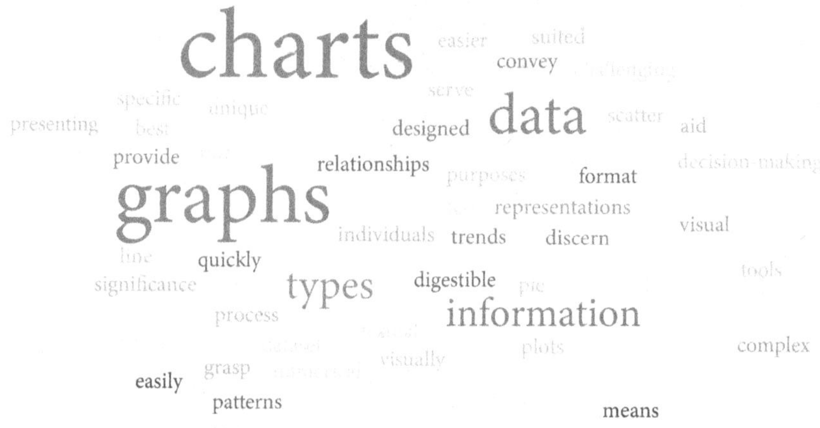

Figure 9.10 Word Cloud

or feedback on social media platforms. As shown in Figure 9.10, more prominent terms are presented in larger fonts and distinct colors, enhancing their visibility.

Word clouds are commonly employed to visually represent the thematic substance of textual information. By emphasizing the most significant words, they are able to efficiently communicate the main ideas of a substantial amount of text. Word clouds are commonly used in textual analytics as an initial analytical tool to uncover prominent themes or visually represent the frequency of specific terms in a dataset.

Although word clouds provide an appealing method to condense textual material, their analytical rigor is restricted. Nevertheless, they can serve as a compelling tool for captivating audiences or for preliminary exploratory analysis to motivate further research.

9.4 Challenges in Visualizing Social Media Data

While the process of visualizing social media data can be fulfilling, it is also fraught with challenges that might impede the extraction of valuable insights. The immense amount of data produced daily by social media platforms presents a major challenge. Visualizing the abundance of posts, comments, shares, and other forms of interactions can be daunting, and the task of sorting through this extensive dataset to extract pertinent information for visualization can be a massive endeavor.

The variety of social data also adds a layer of complexity. A single social media platform has a variety of data types, including text-based posts and comments, images, videos, and pure numerical metrics such as likes and shares. A single data visualization framework may not effectively integrate and compare these diverse data types. Furthermore, qualitative data is hard to visualize unless it is processed into numeric form, after which making its visual representation becomes possible.

The inherent dynamism of social media data introduces complexity to the process of analyzing and visualizing data, especially in marketing and public relations domains. The swift rate at which trends and popular subjects evolve on these platforms implies that what is pertinent today may become outdated tomorrow. The ephemeral nature of social media content necessitates regular revisions to visualizations, posing a substantial challenge in preserving their accuracy and relevance. It is for this reason that AI-supported real-time data analytics and adaptive visualizations become necessary. Furthermore, utilizing algorithms capable of forecasting emerging patterns may also yield advantageous outcomes.

Preserving user privacy in the visualization of social media data is of utmost importance, particularly with the growing global recognition of concerns surrounding data privacy. It is imperative that data visualizations adhere to the privacy of individual users, particularly when handling potentially sensitive audience data. Hence, striking a balance between safeguarding user privacy and maximizing the usefulness of data analytics is crucial.

A vital consideration in data visualization is the significance of contextual relevance. Without the necessary context, a visualization risks misinterpretation (Vegas et al., 2007). For instance, an abrupt increase in brand mentions may initially appear positive. However, without context, it may be easy to disregard that this increase is due to negative feedback or a public relations crisis. Consequently, it is crucial to ensure that visualizations convey the correct message in the appropriate context. In essence, although the visualization of social media data promises valuable insights, the process is filled with challenges that require cautious navigation.

Case Study 9.1 Strategic Multilingual Instagram Analytics for Global Engagement at the Aegean Pearl Luxury Beach Hotel: A Case Study in Data Visualization in Tourism and Hospitality

This case study examines how the Aegean Pearl Luxury Beach Hotel in Fethiye, Turkey, strategically implemented advanced visual and analytical tools on Instagram. By employing advanced data visualization in a multilingual Instagram environment, the hotel intended to refine its content strategy, nurturing deeper connections with a diverse international audience and boosting engagement and bookings. The hotel aimed to develop a nuanced and effective content strategy by analyzing the engagement patterns, preferences, and behaviors of its multilingual (English, German, Turkish) Instagram audience.

Data Gathering and Analysis

The hotel's Instagram strategy included various post types, including images, videos, and carousels highlighting the hotel's amenities, picturesque vistas, local cultural landmarks, and delectable cuisine. This strategy meticulously considered the optimal posting frequency to maximize engagement. Likes, comments, shares, and bookmarks were meticulously monitored to determine the effectiveness of the content. In addition, the demographics of their followers were considered, with a particular emphasis on their linguistic preferences. Finally, textual comments were methodically investigated to determine sentiment and derive thematic insights, informing their content strategy further.

Data Visualization

An innovative visualization strategy was employed whereby the analysts created charts such as multiseries bar graphs, dynamic heatmaps, and word clouds to translate massive amounts of data into coherent insights. All this information was displayed in a dashboard which could be used by managers to make effective decisions. The bar charts displayed monthly engagement trends, pinpointing high-interaction periods and their correlation with specific posts or events. The heatmaps represented the peak engagement times, offering insights into the global audience's active hours. Maps visualized follower demographics by region, emphasizing areas with high engagement. Sentiment graphs showcased positive, negative, and neutral sentiments from comment analysis across the three languages. The visual representations yielded intricate insights into optimal posting times, linguistic engagement patterns, and thematic inclinations across distinct language segments.

Strategic Results

- **Content refinement**—Informed by the multidimensional insights, the hotel adjusted its content strategy, emphasizing aspects that resonated

> with German-speaking followers and cultivating collaborations with relevant influencers.
>
> - **Engagement enhancement**—The strategic realignment significantly increased engagement and appointments, particularly from the German-speaking demographic.
>
> ## Conclusion
>
> When navigating multilingual social media landscapes, the breadth and adaptability of analytic tools are crucial. The Aegean Pearl's use of sophisticated analytics and data visualization transformed complex multilingual data into actionable insights, facilitating the development of a more effective and globally alluring Instagram strategy. The case demonstrates the transformative power of visualization tools for optimizing the content strategy. By incorporating an integrated approach that combines quantitative metrics with qualitative insights, brands will be able to develop communication strategies that are more empathic and culturally sensitive, thereby fostering global brand affinity.

9.5 Key Principles of Effective Visualization

In the field of data analytics, visualization plays a pivotal role. The essence of compelling visualizations resides in their cognitive and perceptual alignment with human comprehension. These visualizations guide the observer, allowing rapid and accurate assimilation of the data's inherent insights. According to Rolandi et al. (2011), the design of any chart or figure must begin with a comprehensive narrative. For those designing visualizations, clarity is paramount, necessitating the removal of superfluous information without compromising the core data. The ultimate objective of data visualization is to create a presentation devoid of redundancy and clutter, to present a focused narrative that speaks for itself (Case Study 9.1).

It is important to understand the fundamental visual properties of a chart to effectively leverage the force of visualization. At the forefront of these are the "pre-attentive visual attributes," which accelerate the processing of visual data by the human brain (Tollner et al., 2011; Clarke, 2022). Pre-attentive visual attributes refer to characteristics of a visual item that can be recognized by the human visual system without requiring conscious attention (Rodriguez et al., 2008). These attributes such as color, size, shape, orientation, weight, and position are crucial in data visualization as they enable designers to effortlessly guide the viewer's attention toward the most significant or pertinent aspects of the display (see Figure 9.11). These characteristics are the foundations of effective visualization, enabling designers to tap into our inherent visual processing abilities and facilitating rapid and cogent data communication. Rolandi et al. (2011) emphasized that utilizing "visual contrast" to emphasize critical narratives or insights by varying visual elements' size, shape, position, orientation, or color is a crucial technique. Let us look further into these characteristics:

1. **Size**: Size is a crucial factor in any visualization, as it can emphasize significance, denote quantity, or convey value. Disparities in scale attract the observer's attention immediately and provide intuitive focal points within the data landscape.
2. **Shape**: Shape is a differentiator, facilitating prompt categorization and recognition. For instance, a solitary square immediately stands out among a collection of circles, emphasizing its uniqueness.
3. **Position**: The spatial arrangement of an element, whether in a flat space or a hierarchical structure, conveys meaning, whether it be rank, chronology, or relational dynamics.
4. **Orientation**: In a context of uniformity, an orientation anomaly catches attention immediately. It is a tool for highlighting differences, delineating categories, and indicating deviations.
5. **Color**: Color offers versatile means to convey distinctions, categories, and hierarchies. It plays a critical role in making specific elements in the visualization distinct and recognizable.

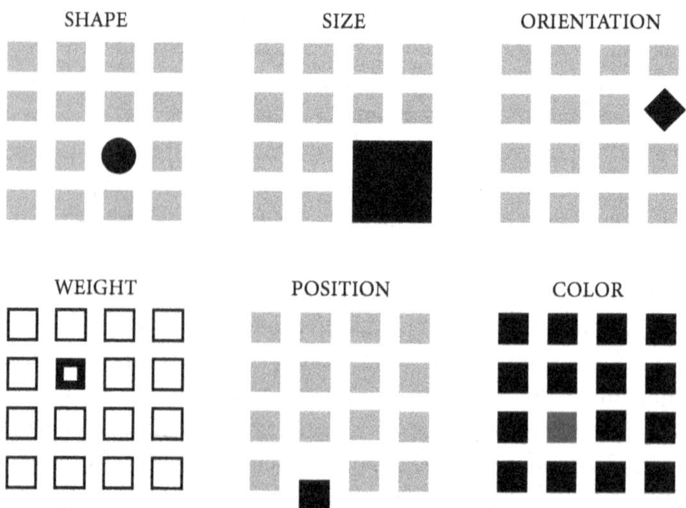

Figure 9.11 Visual Contrast (Rolandi et al., 2011).

6. **Weight**: In the context of visual qualities, the term "weight" pertains to the thickness or boldness of lines and shapes in a data visualization depicting visual prominence. Visual weight is acquired by specific lines or elements within a visualization when they are shown with a bolder or thicker appearance compared to others, thus capturing the viewer's attention.

When employed with discretion, such visualizations, crafted carefully, not only engage but also render intricate data insights accessible and intuitively comprehensible.

Effective data visualization strives to simplify complex data sets and present them in an approachable format. Building on the modern visualization principles laid by Tukey (1977) and Tufte (1983), and on work by various scholars such as Ware (2019), I offer the following six principles for effective data visualization:

1. **Simplicity and clarity**: Focusing on minimalism and directness is the key to a compelling visualization. A concise narrative does not necessitate an excessive use of words to convey its meaning, similarly, a well-crafted visual should not inundate its viewers with unnecessary details. Often, the simplest solutions are the most efficient, and this is particularly important when conveying information. Effective charts and graphs exemplify this by presenting data in a plain and uncomplicated manner. They illuminate the concealed narrative within the statistics, guiding the audience's comprehension without drowning them in complexity. This entails avoiding superfluous embellishments in charts and graphs. In the same way that Edward Tufte advocates for "data-ink ratio" —the amount of ink used to represent and illuminate data as opposed to superfluous or redundant ink—it is essential to avoid unnecessary visual elements that could undermine the primary narrative (Tufte, 1983). In other words, Edward Tufte's concept of the "data-ink ratio" emphasizes using only the ink needed to display meaningful information while eliminating redundant or decorative elements. Similarly, avoiding excessive visuals ensures that the core message remains clear and effective without distractions. Consider a bar chart displaying the GDP of various nations. A straightforward layout with distinct bars and direct labels can provide instant insight. Excessively decorative designs, ornate typefaces, or extra lines and images can obscure the primary message and hinder comprehension.

2. **Appropriateness of representation**: It is crucial to align the visualization type with the character of the data and the intended message. In his extensive work on data analysis, John Tukey introduced the box plot, a visualization ideal for comprehending data distributions. But, while

a box plot may be appropriate for displaying distribution data, a line graph would be more appropriate for displaying trends over time. And to represent quantitative data, it would be wise to employ histograms, scatter plots, or line charts to visually display the distributions. Bar charts or pie charts are suitable for comparing different groups when dealing with categorical data. Hence, matching data with its optimal visual representation ensures that the intended insights are readily and organically discernible.

3. **Consistent and informative labeling**: Labeling is an essential element of any visualization. Accurately designated axes, legends, and data points provide context and eliminate ambiguity. In order to maintain uniform and informative labeling in chart visualizations, it is important to implement a transparent and consistent labeling system throughout all visual components. It is also vital to employ informative headings that succinctly communicate the chart's objective and substance. In a scatter plot comparing the weight and mileage efficiency of automobiles, for instance, the axes must indicate their respective measuring units (e.g., kilograms and miles per gallon). Without such precision, the visualization may be susceptible to multiple interpretations.

4. **Judicious use of color**: Color is an effective means of representing visual information. However, the use of color requires a careful approach. The objective is to utilize color to enhance the data narrative, and improve readability and interpretation, rather than divert attention from it. It is also not wise to employ color combinations that overwhelm the viewer. Consistent color schemes can organize data or highlight differences, distinguish data points, or categorize related elements.

   Equally essential, however, is to be cognizant of color blindness concerns and to avoid color combinations that may be indistinguishable to a portion of the audience, such as red. Consideration for colorblind viewers means avoiding problematic color combinations like green and red. A further example would be in a heat map displaying website user activity; hotter colors like red could signify areas with the most user interaction, while more cooler and professional colors like blue indicate lesser activity.

   When students ask about the optimal or most sophisticated color for charts and graphs, I advise them to take inspiration from the natural world. The natural color spectrum, ranging from the many hues of blue in the atmosphere to the numerous tones of brown in the soil and the shades of green in foliage and grass, presents a visually pleasing and harmonious juxtaposition. Utilizing natural hues in our visual representations, such as the combination of blues with browns and grays or greens with blues, can result in a visually appealing and impactful aesthetic. These color choices not only evoke a strong response from viewers but also contribute to a perception of professionalism and clarity in our charts and graphs.

5. **Proportional and accurate scales**: Accurate data representation necessitates the use of scales that are both proportionate and exact. Skewed or shortened scales might result in inaccurate interpretations. Assume that the vertical axis of a line graph representing a company's stock values does not start at zero or has fluctuating scale. Under such circumstances, it has the potential to amplify or downplay price movements, resulting in potential misinterpretations. Edward Tufte places great importance on maintaining graphic integrity and highlights the risks associated with deliberately or inadvertently distorting data.

6. **Context and integrity**: Visualizations do not exist in an isolated setting. Ensuring context and integrity in visualizations entails presenting data in a manner that is both precise and significant to the viewers. In order to ensure that the viewer comprehends the circumstances, constraints, or special conditions of the exhibited data, it is necessary to provide appropriate context. Although a well-designed visual speaks for itself, it is still important to provide context by the judicious use of succinct titles and bylines.

Data-driven storytelling has the potential to enhance trust or diminish it if is not presented professionally. Given the ease with which data can be manipulated, misunderstood, or misinterpreted, it is crucial to have a reliable and impartial source that is also cited next to the chart or graphic. Acknowledgments, clarifications, and citations to pertinent data points have the potential to augment comprehension and confidence. Furthermore, adhering to accurate dimensions and preventing any manipulation of graphical elements that may deceive the viewer is of the utmost importance. For example, a histogram that illustrates the monthly amount of rainfall could require the inclusion of details about the specific geographical area and any exceptional data points, such as severe weather occurrences. Integrity guarantees that the data have been acquired from reliable sources and are presented in an unbiased manner.

By combining the abovementioned principles, many of which are inspired by or directly derived from the works of titans such as Tufte and Tukey, it is possible to create data visualizations that are aesthetically pleasing, insightful, and truthful in their depiction of data.

Chapter Summary

- The implementation of data visualization techniques can greatly enhance the understanding of social media data.
- Data visualization emphasizes the vital importance of design aesthetics and cognitive psychology in understanding and analyzing intricate datasets.
- Data visualization combines empirical data with experiential elements, facilitating a more comprehensive comprehension of the environment through visual representation.
- The advancement of human creativity, namely in the field of visualization, highlights the collaborative effort of civilizations throughout history. The advancements of each period are based on the knowledge and experience gained from previous ones, demonstrating that human creativity is not limited by geography or culture.
- Effective data-driven storytelling occurs only when it conveys novel insights, provides new perspectives, or elicits actionable responses.
- The ultimate objective of data visualization is to create a presentation devoid of redundancy and clutter, to present a focused narrative that speaks for itself.

Questions for Review

1. What is data visualization? Shed light on its significance.
2. Trace the history of data visualization from ancient times to the 21st century.
3. What are the different types of charts that help visualize information? How should we select the right chart?
4. Describe the six principles for effective data visualization.

10

Spatial Analytics for Social Media

In the previous chapter, we delved into data visualization, tracing its historical development, understanding the principles of effective visualizations, and examining its various forms. Our focus was primarily on charts and graphs as we navigated the complexities inherent in representing social media data and emphasized the fundamentals of creating effective visual displays. These visual elements translate complex data into understandable formats, facilitating nuanced comprehension and informed decision-making. However, data visualization takes various forms in which charts and graphs are only one facet. There exists another dimension, equally compelling and illuminating, situated at the intersection of geography and data representation—map-based visualization. We have already traced the history of data visualization in terms of maps. In this chapter, we will explore modern-day geographical maps and how they can help tell an effective data story.

We explore the visualization of social media data through geographical or spatial analytics, transitioning from the abstract domains of bars, lines, and plots to the world of maps. Utilizing the geographical or spatial information inherent in social media data, spatial analytics reveals patterns, insights, and trends not otherwise discernible using conventional visualization formats. We investigate the significance of maps in data visualization, the fundamentals of spatial data, and the relationship between geography and social media data. In addition, we delve into the various sources of spatial data in social media and investigate various spatial analytic techniques and visualization tools, demonstrating the importance of data visualization in various career trajectories.

As we venture deeper into the spatial visualization of social media data, we investigate not only the aesthetic and functional aspects of map-based representations, but also their unique value in interpreting social phenomena, behaviors, and interactions that occur across geographical landscapes. Spatial analytics provide nuanced layers of context and meaning to the digital footprints we leave in the virtual world, such as location-based posts on Instagram and Facebook (Tsou, 2015). This forms the foundation of our exploration in this chapter, weaving through the intricate connection between spatial data and social media analytics to disclose unprecedented patterns and trends rooted in geography.

10.1 Understanding Spatial Analytics

Maps are a generally recognized media that have been used throughout the ages. They serve as a testimonial to the inherent need that humans have to comprehend the world in which they live and make sense of their existence on Earth through points or landmarks. Some of our earliest visual representations also resembled primitive maps, contributing to their widespread recognition. Human ancestors marked the beginning of our endeavor to give form to the intangible and to navigate our environment, highlighting our age-old fixation with spatial representation. Hence, our current reliance on maps for data visualization is not a modern-day occurrence, but rather a continuation of an ancient custom. This heritage elevates maps beyond basic tools, making them a potent medium for distilling complex data into insights that resonate with both expert and nonexpert audiences.

Spatial analytics is a multidimensional field that combines methodologies and techniques to refine geographic or locational data into actionable insights and useful knowledge (Awange & Kiema, 2013; Murray, 2021). Spatial data, also known as geospatial data, is characterized by its capacity to reference information geographically (Longley et al., 2015). Spatial analytics combines geographic information science, data science, and statistics (Waller, 2022). Spatial analytics is also known as location analytics or geoanalytics. By displaying geographic data on maps, spatial analytics reveals previously concealed insights and adds a new level of comprehension (Longley et al., 2015).

Cartography, or the creation of maps, is often regarded as one of the earliest forms of information or data visualization. For thousands of years, maps have been used to visually represent spatial information, depicting geographical locations, relationships between places, and other data (Crampton, 2009). Ancient civilizations created maps to comprehend and navigate their respective worlds. While there were other primitive forms of data representation in ancient times, cartography stands out due to its complexity, the scope of information it conveys, and its persistence and evolution throughout history. The concept of data visualization in the digital age incorporates a much broader variety of tools and techniques, particularly with the advent of statistical graphics and interactivity.

The abundance of location data generated by social media platforms presents unique opportunities to analysts and researchers for in-depth exploration (McKitrick et al., 2023). The ubiquity of smartphones, enhanced internet connectivity, and the omnipresence of social media have culminated in a bounty of rich, location-based data. This massive data repository can be converted into spatial maps by integrating tabular, graphical, and cartographic techniques (McKitrick et al., 2023). The potential and applications of spatial analytics are increasingly expanding, altering our understanding of geographic information continuously.

Geographic information systems (GIS) serve as the foundation for managing and visualizing this spatial data, assisting professionals varying from environmental scientists to engineers in understanding spatial phenomena (McKitrick et al., 2023). Spatial analytics helps extract meaningful insights from location data collected from a variety of sources such as GPS and cellular networks. Location or spatial analytics, a subset of the broader GIS field, is instrumental in analyzing movement patterns, monitoring phenomena such as disease outbreaks, and determining activity-rich customer locations.

Spatial analytics plays a crucial role in social media analytics by leveraging the vast quantity of user location data to comprehend user behaviors, monitor information dissemination, and identify impact zones where social media intersects with the real world. Consider a social media analyst who meticulously investigates the spread of misinformation on platforms such as X (formerly Twitter). Every post (formerly tweet) emanates from a particular location, and the primary objective is to gain a comprehensive understanding of the mechanisms underpinning the dissemination of misinformation across diverse locales. In such circumstances, spatial analytics helps unearth areas with concentrated misinformation and reveal the relationship between the dissemination of misinformation and various socioeconomic and demographic variables.

10.2 Application of Spatial Analytics in the Social Media Domain

The very nature of maps permits us to visualize the spatial dynamics of our data. Consider them the link between basic data elements, such as an address or crime scene, and discernible patterns. Through the lens of a map, one can identify areas with high consumer density, regions rife with crime, or the path of a disease's spread—insights that are frequently obscured by conventional visualizations such as bar or pie charts. Spatial data from social media has applications in tourism, public health, and even politics, in addition to crisis management. For example, location information from Twitter data was used to map the 2015 floods in South Carolina (Li et al., 2018).

Given the prevalence of location data especially on social media, maps possess an inherent advantage in terms of communication. Their capacity to clarify spatial relationships guarantees that they continue to be unrivaled presentation tools, facilitating comprehension among diverse audiences. These geospatial visualizations weave narratives about humanity, from disease and resource tracking to customer identification by region, to the simplification of navigation routes. They can even identify correlations between seemingly unrelated phenomena.

Crime mapping. Through the utilization of spatial analytics, it has become possible to thoroughly investigate the underlying factors behind societal issues, therefore enabling us to develop focused and impactful solutions. Within the context of social media, the geographical aspect of data provides significant opportunities for comprehending and tackling intricate social problems. Spatial analytics offers a powerful lens through which we can decode the intricate relationship between social media interactions and their geographical context. It allows us to discover concealed patterns and connections that link social media dynamics with other crucial spatial datasets, such as demographic profiles and crime statistics. Researchers can employ spatial analytics to examine correlations between social media utilization and crime rates (Bendler et al., 2014; Malleson & Anderson, 2015), thereby contributing to the creation of more effective crime prevention strategies.

Public relations. Monitoring the geographic spread of a trending hashtag provides public relations (PR) professionals with invaluable information about emergent trends. In other words, the viral dissemination of a particular post or hashtag can be mapped. This enables them to identify areas of increased activity, which can be invaluable for public relations responses and gaining a geographical understanding of trends.

Marketing and advertising. A business could use spatial analytics to determine popular locations from its social media postings to refine its advertising strategies or identify potential store locations. With this deep understanding, organizations can create marketing efforts that are not only focused but also deeply meaningful to the lives, tastes, and wants of certain consumer segments. By strategically aligning marketing strategies with the local context of their target audience, businesses may effectively establish more meaningful connections with consumers, resulting in increased engagement and increasing the effectiveness of their marketing endeavors. This focused approach not only maximizes the allocation of resources but also enhances the consumer experience, promoting loyalty and facilitating sustainable business expansion in a competitive digital environment.

Public health. Contemporary public health officials could utilize social media data to map mentions of disease symptoms to identify and manage outbreaks proactively. Using spatial analytics, a public health official might leverage it to trace the trajectory of a disease outbreak, facilitating targeted interventions in at-risk areas (Hossain & Househ, 2016; Boulos & Geraghty, 2020). Based on social media mentions and geotagged posts signifying symptoms or illness, a public health official can use maps to visualize the spread of disease. This expedites their ability to identify prospective concentrations and areas of concern. By correlating these data with conventional reporting mechanisms, resources can be allocated more precisely, and public health interventions can be more well-informed and timelier.

Tourism and hospitality. In the realm of tourism and hospitality, geotagged images and GPS information via social networks enabled analysis of visitor behavior in US national parks (Barros et al., 2020). Businesses have also utilized platforms such as TripAdvisor and Yelp to identify popular tourist destinations. The use of spatial data provides businesses with a unique and powerful advantage, especially in the field of location-based targeted marketing, surpassing conventional marketing methods. This method is based on a comprehensive understanding of customer behaviors and attributes that are closely associated with certain geographic areas. Using a map, a digital marketing analyst can visualize location-based regional social media engagement data. This can help them determine which geographic regions have the highest interaction with specific content, allowing them to create more targeted campaigns.

10.3 Harnessing the Power of Spatial Data

Spatial data can represent physical entities such as buildings, roads, and rivers, as well as abstract concepts like population density, enabling users to locate them on maps or globes (O'Sullivan & Unwin, 2003). Combining location, attribute, and occasionally temporal information, spatial data provides a comprehensive view of objects, events, or phenomena concerning their location on the Earth's surface. Obtaining spatial data is essential for the creation of these insightful maps. The digital age offers an abundance of sources, from government databases and sensor networks to social media platforms themselves.

Before the advent of the internet and social media, spatial data was limited to traditional sources such as satellite imagery and aerial photography. In the current era of digital technology, we have gained access to an unparalleled range of information sources. Among them, social networks have emerged as particularly abundant sources of spatial data. This evolution not only enhances our ability to acquire a wide range of data but also enhances our capacity for analysis, thereby expanding our understanding and interaction with the world.

The process of acquiring and examining data from social media that is based on location is also referred to as spatial data mining (Li et al., 2015). Spatial data mining in the context of social media involves the retrieval and analysis of geotagged or georeferenced information from widely used platforms like X, Facebook, Instagram, and Yelp. This methodology empowers analysts and researchers to unveil patterns, correlations, and trends by examining the geographical locations linked to postings, images, reviews, or other types of material. By employing these geospatial indicators, experts can acquire a more comprehensive understanding of user behaviors, regional preferences, and diverse socioeconomic dynamics that would otherwise be concealed by traditional data analysis.

Every hour of the day, a vast number of individuals on popular social media platforms like Facebook, X, YouTube, and Instagram share posts that are labeled with geographical information. The combination of interpersonal communication and geospatial data has created a very suitable environment for spatial analysis. However, the process is not simple; it encompasses a sequence of careful steps, ranging from gathering data to visualization. More precisely, geotagged or georeferenced posts are retrieved from these platforms by utilizing APIs or web crawling techniques. Additionally, there are problems about the quality and veracity of the data, as well as ethical concerns. Furthermore, the preservation of user privacy, the expansion of capabilities to handle extensive data streams, and the careful consideration of ethical ramifications associated with data utilization all require significant focus.

10.4 Sources of Spatial Data for Social Media

Social media platforms employ diverse techniques to collect location data. Geo-tagging is a prominent and direct method for incorporating location information into social media content. Facebook, X, and Instagram, for example, permit users to attach GPS coordinates to their postings. Users can specify their location when tweeting on X, adding geographical context to their narratives. Instagram, on the other hand, allows its users to identify their images with precise location information, creating a geospatial representation of shared visual narratives.

Utilizing GPS or other location-based services on users' devices is the most prevalent method. In addition, social platforms may also use IP addresses to approximate the location of a user. In some instances, these platforms even acquire data from third-party location data suppliers. Most users are unaware that even if they opt out of direct location monitoring, their location can still be determined through indirect methods such as IP address tracking. As the pervasive use of social media continues, the spatial data it generates presents unprecedented opportunities for diverse applications.

Intriguingly, the quantity of geotagged posts is a small percentage of the overall social data. According to some estimates, only about 1% of tweets posted on Twitter (now X) were geotagged (Morstatter et al., 2013). Similarly, other social platforms, such as Facebook, may not provide location-based information. Nevertheless, the sheer number of users means we still have an enormous quantity of spatial data to gather, analyze, and visualize via maps. As discussed earlier, social media data can be accessed via two primary methods: (1) application programming interfaces (APIs), and (2) location data inferred from the user content/profile.

1. **Location data through APIs**. Data gathered through the APIs permits customized queries to retrieve specific posts based on parameters such as location, time, and content. For example, data from X can be obtained through the X's API. Tweets include metadata that indicates the publication time. Moreover, some tweets contain geolocational information that specifies the location from which the message was sent. Depending on a Twitter user's preferences, these spatial data may appear as place names (e.g., Dublin, Ohio) or latitude/longitude coordinates (Li et al., 2018).

   Data can be considered "location-based" if it contains locational metadata. This can range from precise latitude and longitude coordinates to more general indicators such as place names and postal codes. Consider user profiles as an example. They frequently specify specifics such as city, state, province, or country of domicile, thereby providing a geographical context. Metadata associated with user activity reveals increasingly subtle clues as one digs deeper.

2. **Location data inferred through user profile**. This method entails deducing location details from social media profiles in cases where direct data is not accessible through APIs. It serves as an essential fallback strategy for obtaining geographical insights through the analysis of user-provided profile information. However, this method faces significant challenges: some individuals do not reveal their location. Innovative methods are needed to accurately infer location data for researchers to extract significant spatial insights when direct location information is unavailable.

   The concept of location in social media can be understood from three distinct perspectives: the user's profile location (indicating where they reside); the tweet's location (indicating where the message was posted); and message context (referring to the location which the message discusses) (Ajao et al., 2015). The "user's location" refers to the user's domicile or the address specified in their profile. The "location field" mentioned in a user's profile, URLs in their biography (suggesting a possible country of origin), and the user's selected time zone were used to infer the actual location of users in a study by Schulz et al. (2013).

In the study by Mahmud et al. (2014), additional data, such as patterns in a user's posting times and frequently cited locations of interest, are considered in addition to this heuristic methodology. Furthermore, Morstatter et al. (2015) developed an algorithm to identify users in crisis-affected regions. By concentrating solely on determining whether a user is within or outside a specified region, their method attains a more refined performance than conventional techniques. Therefore, location inference can either be done manually or via automated techniques. Within the automated techniques of location inference, machine learning and natural language processing (NLP) techniques can be employed (Ajao et al., 2015).

10.5 Spatial Data Representation

Understanding the methods of representing geographical data is just as important as gathering it. Social media encompasses various spatial data types that accurately represent geographical things. Vector data (points, lines, polygons), and Raster data are used in mapping and analysis to accurately represent the spatial aspects of the data (Longley et al., 2015).

1. **Points.** Points denote precise positions on the Earth's surface. This includes user locations, landmarks, or events tagged in social media posts. Every point is determined by its coordinates, often consisting of latitude and longitude information. A study by Steiger et al. (2016) analyzed tweets tagged with specific geographic coordinates to uncover hidden relationships and information that shed light on the usefulness of point data in comprehending urban layouts.

2. **Lines.** In geospatial analysis, "lines" data, also referred to as "linear" data or "polylines" are abstract representations of lines or connecting points, crucial for charting routes, trajectories, and connections. The lines can represent natural and artificial features including highways, rivers, footpaths, utility lines, and migratory routes. Lines symbolize the movement of information, social interactions, and cultural influences as they traverse physical space. This enhanced cartographic viewpoint provides useful information for urban planners, transportation specialists, and environmental scientists. A study by Chen et al. (2018) demonstrated how combining geotagged tweets with conventional GIS technology may generate dynamic and intricate maps that accurately depict the represented surroundings.

3. **Polygons.** Polygons are essential in geographic data representation for depicting area-based properties and outlining enclosed regions like city boundaries, administrative divisions, or activity zones discovered through social media data (Ricov & Pripuzic, 2022). Polygons serve analytical goals in fields such as urban planning, environmental research, and public health. Polygons are useful for visually representing spatial phenomena in a structured manner, enabling detailed investigation of area usage, demographic characteristics of regions, and environmental features of specific locations. Polygons can be utilized in social media data to delineate zones of intense activity or significance, like locations with regular social events, political demonstrations, or cultural celebrations, based on the compilation of geotagged posts or tweets.

4. **Raster Data.** Raster data is a type of geographic data that is stored as a grid of uniformly sized pixels, each containing attribute data (McInerney & Kempeneers, 2015). A raster is a grid structure composed of cells (or pixels) arranged in rows and columns, with each cell holding a value that represents data, like temperature, topography elevation, or social media activity intensity. The pixel values of raster data allow for the examination of gradients, densities, or spatial patterns. Rasters are ideal for depicting data that exhibits continuous variation across a terrain. MrSIDs, GRIDs, TIFFs, and ERDAS Imagine files are all types of raster files.

Vector data is scalable, provides accurate measurements, and is adaptable for editing and analysis (Longley et al., 2015). However, vector data has constraints in managing extensive file sizes and in displaying continuous data. On the other hand, raster data is efficient for representing continuous data and is visually pleasing (Longley et al., 2015).

The decision to use vector (points, lines, polygons) or raster data depends on the individual data, analysis requirements, and desired level of precision. Both types are frequently used in combination in different applications. These spatial data representation types are essential for comprehending and examining the geographical dimension of social media data. Researchers can discover patterns and trends in the large amounts of data produced by social media users by using advanced approaches and combining different forms of geographical data.

10.6 Spatial Analytics Techniques

Spatial analytics techniques provide effective tools for examining and comprehending location-based patterns and trends seen in social media data. Stakeholders can make better-informed decisions and obtain a deeper understanding of spatial behaviors and trends by viewing spatial data from social media. Important methods in spatial analytics for social media comprise hotspot analysis, geovisualization, geofencing, spatial regression analysis, and mobility and trajectory analysis. These tools enable analysts to analyze and understand the intricate geographical aspects of social media data. We will discuss each of these methods in further detail below.

1. **Hotspot analysis**
   Hotspot analysis is a crucial spatial analytics technique that identifies spatial concentrations of statistically significant high and low values (Barthel et al., 2015). For instance, when a global event such as the Olympics is trending on X, an analysis utilizing a visualization tool such as Tableau can identify the areas or regions with the highest concentration of related tweets. A study by Kumar et al., (2022) analyzed crime data with Tableau. Hotspot analysis not only exposes areas of heightened interest or engagement, but it can also help determine where promotional activities or advertisements are most likely to be effective.

2. **Geovisualization**
   Geovisualization or cartographic visualization emphasizes the visual representation of spatial data, transforming complex geographic datasets

into understandable visual graphics. The tourism industry demonstrates its application. Businesses in the hospitality and tourism industry could use Datawrapper to display the locations from which the majority of Instagram users post while touring a particular tourist destination. This not only provides demographic insights but also can aid in the customization of region-specific advertising campaigns. A study by Vu et al. (2015) researched the behavior of tourists coming to Hong Kong by analyzing geotagged images and hence provided vital insights for improving destination development and transportation system planning.

3. **Geofencing**

Geofencing enhances spatial analysis by erecting virtual boundaries around a particular geographic region (Shevchenko & Reips, 2024). This technology is extensively utilized in diverse applications such as marketing, security, and resource management. Brands might deploy this approach to establish virtual perimeters around competitors' locations on platforms like Snapchat. By doing so, they can gain insight into user preferences and behaviors within these zones. Moreover, businesses can utilize geofencing to broadcast promotional messages to potential customers who reach a specified area around their store or a competitor's site. This is a task that can be made more intuitive by employing Tableau's spatial visualization capabilities.

4. **Spatial regression analysis**

Understanding and evaluating the relationship between a particular set of data and its spatial characteristics is the essence of spatial regression analysis. Spatial regression analysis involves statistical methods for modeling spatial connections between variables (Gibbons et al., 2015). This technique could be used in a health-related application to identify correlations between regions with low vaccination rates and regions with a high concentration of flu-related tweets. To conduct spatial regression analysis, precise geocoded data and comprehension of spatial relationships between data points are essential. Various software packages and tools that facilitate spatial regression analysis are R (with spatial packages such as spdep), Python (PySAL), and specialized GIS software like ArcGIS with spatial analysis plugins.

5. **Mobility and trajectory analysis**

Mobility and trajectory analysis expands the use of geovisualization by studying the movement patterns of persons using geotagged data. Within the tourism sector, this analysis is crucial for pinpointing popular tourist routes and sites using geotagged images on social media platforms such as Instagram. Tourism boards and agencies can identify the most frequented tourist routes and locations. For example, Crivellari and Beinat (2019) presented an innovative way for analyzing mobility and trajectories using a machine-learning approach. Visualizing these routes using tools such as Datawrapper or Power BI can also provide insights into travelers' preferences, leading to more effective promotional endeavors and infrastructure planning.

10.7 Types of Maps for Visualizing Social Media Data

Different mapping approaches can be used to visually display the large amounts of data that are accessible. Visualizing location-based data on maps can reveal patterns and trends that may be hidden inside large amounts of textual information. Not all mapping approaches are appropriate for visualizing social media data due to the varying applicability of spatial maps based on the unique data features. Given the nature of data and insights typically gleaned from social media platforms, the following categories are the most relevant spatial maps:

10.7.1 Choropleth Maps

"Choros" is the Greek word for region or area, whereas "plethos" stands for multitude, or a large group of people (Wiktionary, 2024). Choropleth maps are specialized geographical visualizations in which regions are shaded or patterned based on the statistical measure they represent (Tobler, 1973). These maps are especially useful for providing a spatial comprehension of the distribution of data across diverse geographical boundaries (see Figure 10.1).

Imagine analyzing engagement rates on social media from various regions of the country. A choropleth map could highlight regions based on the intensity of user engagement, offering a fast visual insight into areas with the highest social media activity or viral content spread. A further application could be to display the majority of mentions of a specific hashtag or trend across various states or cities, providing marketers or analysts with a clear picture of regional interest or influence. These maps can also be useful for visualizing regional sentiments or trends based on aggregated social media data (Case Study 10.1). A choropleth map can color-code regions based on their average sentiment scores, allowing a brand, for example, to determine which states or countries have the most positive sentiments about their product.

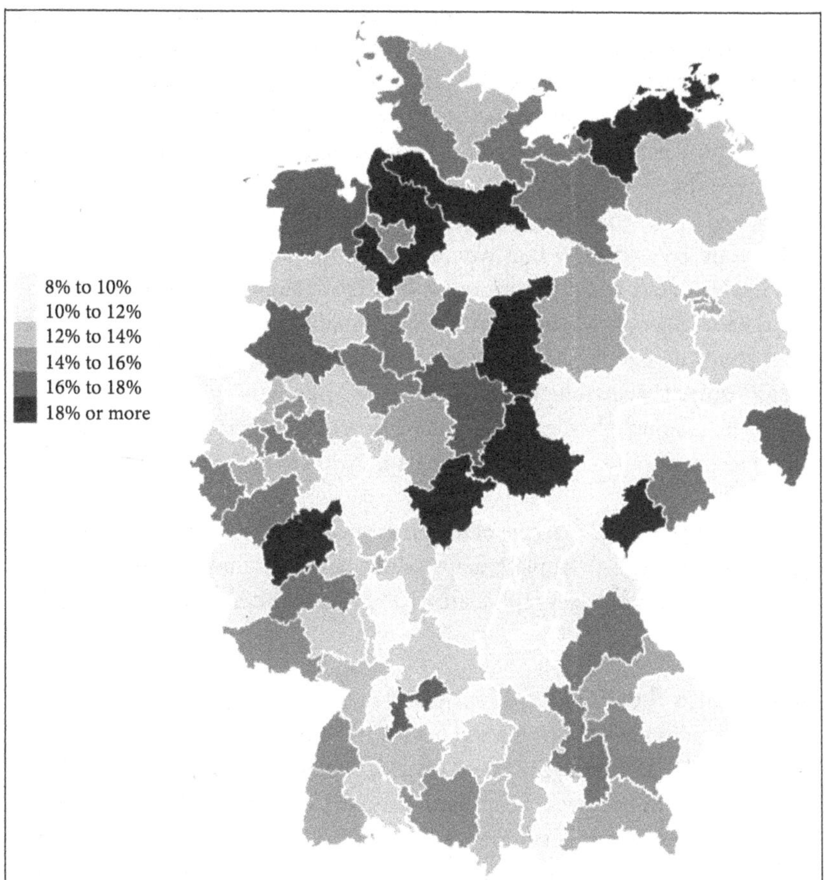

Figure 10.1 Choropleth Map

Case Study 10.1 Andy's Journey into Spatial Analytics with US Election Data

Andy, an undergraduate student in a social media analytics course, was always fascinated by how data could tell a story. He'd spent hours scrolling through social media feeds, analyzing trends, and seeing how influencers used engagement metrics to tell compelling narratives. His professor had tasked him with a new challenge: use spatial analytics to tell a compelling story using US election results data.

The assignment sounded daunting at first. Spatial analytics? Election data? Maps? But Andy was no stranger to tackling complex problems. He had always loved puzzles, and this felt like one big analytical puzzle. His professor's instructions were clear: "You need to weave election data into a narrative, and spatial analytics should be the vehicle. You're telling a story about voting patterns, shifts, and demographic trends—so think of the data as the backbone of your story."

Excited by the challenge, Andy dove right into the task. Little did he know, this would be a journey that would change the way he viewed data—and stories. He had learned in the course that spatial analytics involves analyzing data in a geographical context, often visualized on maps. By overlaying data points on geographic locations, you can uncover patterns, trends, and relationships that are often hard to see in raw numbers.

His first thought? "Election results are perfect for this. States, counties, and districts are already divided—why not use those divisions to show voting trends?"

He also discovered that one of the most effective ways to visualize election results was through choropleth maps, which use color gradients to show variations in data across geographic areas. This would be his tool for telling the story.

Diving into the 2024 US Election

To create an impactful story, Andy needed reliable, up-to-date election data. He started by gathering the latest US election results. The data came in—votes by state, by county, and by district, as well as demographic breakdowns (age, race, income) and historical trends. Andy knew he would need to clean and structure the data before it could be used for analysis, but he didn't mind the work. This was part of the fun.

Telling a Story with Election Data

As Andy explored the election data, he realized he needed a compelling narrative to tie it all together. The story had to be more than just a static map of who was winning or losing; it had to be about why certain areas were swinging in one direction or another. The narrative had to explore voter behavior, demographic shifts, and regional patterns.

For example, he was particularly intrigued by the battleground states—those key swing states like Florida, Michigan, and Pennsylvania that could decide the election. But Andy also wanted to dig deeper. He thought about the rural versus urban divide and how different regions might vote based on economic factors, education levels, or cultural influences.

He sat back and thought about the story he wanted to tell. The narrative would focus on voter shifts—how different regions were changing their political affiliations over time—and demographic trends—how shifts in population, age, and race were impacting voting patterns.

The Tool: Datawrapper

Andy's next step was employing the assigned Datawrapper tool to create his maps. He had experience with Excel and some GIS software, but for this project, he decided to use Datawrapper, a simple, web-based tool that allowed him to create beautiful, interactive choropleth maps.

He uploaded his cleaned data into Datawrapper, which automatically identified geographic regions (states, counties) and corresponding election results. Datawrapper instantly turned his raw data into an interactive map. But Andy knew the real work was still ahead: he had to choose the right colors, labels, and filters to make the map visually compelling and easy to understand.

Andy decided to use a diverging color scheme—shades of red for Republican and blue for Democrat—and adjusted the color intensity based on the percentage of votes each candidate received. For states with narrow margins, he used lighter shades, and for states with clear wins, he used darker, more saturated colors.

Next, he added hover-over tooltips, so when viewers hovered over a state, they could see the exact percentage of votes for each candidate, along with a breakdown of key demographic trends, like race, age, and education levels. He also gave the map a compelling title and a byline.

The Story Unfolds: Regional Shifts and Voter Trends

As Andy put the finishing touches on his map, he started to see the story come together. For instance, in Florida, he noticed that the map showed a sharp increase in support for conservative candidates in rural areas, while urban centers like Miami and Orlando were leaning more liberal. This was no surprise—Florida had long been a battleground state, but now Andy could see just how deep the divisions ran, even within the state.

When Andy presented his project to his professor, he didn't just show a map. He told a story about how shifting demographics and regional differences were influencing the election. He explained how voters in urban centers were more likely to support progressive candidates, while those in rural areas tended to favor conservative ones.

The choropleth map wasn't just a data visualization; it was a tool for storytelling, helping Andy weave complex political trends into a narrative that was not only visually engaging but also informative.

> ## Conclusion: The Power of Data Storytelling
> Through this assignment, Andy learned that spatial analytics was much more than just drawing maps—it was about telling powerful stories. By using Datawrapper to visualize election results and demographic data, Andy was able to create a clear, interactive narrative about the 2024 US presidential election. The assignment opened his eyes to the potential of data visualization as a storytelling tool. By combining data, spatial analysis, and a compelling narrative, Andy discovered how data could not only inform but also captivate an audience. It was a skill he would continue to hone in his future career in social media analytics—and one he would carry with him as he explored how data could shape the stories of tomorrow.

10.7.2 Dot Density/Distribution (or Point Distribution) Maps

Dot density maps are renowned for their simplicity since they show each data point as a dot, making them a useful tool for depicting variances in density. Highly dotted areas on such a map denote high-density regions, whereas zones with few or no marks indicate areas with limited data (see Figure 10.2).

Dot density maps are a powerful tool for visualizing huge quantities of geospatial data across vast geographical areas. Imagine a map of North America where each dot represents one town or city. This illustration facilitates comprehension of the vast quantity and distribution of these urban population centers. In addition, the inherent simplicity of these maps makes them ideal for black-and-white print or presentations, ensuring that the information is legible without the need for color distinction. Dot distribution maps can also be particularly useful for visualizing individual social media posts or check-ins. Each dot could represent a tweet or an Instagram post, revealing where users are the most active.

10.7.3 Symbol Maps

A symbol map, also known as a point symbol map or a proportional symbol map, employs symbols such as circles, squares, or other shapes to represent quantitative data at specific geographic locations (Dent et al., 2009). The size (or sometimes the color) of the symbol varies proportionally to the magnitude or frequency of the phenomenon it represents. For instance, a symbol map could depict the population of cities throughout the globe.

Created with Datawrapper

Figure 10.2 Distribution of the tourist accommodations in Turkiye 2023

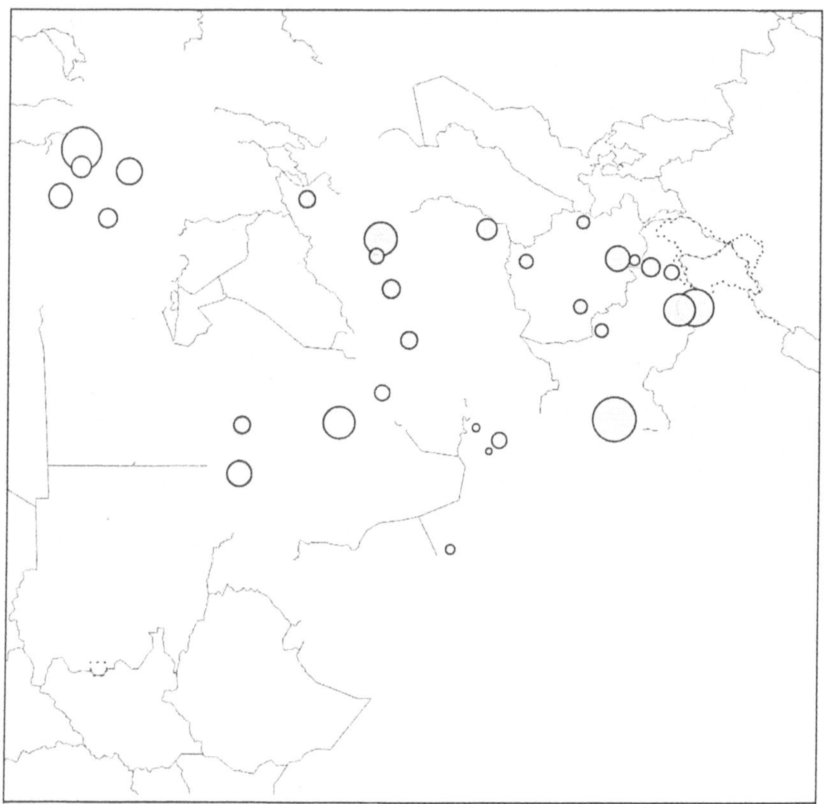

Figure 10.3 Symbol Map (Created with DataWrapper)

As depicted in Figure 10.3, on a symbol map, larger symbols would represent cities with larger populations, while smaller symbols would represent cities with smaller populations. This provides a distinct visual comparison, allowing viewers to promptly distinguish between cities with larger and smaller populations. If a brand is monitoring mentions of its name or a specific hashtag, this map can use symbols (such as circles) of proportional size to depict the volume of mentions across various cities or countries.

10.7.4 Spatial Heatmaps (or Density Maps)

A spatial or geographic heat map is a spatial representation of data in which individual values are represented by colors, facilitating the visualization of patterns, trends, and concentrations on a map (see Figure 10.4). The term "heat map" derives from the gradation of colors used, which typically

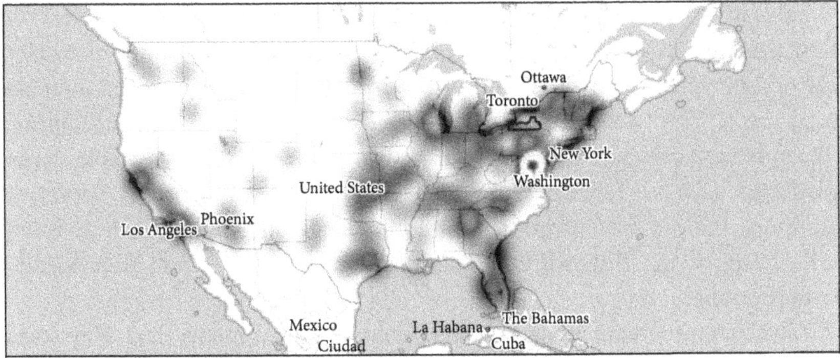

Figure 10.4 Spatial Heatmap generated with Python

transitions from chilly to warm colors to represent increasing values or concentrations.

When attempting to identify where discussions about a particular topic are most concentrated, spatial heatmaps (or density maps) can visualize the concentration. For instance, a spatial heatmap can indicate where a viral news story or meme is generating the most discussion. While the choice of map depends on the specific objective and data, these varieties are particularly well-suited for transforming the vast and diverse landscape of social media data into visual insights.

10.8 Data Visualization Tools

The spatial visualization of social media data necessitates the use of specialized tools and techniques for the management, analysis, and representation of large datasets. In this context, it is relevant to highlight several well-known spatial visualization tools that are instrumental in facilitating these processes.

1. Tableau (https://www.tableau.com/)

Tableau is a leading platform for data visualization and business intelligence, known for creating engaging charts, graphs, maps, dashboards, and narratives (Batt et al., 2020). Established in 2003, Tableau Software has become a prominent player in the field of data visualization. In 2019 Tableau was acquired by Salesforce for approximately $15.7 billion. Tableau's features provide value when analyzing spatial data, improving the usefulness of geographic information by allowing users to delve into the spatial component and reveal the reasons behind spatial trends.

Tableau offers various functionalities that businesses and organizations find useful. It is equipped with immediate geocoding through which users can automatically convert existing location data into interactive, multilayered maps. Users can also navigate global data landscapes within Tableau's dynamic visual ecosystem, where data insights are easily shareable across platforms such as Tableau Online, Tableau Public, and Tableau Server. In addition, Tableau can integrate geographic data from sources such as R and GIS, bridging the distance between complex spatial files and user-friendly visualizations.

Tableau can be equally useful for visualizing social media data. Key social media metrics can be easily visualized into charts, graphs, and intricate geographical maps. Tableau provides a variety of map creation options to accommodate diverse needs. Users can generate proportional symbol maps, choropleth or filled maps, point distribution maps, heatmaps to depict data density, and flow or path maps to visualize directional data.

2. Microsoft's Power BI

As a component of the Microsoft Power Platform portfolio, Power BI (https:// powerbi.microsoft.com/) is a dynamic visualization tool with a strong emphasis on business intelligence. It features functionalities such as multisource data connectivity, data modeling, and the generation of actionable visual graphics. Microsoft's Power BI features powerful geographic visualization capabilities. It provides flexible data representation, including maps, graphs, scatter plots, and more. This adaptability ensures that social media datasets can be converted into georeferenced, clear visual insights without difficulty.

3. Datawrapper

Datawrapper (https://www.datawrapper.de) is well-known for its ease of use to generate basic interactive visualizations. Datawrapper facilitates the creation of sophisticated maps, charts, and diagrams. The online tool is an excellent choice for anyone who wants to visualize data effectively. Datawrapper is considered a valuable resource for journalists and media professionals who are often tasked with timely reporting on various events. In addition, businesses without specialized data analytics expertise can use Datawrapper to rapidly gain insights without the need for complex software or extensive training. Datawrapper essentially accommodates those in need of swift, efficient, and uncomplicated geographic data visualization, enabling even those with rudimentary data skills to chart social media insights with proficiency. By importing a CSV dataset, users can create and incorporate a variety of visuals, including pie and line charts as well as various mapping visuals.

4. ArcGIS

ArcGIS is at the forefront of geographic information system (GIS) technology, providing wide-ranging administration, visualization, and analysis of geographic data. It enables the creation of layered or spatial maps that can depict a variety of datasets, from climate trends to trade routes. These layers, when precisely superimposed, produce maps that are exhaustive and information-dense. Typically, the foundational layer is a geographical map, whether derived from satellite images or standard road maps. Given its exhaustive toolkit and diverse applications, ArcGIS is the go-to platform for many enterprises, educational institutions, and governmental bodies involved in geographic data exploration.

10.9 Selecting the Right Visualization Tool for Location Analytics

In today's dynamic digital era, it can be difficult to identify the data visualization software that best meets one's specific needs. This is especially true given the vast variety of available options, which range from readily accessible browser-based solutions to sophisticated platforms designed for enterprise-grade application integration. To effectively navigate this vast domain, it is essential first to define the specific objectives and data assets. The ideal tool should seamlessly integrate business intelligence, advanced analytics, and in-depth reporting functionalities, equipping you to meet both your current and prospective analytical demands.

The seamless integration of data into a visualization platform significantly influences its adoption (Heer et al., 2010). Accessibility and ease of use is also a crucial factor in the choice of a visualization tool. It is important to choose tools that guarantee universal access to data visualizations and their interfaces. It is also important to take into account the desired medium for showcasing these visualizations, which may vary from a company website to specific blogs or digital news outlets. Every tool in the visualization field offers distinct advantages. Tableau, ArcGIS, Datawrapper, and PowerBI are prominent industry leaders that offer specialized features.

Datwrapper's emphasis on simplicity and speed enables users to rapidly depict social media trends on maps, making it especially useful for journalists and businesses desiring quick insights without engaging in complex manipulations or enduring precipitous learning curves. Its ability to rapidly convert vast quantities of data into comprehensible visual representations enables users to efficiently distill complex information, making it a go-to resource for those who require fast, uncomplicated, and clear insights.

Microsoft's PowerBI is capable of transforming large social media datasets into intuitive geographical visualizations. It is especially beneficial for brands and businesses seeking to measure regional engagement or evaluate the effectiveness of advertisements. With its comprehensive range of visualization capabilities and the integration of advanced analytics, it enables users to discern patterns and make data-driven decisions with confidence.

In a scenario with multiple requirements, it is crucial to select the tool that correlates best with the desired outcomes. Datawrapper excels at simple, quick visualizations, while ArcGIS is unmatched for robust, in-depth geographical analyses. When fast, interactive, and user-friendly visualizations are required, Tableau is the best option, whereas PowerBI excels at intuitive geographical representations of large datasets and robust analytics.

Most of these tools offer a comprehensive suite of options for professionals seeking to harness the power of spatial data and analytics to draw insights, inform strategies, and make decisions in a world that is becoming increasingly data-driven. Users will be able to maximize analytical outcomes in the domain of spatial and location analytics by balancing and leveraging the unique strengths of these tools, based on the specific requirements and complexities of the tasks.

Chapter Summary

- Spatial analytics is a multidimensional field that combines methodologies and techniques to refine geographic or locational data into actionable insights and useful knowledge.
- Cartography, or the creation of maps, is often regarded as one of the earliest forms of information or data visualization.
- The abundance of location data generated by social media platforms presents unique opportunities to analysts and researchers for in-depth exploration.
- Location or spatial analytics, a subset of the broader GIS field, is instrumental in analyzing movement patterns, monitoring phenomena such as disease outbreaks, and determining activity-rich customer locations.
- Social media platforms employ diverse techniques to collect location data.
- Important methods in spatial analytics for social media include hotspot analysis, geovisualization, geofencing, spatial regression analysis, and mobility and trajectory analysis.
- Different mapping approaches can be used to visually display the large amounts of data that are accessible.

Questions for Review

1. What is spatial analytics? Why is it important in social media analytics?
2. What are some of the different fields in which spatial analytics is applied in the social media domain?
3. What are the different types of charts that help visualize information? How should we select the right chart?
4. What are the different mapping approaches for visualizing social media data? In what ways are spatial heat maps different from dot density maps?

11

Integrating Design Thinking into Dashboards and Reports

Chapter Outline

11.1 Introduction to Dashboards and Reports
    11.1.1 Dashboards
    11.1.2 Reports
11.2 Integrating Design Thinking into Data Visualization
11.3 Exploring Dashboard and Reporting Tools
11.4 Leveraging the Power of Data Storytelling in Social Media Analytics
11.5 Social Media Analytics Centers and Labs
11.6 The Value of Data Visualization Across Careers

In previous chapters, we explored the processes of gathering, refining, integrating, and visualizing social media data. In this chapter, we have reached the final stage of our social media analytics DAV Framework, in which we conclude the Visualization stage. We now shed light on the importance of an integrated approach where all data visualizations can be displayed together.

It is essential to have a centralized interface that effectively captures the totality of social media endeavors so that senior management can make informed decisions. Such an interface is in the form of a dashboard, which can display real-time data, and provide instantaneous access to key metrics, allowing for speedy adjustments in response to changing circumstances. A dashboard can provide a holistic view of data and can facilitate interactivity and real-time synthesis of data.

Consider the semester-long efforts of a student culminating in a coherent final report. In the health sector, dashboards facilitate instantaneous surveillance of patient metrics, allowing for immediate response to any deviations in vital signs, whereas reports enable more comprehensive evaluations of patient health trends and treatment outcomes. Hence, dashboards are widely acknowledged as a key application of data visualization.

The Data Analytics Advantage. Laeeq Khan, Oxford University Press. © Oxford University Press (2025).
DOI: 10.1093/oso/9780197814222.003.0011

Dashboards can differ greatly in design and usage contexts from other exploratory visualization tools (Sarikaya et al., 2018). These visualization dashboards are employed in a wide variety of industries, nonprofit organizations, and service organizations to assist in making decisions that are data-informed. Keeping in view the value that dashboards provide, I felt it necessary that dashboards and analytics reports be discussed in greater detail within the wider field of data visualization. Therefore, a separate chapter was needed to elaborate on the importance and rationale of the dashboard and the associated reports. Also important is to comprehend how best these dashboards can be effectively created in the context of social media analytics from a design thinking perspective.

Social media analytics reports and dashboards are vital tools that enable the measurement and monitoring of social media campaigns and activity. Dashboards and reports are more important than ever in today's swiftly advancing digital era, as these allow for the development of informed social media strategies, the measurement of the effectiveness of campaigns, and the identification of areas that need improvement. These tools deliver an all-encompassing summary of social media analytics, which includes an evaluation of the reach, engagement, and audience demographics, among other metrics. These visual interfaces synthesize immense information repositories, transforming unprocessed data into comprehensible insights, thereby enabling organizations to steer their strategies with precision and agility.

11.1 Introduction to Dashboards and Reports

11.1.1 Dashboards

At their essence, dashboards serve as an integrated collection of widgets—essentially, concise reports that visually represent data in diverse formats. Dashboards usually feature a grid layout with straightforward displays of prominent numbers, charts, and maps. Advanced dynamic dashboards offer additional capabilities and can be equipped with features that enable real-time, dynamic data monitoring (Sarikaya et al., 2018). Dashboards can incorporate elements of infographics or visual storytelling and serve as a graphical representation of data, aiding in monitoring specific conditions and enhancing comprehension (Wexler et al. 2017; Sarikaya et al., 2018). In terms of design, when a set of charts and data visualizations are boxed within a typical computer screen dimension, these may be classified as a dashboard.

As our world becomes more digital, the prevalence of interfaces in our daily existence increases. Beyond the realm of business, we encounter dashboards in our personal lives, whether for monitoring our bank accounts or our home appliances. The most ubiquitous example is the car dashboard, a fixture many of us see on an everyday basis. A car dashboard displays vital information such as vehicle speed, fuel level, and engine temperature in strategic locations, ensuring that drivers remain informed and vigilant. On a digital dashboard, visual elements such as gauges and maps are meticulously curated to provide immediate insights. For example, an operations manager in a manufacturing facility could quickly assess production rates, machine efficiency, and inventory levels, allowing for opportune managerial interventions.

Dashboards facilitate the evaluation of the efficiency of websites or social media platforms by providing a snapshot of the user's most pertinent metrics and reports. According to Sarikaya et al. (2018), dashboards provide several advantages over alternative techniques of data visualization for presentations and exploration. These advantages include quick readability, synchronized views, continuous data monitoring, and both individual and group awareness. By aggregating data elements such as conversions, visits, likes, and comments, they serve as the control panel of a business, providing a comprehensive or detailed view of organizational performance at any given time. Moreover, these dashboards are proficient at capturing and displaying key performance indicators (KPIs), metrics, and a myriad of other data points, monitoring, and quantifying progress over time. Their value resides in their ability to monitor multiple metrics simultaneously, allowing for rapid account evaluations and the identification of potential inter-data correlations.

Dashboards are central to social media analytics, where they can be termed "social dashboards" (Sarikaya et al., 2018). These social dashboards have emerged as centralized platforms for administering and analyzing an organization's digital presence in the social media landscape (see Figure 11.1). Hootsuite, Buffer, and Sprout Social provide powerful social dashboards, as they aggregate analytics, engagement metrics, and scheduling functionalities in a visually cohesive format. The displays offer several advantages in the form of procedural improvements, consolidation of insights, and supporting data-driven decision-making.

Data-driven decision-making is essential in the modern business environment. Dashboards in the social media analytics realm transform enormous amounts of data into actionable insights, thereby improving the overall efficacy of the overall data analysis. They expedite the analysis process by presenting data in an easily understandable visual format. Moreover, with the advent of real-time report generation and advanced predictive capabilities, analytics dashboards will play an increasingly crucial role in directing organizational success.

An effective and well-designed social media analytics dashboard possesses essential characteristics that allow organizations to easily monitor, evaluate, and

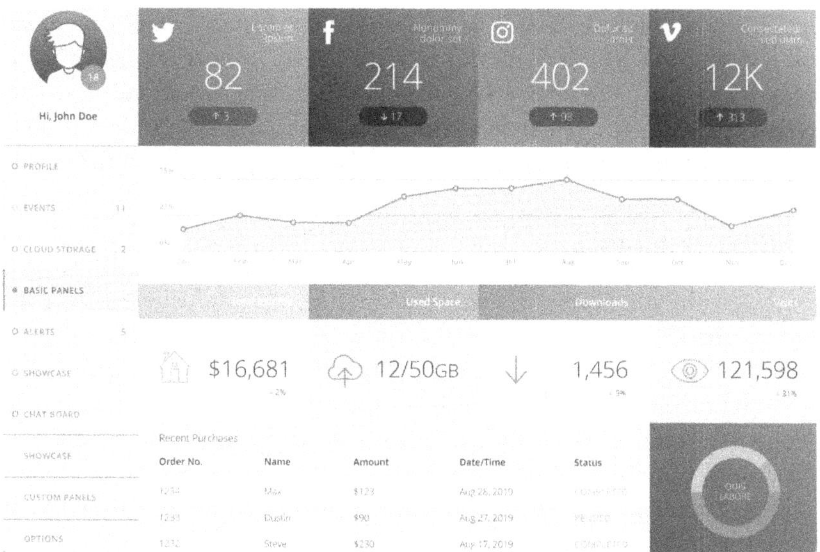

Figure 11.1 A sample Social Dashboard

derive strategic actionable insights from their social media activities. The dashboard should feature a user-friendly layout that is straightforward to navigate, catering to users of varying skill levels and enabling quick access to necessary information. A quality dashboard should offer real-time data updates, allowing users to monitor social media indicators as they fluctuate and react immediately to any new trends or difficulties. Users should have the capability to personalize the dashboard to emphasize metrics that are most pertinent to their aims, enabling a customized analysis that corresponds with particular goals.

In line with this user-centered approach, Cahyadi and Prananto (2015) maintained it was very important to make sure that dashboard designs were in line with the overall goals and ideals of a company. By integrating the interface into the organizational strategy, users will have a more compelling reason to adopt and utilize it. This is more than a simple user-interface enhancement or functionality upgrade; it is a holistic approach to dashboard creation. According to Cahyadi and Prananto (2015), it is essential to delve deeply into the multifaceted dimensions of designing an effective interface.

A powerful dashboard also integrates data from several social media platforms to provide a comprehensive overview of social media performance across all channels. Modern dashboards also offer interactive charts and graphs used to visually represent data, making intricate information easier to understand and more interesting. Furthermore, a dashboard should be capable of displaying historical data to recognize trends, assess campaign effectiveness, and develop well-informed future tactics. Whenever important events or milestones take place, dashboards can have the added functionality of notifying users about major changes, to allow for prompt action. A well-designed social media analytics dashboard can greatly improve an organization's capacity to make decisions based on data, refine social media tactics, and accomplish marketing goals.

11.1.2 Reports

Reports provide a more comprehensive and structured overview of data in the form of tables, charts, text, and graphs, which is conducive to in-depth analysis and reflection. While both reports and dashboards may contain comparable components, such as charts and tables, their structures and intended uses are significantly distinct. A report provides comprehensive information, whereas a dashboard is intended to provide immediate answers at a glance by distilling the essence of real-time data.

In terms of duration and presentation, there is a stark contrast between the two. Typically spanning multiple pages or even volumes, reports are replete with tables, figures, and detailed narratives. The navigation of a report, particularly in digital formats, may require extensive scrolling or page transitions. On the other hand, dashboards are typically concise and created for rapid consumption, usually fitting in the rectangular screen space.

In contrast with a dashboard, which provides minimal explanations, a report delves deeply and is frequently accompanied by detailed explanations, summaries, and future recommendations (Fitzpatrick & Weissman, 2021). Dashboards are designed for speed and immediacy, while reports are intended for depth and reflection. In addition, reports are structured compilations that seek to provide comprehensive analyses. In contrast to the instantaneous nature of dashboards, reports typically concentrate on particular time intervals and provide detailed insights into data trends, anomalies, and evolving patterns. For instance, a corporation's annual financial statement would meticulously detail numerous financial metrics, providing stakeholders with a deep understanding of fiscal health and trends.

In the realm of social analytics and data visualization, dashboards excel in situations requiring real-time monitoring and swift decision-making, such as emergency centers, stock trading arenas, and e-commerce platforms monitoring real-time user behavior. Conversely, reports find their efficacy in scenarios that demand exhaustive analyses, periodic reviews, or extensive data presentation (see Figure 11.2). An academician, for example, would rely on detailed reports to explicate research findings, while an auditor would rely on them for comprehensive financial evaluations of businesses.

ANALYTICS REPORT

The advent of social media has transformed the landscape of business engagement, offering unprecedented avenues for interaction with customers. However, the vast amount of data generated poses a challenge for businesses in extracting actionable insights. This study employs advanced analytics techniques to dissect social media data, aiming to uncover patterns that can inform strategic business decisions. The findings underscore the critical role of social media analytics in informing business strategies.

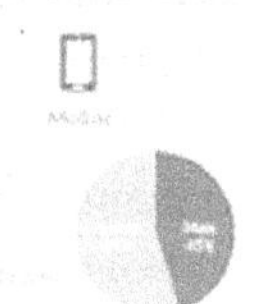

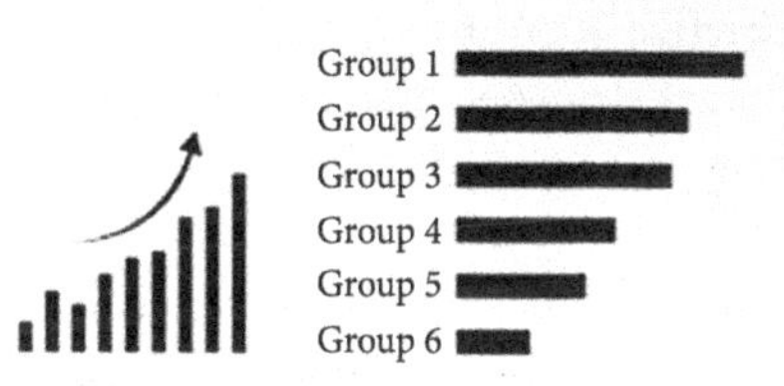

Engagement Metrics Correlation: The study found a significant correlation between engagement metrics {likes, comments, shares) and positive business outcomes, particularly in customer acquisition and retention. Predictive Analytics for Strategy Optimization: Predictive models were developed to forecast future trends in customer behavior, enabling businesses to tailor their strategies proactively.

This report presents the findings of a comprehensive study aimed at understanding how businesses can leverage social media analytics to refine their strategies for improved customer engagement and increased revenue. By analyzing data from various social media platforms, the study identifies key metrics that correlate with successful business outcomes and offers strategic recommendations for leveraging these insights.

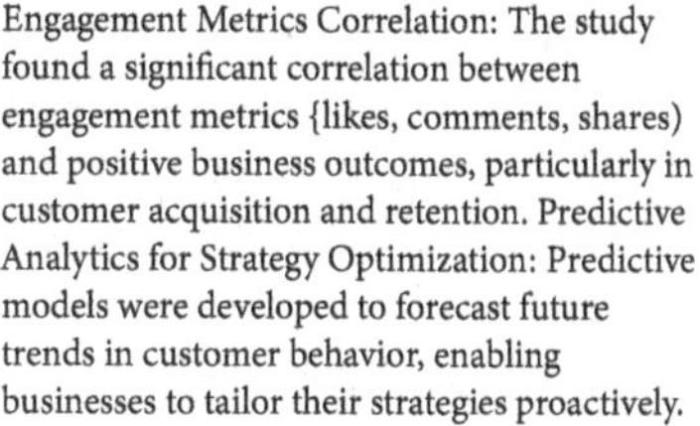

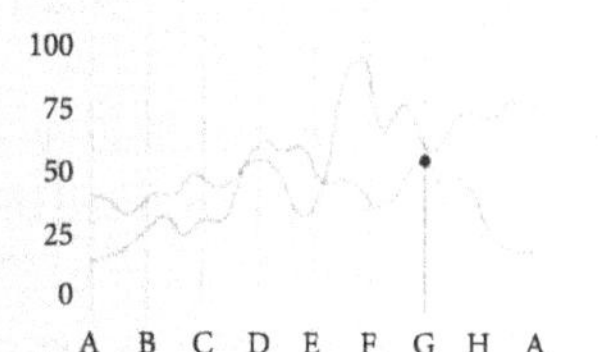

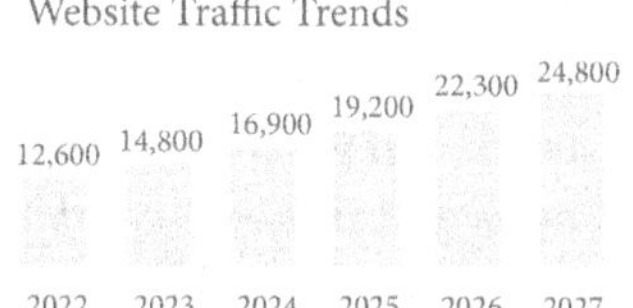

Website Traffic Trends

This report demonstrates the indispensable value of social media analytics in crafting effective business strategies. By harnessing the power of data, businesses can gain a competitive edge, fostering stronger customer relationships and driving sustainable growth.
Further research is suggested to explore the integration of artificial intelligence and machine learning techniques in analyzing social media data, potentially offering even more nuanced insights into customer behavior and strategic opportunities.

Figure 11.2 Sample Analytics Report

Effective reporting methods are crucial for the success of data visualization and social media analytics. Modern analytics platforms provide both dashboards and advanced report-generating features. These could range from basic metric summaries to extensive descriptive analyses that highlight significant occurrences throughout certain time frames.

Reporting tools are vital for creating customized reports that track specific metrics and narratives. Social media management platforms such as Hootsuite, Buffer, and Sprout Social enable organizations to efficiently manage multiple social media accounts, schedule content in advance, assign tasks to team members, and generate detailed analytics reports to measure their social media engagement impact (Tam & Kim, 2019).

Beyond the technologies or mediums, the success of a report depends on its ability to convey the intended message, thereby bridging the gap between the communicator and the audience. Effective reporting not only motivates action but also integrates analytical insights into broader strategies without friction. Emphasizing comprehensive reporting is not just a hallmark of successful analytics but also its driving force.

Effective reporting requires that the intended message resonates with the intended audience. Although this may appear simple, it is frequently complicated by both technical factors and the inherent subjectivity of human interpretation. Hence social media analytics reports provide a detailed overview of the health of an organization's social media presence (Fitzpatrick & Weissman, 2021). While a report follows a typical format with text, charts and images juxtaposed for effective storytelling, it is also important to recognize the importance of tailoring our methods and reporting structures to suit various objectives, audiences, and mediums. Hence, there are various ways reports can be structured. The approaches to data storytelling employing reports will be discussed in the later part of this chapter.

Hence, dashboards and reports need to be properly designed. Well-designed dashboards and reports function as visual interfaces between unprocessed data and its users and translate complex information into actionable insights. The synthesis of aesthetics and functionality guarantees that data is not only viewed but also grasped and utilized. Elements such as color and layout enhance visual clarity, reduce cognitive burden, and direct the viewer's attention to crucial metrics and trends. The effectiveness of a dashboard and a report is determined by the quality of its design, which should be informative, interesting, and user-friendly.

11.2 Integrating Design Thinking into Data Visualization

Effective data visualization is about more than just display; it involves communication, message resonance with the audiences, and the efficient delivery of information. At the core of effective data visualization is the concept of design thinking. Design thinking is a methodology based on empathy and comprehension (Köppen & Meinel, 2014). This method, when combined with data visualization, facilitates the development of deeper insights and more compelling narratives. Design thinking is essentially a user-centered approach to problem-solving. Combining this with the complexities of data visualization will produce more fruitful results.

Design thinking emerged as a way of thinking to tackle complex problems that could not be solved using conventional methods by incorporating human-centered requirements, technological possibilities, and strategic business objectives. Since its inception in the 1960s, this concept has evolved from a theoretical notion to a widely acknowledged and utilized practical method in several fields (Chongwatpol, 2020). The design thinking creative strategy is centered around an iterative, user-focused methodology that includes stages including problem identification, idea generation, reflection, brainstorming, and continuous refinement of design concepts (Brown, 2009; Seidel & Fixson, 2013). This method represents a shift from conventional, sequential business models that emphasize milestones, providing a more adaptable and fluid process designed to encourage creativity and innovation (Chongwatpol, 2020).

While design thinking and data visualization may appear distinct, they intertwine to enhance the narrative quality of data, guiding us in the creation of impactful, audience-focused data narratives. An interesting investigation into the field of data visualization by Parsons (2021) indicated that practitioners frequently avoided systematic approaches when asked about their design journey. They favored adaptive methods, making decisions in real time based on the situation and previous experiences. This exemplifies a fundamental design thinking tenet: problem-solving flexibility.

To illustrate the concept further, we will focus on the design thinking framework presented by Stanford's Hasso-Plattner Institute of Design, also known as the d.School (Plattner, 2011). This framework consists of five iterative stages and how they relate to data visualization:

1. **Empathize**: Empathy, the foundation of design thinking compels us to consider the perspective of our audience. This phase involves immersing oneself in the user's universe and attempting to comprehend their wants, needs, and obstacles (Chongwatpol, 2020). In the context of data visualization, this means understanding how distinct groups perceive and interact with visual data. For example, while policymakers may benefit from complex data visualizations, schoolchildren may require simplified and more engaging images. Effective data visualization addresses both the cognitive and emotional needs of its audience.

2. **Define**: Building on the findings and synthesis from the empathy stage, this stage of design thinking focuses on problem definition (Chongwatpol, 2020). An example of this would be posing the question, "How

can we design visualizations that resonate with seniors who may not be tech-savvy?"

3. **Ideate**: The ideate stage involves the generation of diverse solutions, always tying them back to the identified problem. This is often in the form of out-of-box thinking (Chongwatpol, 2020). For visualization, brainstorming sessions might investigate various methods to depict data effectively.

4. **Prototype**: Bring concepts to life by creating physical versions or prototypes. It is like a test stage where team members can understand the details of the design and simply get a better sense of how the prototype may appear to the end-users (Chongwatpol, 2020). To appeal to its intended audience, a visualization prototype may favor more straightforward color schemes or more prominent text.

5. **Test and Refine**: In this fifth and final stage of design thinking, after constructing the prototype, the focus is on collecting feedback and using this information to make any necessary adjustments. A prototype is regarded as a step toward the final product, as opposed to the final product itself.

Having outlined the five stages of design thinking, it is possible to view the relationship between design thinking and effective data visualization. When applying design thinking to the process of data visualization, it is necessary to connect the two techniques seamlessly. The following list of three key general guidelines builds on and embeds design thinking principles into data visualization, offering a convergence of both methodologies:

- **Know your audience**. The first and most important step is to identify the requirements of your audience. For example, dashboards and reports designed for the ordinary user should emphasize being as straightforward and understandable as possible. Understanding the target demographic allows for more effective communication, which in turn leads to more actionable insights. The visual and functional design of a dashboard needs to be audience-centric, and tailored to their literacy levels. Social dashboard design needs to consider audience domain knowledge, experience with visualizations, and connection to the data. Sarikaya et al. (2018) classified levels of visualization literacy of the audience that can dictate the design of social dashboards: Low literacy encompasses a basic dashboard that may display simple bar and line graphs. Included in medium literacy audience dashboards are dual axes, scatterplots, cumulative measures, and heat maps. High literacy refers to advanced visualization techniques, such as radar, tree map, network visualizations, connected scatter plots, and custom visualizations.

- **Ideating and setting clear objectives**. After gaining an in-depth comprehension of the requirements of the user and the environment in which they operate, the next step is to establish goals that are unique and clear. Think about the information that you want to convey with the visualization, whether it be in a dashboard or a report. It is essential that the purpose be clear, particularly during the phase of ideation; it does not matter if the audience comprises policymakers or industry professionals. A useful tip would be to set out clear objectives and ideate the design of the dashboard on paper.
- **Balancing aesthetics with function**. Although there is no denying the significance of a design's aesthetic appeal, it is of the utmost importance to strike a balance between the design's attractiveness and its practicability. This point is driven home by Edward Tufte's "data-ink ratio" notion, which highlights the importance of data above simply aesthetic aspects of a presentation. The process of making a data visualization is an iterative one, and it requires numerous rounds of refining to make a captivating and engaging visual tale. Moreover, effectively designed dashboards should juxtapose and present visual data and charts holistically.

When developing dashboards, those responsible should understand visual literacy, select context-relevant visual representations, and consider the social context as high priority (Case Study 11.1).

Case Study 11.1 Increasing the Effectiveness of the Messaging for Green Initiatives via Dashboard and Report Design at a Government Department

---

A government agency launched several marketing campaigns across a variety of social media platforms to raise awareness about environmentally conscious programs and policies. A dashboard and report were built with three core objectives in mind: understanding the audience, setting clear objectives, and striking a balance between aesthetics and functionality. These were used to analyze the effectiveness of these efforts and to make data-driven choices for future initiatives.

Comprehension of the Target Audience

The core audience for this evaluation consisted of government officials, policymakers, and environmental strategists. The dashboard was designed with an emphasis on clarity and simplicity, since its creators recognized how important it was to provide these stakeholders with insights that could be quickly digested and acted on. Simple visual representations of sophisticated social media indicators, such as engagement rates and share percentages, were selected from among a variety of charts and graphs. The dashboard guaranteed that even people without an in-depth grasp of social media analytics could comprehend the findings and understand the consequences of those results by catering to the unique demands of this audience.

Ideation and Establishing Clearly Defined Objectives

Before beginning the design process, the major aim was outlined, which was to determine how successful the social media message campaigns were in terms of supporting environmentally friendly projects. Both the dashboard and the report were consequently adapted to provide answers to particular questions:

- How many people did the communications about the green effort get through to?
- What was the percentage of people who engaged with each campaign?
- Which social media outlet did you find to be the most successful in conveying your message?
- After the campaign, was there an increase in the public's support for environmentally friendly initiatives?

The dashboard would be able to provide direct insights into each question if these objectives were clear, and the accompanying report would be able to dive deeper into the intricacies and make recommendations.

Striking a Balance Between Aesthetics and Function

The layout of the dashboard was quite important. It was vital to make it aesthetically appealing to interest the citizens; yet, functionality was the major focus of attention. The use of Edward Tufte's "data-ink ratio" framework allowed for the elimination of superfluous ornamental components. Designers utilized pie charts, bar graphs, and heat maps to represent platform-wise engagement, sentiment analysis, and geographical reaction, respectively. The iterative design approach included multiple changes based on the feedback from the various stakeholders, which helped to ensure that the final dashboard was both user-friendly and informative.

At the end of the assessment period, the government department had a clear grasp of the reach and impact of the messaging that they had been posting on social media regarding their environmentally friendly activities. During this evaluation, the dashboard and report that were developed bearing the aforementioned goals in mind were of great assistance. Not only did they give a full picture of the performance of the campaign but also they opened the way for more focused and effective messaging strategies in the future. This highlights the crucial role that well-designed data visualization tools play in the evaluation of policies and the creation of strategies.

11.3 Exploring Dashboard and Reporting Tools

Various software alternatives are accessible to help create effective dashboards and improve reporting capabilities. This encompasses both free and paid premium options. Microsoft Excel, Power BI, and Tableau, as mentioned previously in this volume, allow the creation of informative dashboards. Moreover, Microsoft Word may be used to generate reports by combining text and pictures to create a persuasive story. The following is a selection of tools that can facilitate the production of reports and dashboards:

1. **Looker Studio**: This web-based product, formerly known as Google Data Studio, was initially released by Google as part of the business Google Analytics 360 package. Its primary function is to convert raw data into individualized reports and dashboards. It emphasizes the necessity of flexible dashboards and asserts that the effectiveness of a dashboard should not be compromised, regardless of its complexity. The capacity to adapt guarantees that a dashboard provides more than simply a collection of static facts.

2. **Hootsuite**: This is a well-known social media management platform that has over 15 million users and delivers an all-encompassing experience to its customers. Users with the free plan can combine three different social media accounts and have limited post-scheduling capabilities. A business account is required for Instagram's scheduler, in addition to the ability to create ads and generate ROI data. Included in the features are post publishing and scheduling, as well as suggestions for hashtags and Canva templates.

3. **Sprout Social**: Sprout Social is a social media management platform that caters to social media teams and provides a wide range of capabilities, from the ability to create and schedule posts to comprehensive social listening tools. Because of its comprehensive and ready-to-share information, it is a potential challenger for businesses that place a high priority on analytics.

11.4 Leveraging the Power of Data Storytelling
in Social Media Analytics

Exploring the multifaceted realm of social media analytics presents many opportunities and notable obstacles. The vast number of people leaving digital footprints on social media presents a significant potential to extract valuable knowledge. However, without the practice of data storytelling, these insights may be overlooked in the middle of other information. This essential talent of integrating information into engaging stories is a guiding light in the intricate field of social media analytics.

The essence of data storytelling is the integration of data, images, and narrative to communicate profound insights (Ojo & Heravi, 2018). When it comes to social media analytics, ephemeral trends and the complexity of unstructured data underline the necessity for captivating storytelling. A simple spreadsheet can show how popular a hashtag was over a month, but a data narrative can explain "why" it was so popular, providing a deeper level of context and helping users make more educated choices in the ever-changing world of social media. Merely presenting data isn't enough. Explaining the context is also crucial. Without context, audiences may become overwhelmed, misconstrue the message, or delay decision-making.

The use of design thinking concepts transforms data storytelling from a simplistic depiction into an interesting story that is centered on the end user. We can build narratives that are specific to the requirements of our audience by empathizing with them, whether they be brand managers or lawmakers. A brand manager, for example, would be interested in learning how consumers' attitudes have shifted in the wake of a social media marketing campaign. The story would highlight the campaign's ripple effects when using design thinking, which would make it relevant and resonant.

There is more to data storytelling than just charts and graphs (Knaflic, 2015). It is the story you tell about your data that helps put it in context and makes it more understandable (Lund, 2022). In the same way that an oral story does so through the use of words, data storytelling does it via the use of images to convey information. Data storytelling is a tool that may help bridge the gap between raw data and actionable tales in the modern digital era by offering context, clarity, and motivating action.

Imagine a social media marketing report that goes beyond a simple dashboard to present levels of interaction, strategic movements, engagement peaks, product background, and competitor insights all woven together as a compelling story. A holistic data story combines numerical information with a narrative to provide a presentation that is unmistakable and captivating, resonating with the user. Data on its own might be impenetrable, but a narrative can give context and explain why measurements are significant in a way that goes beyond simple numbers and charts.

For effective data-driven storytelling, it is vital to create clear goals, ensure that everyone involved understands the aim of your narrative, know the audience you are trying to reach, and elaborate on the primary message that you intend to express. Your narrative may have more of an impact on the audience if you tailor it to the interests of your audience and tell it convincingly. Adding depth to a story requires engaging in essential parts of storytelling, such as plot, context, and characters, and crafting a conclusion that has significance. Keeping one's neutrality is of the utmost importance, and the visualizations you create should always represent the integrity of the data (Lund, 2022).

It is also essential to personalize your story by providing material that is both approachable and condensed in a way that maintains and piques attention. It is possible to dramatically improve the narrative by fluidly incorporating consistent and supporting data-driven charts. In the end, while the statistics serve as the structural backbone of your tale, the narrative is what gives it life and brings it to life. A tale that is appealing and informative may be crafted through an artful blending of the two, which can guide educated decision-making.

An analytics report that adheres to the principles of effective storytelling and design thinking, provides comprehensive insights into the performance of a period. It records significant events, including offline initiatives, and ties social media activity to the organization's broader goals. Moreover, since humans are naturally drawn to narratives, it is important to create a narrative that contains obstacles, resolutions, and latent conflicts (Ojo & Heravi, 2018). Structuring a report as a narrative, beginning with an introduction, followed by an initial climax, development, and a final climax, keeps the audience interested (Lund, 2022). This Hollywood-familiar dual-climax technique has proven effective in business reporting, including social media analytics. By employing this narrative structure, the report becomes more than just a collection of facts; it becomes a journey that captivates the readership (see Report 11.1).

Report 11.1 Sample Social Media Report Format

1. **Title and Executive Summary**: A brief review of the report, summarizing important findings, successes, and areas for improvement.
2. **Introduction**: In the introduction, provide a summary of the report's goals and the time period that it covers.

3. **Social Media Goals and Objectives**: Compile a list of the aims and goals that were established in advance for the reporting period. This might include goals such as generating interaction, driving traffic to a website, or influencing the feeling associated with a brand.

4. **Platform-Wise Performance**:
   a. Facebook: Total followers, new followers, post reach, and engagement rate are the metrics that make up "reach and engagement." Showcase the post that has received the most attention by highlighting it as the "Top Performing Post." Performance of Paid Advertisements: The click-through rate, the conversion rate, and the return on ad expenditure are all important metrics.
   b. Instagram: Total followers, new followers, and engagement rate are the metrics that makeup growth and engagement. Highlighting the best-performing posts and stories based on the number of likes, comments, and shares.

   [Repeat for additional platforms such as X, LinkedIn, and Pinterest, among others.]

5. **Analytics: Metrics and Key Performance Indicators**: Engagement metrics such as likes, shares, comments, and total engagement rate. Traffic metrics can include the number of referrals to the website, the bounce rate, and the average length of each session. Lead generation, conversion rate, and client acquisition cost are all examples of conversion metrics.

6. **Competitor Analysis**: Conduct a competition analysis by comparing your performance metrics to those of significant rivals, identifying areas in which you excel and those in which you might use some work, and determining a course of action to address any deficiencies.

7. **Audience Insights**: Demographics such as age, gender, and location, etc. Insights on behavior, such as times of activity and patterns of engagement, etc. Track the rate of audience growth in the form of followers and evaluate the results in comparison to earlier time periods.

8. **Content, Themes, and Sentiment Analyses**: Determine which sorts of material (video, photos, articles) are the most popular by content analysis' content reach and engagement metric. Also, gauge the sentiment on different social platforms. For example, what is the audience saying in the comments, messages, and reviews?

9. **Recommendations**: Provide actionable steps for the upcoming period based on the facts and insights from the previous quarter.

10. **Conclusion**: Provide a concise overview of the report's findings as well as its recommendations for the future. In the appendices, you can attach any additional charts, raw data, or specific metrics for future reference.

11.5 Social Media Analytics Centers and Labs

Social media analytics centers and labs are specialized physical facilities that give social media teams a customized environment in which to disseminate the best content and gather useful insights. These centers are equipped with one or more dashboards that show data in a manner that every team member may see and utilize at any time. In certain instances, rather than a single dashboard, the command center may consist of a series of panels, each of which displays a single massive metric. Social media command centers may also contain a specialized room for social media customer care, allowing customer support professionals to be placed closer to the social media team than to the main support hub of the organization.

In the same way that a war room is intense and focused on its mission, a social media command center functions as the nerve center for digital engagements. These facilities are outfitted with large-screen dashboards that graphically display live streams of processed data that have been gathered via the use of social listening tools. These screens, which are frequently as large as walls, are more than simply aesthetic decorations; they turn complicated data into visually consumable formats, which makes it easier to gain real-time insights and make strategic decisions.

A configuration where a room has large screens with live data visualizations helps to cultivate an atmosphere that is conducive to the convergence of information from a wide variety of digital sources, which results in an immersive analytics experience. It is much simpler for experts to see trends, keep an eye on live campaigns, and evaluate public mood when varied data streams have been curated and presented in such an all-encompassing manner. It is not enough to simply observe the facts; rather, one must experience it. Teams can work more effectively, dynamically strategize, and completely comprehend the holistic perspective of their digital footprint in this immersive environment, which ensures that they are constantly one step ahead in their digital engagements.

The Social Media Analytics Research Team (SMART) Lab at Ohio University's widely known Scripps College of Communication, one of the first command centers dedicated to social media, opened its doors in 2015. The

Figure 11.3 SMART Lab, Scripps College of Communication, Ohio University

SMART Lab is not only a center of technical excellence but also a platform that encourages academic development (see Figure 11.3). It serves as a center for research in the field of social media analytics. The research lab promotes academic–industry collaborations, creating research teams across disciplines to foster digital analytics research.

Regardless of the size of a firm, establishing a social media command center can be an efficient choice when working with social media analytics. While analytics may be accessible from any location, a command center provides a strategic and concentrated space that can be a game-changer for the organization.

In addition to social media command centers, analytics labs are specialized organizational units designed to analyze and model data. Using advanced statistical and computational techniques, analytics labs engage in meaningful analytics research involving social media data. Data scientists and analysts with experience in data mining, machine learning, and predictive analytics staff these laboratories.

In today's fast-paced and dynamic digital market, organizations and businesses that wish to remain competitive must have social media command centers and/or analytics labs. Such facilities provide real-time insights into customer behavior and preferences, enabling businesses to make data-driven decisions, adapt swiftly to changes in the market, and build competitive advantage.

11.6 The Value of Data Visualization Across Careers

Data visualization goes beyond its usual boundaries in STEM fields, becoming essential in various industries such as banking, government, marketing, sports, and education, among others. The great acclaim it receives is due to the practical benefits it provides in various professional settings. The rising need for skilled professionals in data visualization in the current job market highlights its crucial significance and expanding relevance.

The effectiveness of a well-designed visualization in improving understanding of transmitted information is crucial. As the professional landscape changes, combining analytical expertise with engaging storytelling skills is becoming essential. Data visualization is a crucial means for bridging the gap between in-depth analysis and compelling communication. Several important factors highlight the importance of data visualization across all industries:

- **Clear communication**: Complex data is turned into images that are easy to understand, which ensures clarity in conversations with a wide range of audiences, from stakeholders to the average individuals.
- **Making educated decisions**: Visualizations highlight patterns and trends, allowing decision-makers to draw out educated plans founded in real evidence.
- **Effectiveness**: The process of data analysis is made more simplified via the use of visual representations, which saves significant time and resources.
- **Discovering previously unnoticed patterns and insights**: Beyond the scope of standard analysis, visualization provides new perspectives, which enables the discovery of previously hidden patterns and insights.

Professionals skillful in the art and science of data visualization will have a competitive edge in their respective fields. A strong grasp of data visualization allows individuals and businesses to make informed decisions, convey ideas effectively, and maintain a competitive edge across several professional sectors. This knowledge is invaluable for analyzing intricate data obtained from social media and converting it into visual stories that can be implemented.

Chapter Summary

- Social media analytics reports and dashboards are vital tools that enable the measurement and monitoring of social media campaigns and activity.

- Dashboards, at their essence, serve as an integrated collection of widgets— essentially, concise reports that visually represent data in diverse formats.
- Reports provide a more comprehensive and structured overview of data in the form of tables, charts, text, and graphs, which is conducive to in-depth analysis and reflection.
- Design thinking is essentially a user-centered approach to problem-solving.
- While design thinking and data visualization may appear distinct, they intertwine to enhance the narrative quality of data, guiding us in the creation of impactful, audience-focused data narratives.
- For effective data-driven storytelling, it is vital to create clear goals, ensure that everyone involved understands the aim of your narrative, know the audience you are trying to reach, and elaborate on the primary message that you intend to express.
- Social media analytics centers and labs are specialized physical facilities that give social media teams a customized environment in which to disseminate the best content and gather useful insights.
- Professionals skillful in the art and science of data visualization will have a competitive edge in their respective fields.

Questions for Review

1. In what way are dashboards different from reports?
2. What is design thinking and how does it relate to data visualization?
3. How can the power of data storytelling be leveraged for social media analytics?
4. What is the reason for having social media command centers and labs?

12

Artificial Intelligence and the Future of Social Media Analytics

---

Chapter Outline

12.1 Current and Future Trends in Social Media
12.2 Future Developments in Social Media Analytics
12.3 AI Insights
12.4 Applications of AI in Social Media
12.5 AI in Social Media Analytics
    12.5.1 AI for Discovery
    12.5.2 AI for Analysis
    12.5.3 AI for Visualization
12.6 Conclusion

Social media analytics exemplifies the continuous quest of learning, adapting, and innovating in the ever-changing digital landscape. Organizations and businesses are presented with possibilities and challenges because of the quick rate at which technological trends and user behaviors are shifting. The capacity of social media analytics to harness these developments, turning huge amounts of data into usable insights, enabling informed decision-making, and permitting preemptive actions to emerging patterns is at the heart of its transformational promise.

At the outset of this book, in Chapter 2, readers were presented with a systematic and succinct approach to social media analytics, distilling the complex web of metrics, methods, and methodologies into a clear and coherent structure. The heart of this approach is the DAV (Discovery, Analysis, Visualization) Framework of Social Media Analytics, a model that effectively encapsulates the necessary processes for conducting a comprehensive social media analysis. The DAV Framework of Social Media Analytics encompasses the required procedures for performing a full social media analysis. Each chapter in this

The Data Analytics Advantage. Laeeq Khan, Oxford University Press. © Oxford University Press (2025).
DOI: 10.1093/oso/9780197814222.003.0012

book unpacked a comprehensive understanding of social media analytics based on the DAV architecture, illuminating its applications, unraveling its complexities, and demonstrating its adaptability across a wide range of domains and use cases.

As we begin the final chapter, we look to the horizon, where we ponder the bigger picture. In this chapter, we will use the information and comprehension that we have gained from the previous chapters to take a glimpse into the future of social media analytics. Which upcoming technology will cause fundamental changes to the environment? How will changes in the norms and behaviors of society affect the data that we collect and the insights that we draw from it? And perhaps most importantly, how can organizations ensure that their analytics strategies continue to be both relevant and strong in the face of rapid change, therefore staying one step ahead of the curve?

In line with the robust growth of social media, social media analytics is also growing at a fast pace. In the following section, let's look at some statistics and current and future trends that bring to light the pervasiveness of social media use and how measuring audience interactions is vital for the success of organizations and businesses.

12.1 Current and Future Trends in Social Media

The scope of social media extends beyond that of individual solutions and platforms; rather, it is a revolutionary digital environment that is redefining the parameters of marketing and business. TikTok, Instagram, X, Facebook, and YouTube are some of the most important platforms that have emerged as crucial routes via which companies can make meaningful relationships, actively interact with consumers, and extend their reach to those audiences. The key social media trends shaping 2025, include AI-driven content creation, personalized user experiences, emerging platforms, and evolving privacy regulations (Garlin, 2025).

By 2024, the global count of internet users stood at an impressive 5.35 billion, translating to 66.2% of the entire global populace (Petrosyan, 2024). In terms of regional Internet utilization, northern Europe occupied the top spot. Further testament to this digital proliferation, countries such as Norway, Saudi Arabia, and the United Arab Emirates reported an astounding 99% internet penetration rate (Petrosyan, 2024). In 2024, the number of social media users worldwide reached 5.24 billion (Statista, 2025). By 2027, this population is projected to increase to approximately 6 billion people.

The United States and China stand out as the leading players when it comes to major social networks. Chinese platforms such as WeChat, QQ, and the video-sharing application Douyin have gained significant traction in their home regions due to their locally tailored content and context. Notably, Douyin's extensive acclaim prompted the launch of its international equivalent, TikTok (Dixon, 2023).

On the business front, 77% of organizations utilize social media to engage with their target audience (Wong, 2023). As a result of the ubiquitous digital transformation, it is not surprising that 77% of businesses use social media for outreach. Beyond brand visibility, which accounts for 44% of these businesses, 41% consider social media to be a crucial channel for revenue generation (Wong, 2023).

Based on the current developments, it is possible to extrapolate the future developments in social media that will impact how human interaction is measured within social media analytics. Following is a snapshot of the future developments:

1. **Increased visual content**: The success of tools such as Facebook Live, Instagram stories, and Instagram reels exemplifies how the dynamics of social media are always shifting. The demand for images and videos is on the rise, and marketing and public relations experts need to adapt their strategies not only to cater to this specific sort of content but also to embrace new forms that successfully communicate brand storylines. Alongside this move toward visual material is an increasing fascination with augmented reality (AR), which is represented by features such as Snapchat filters that can be placed on both still photographs and videos. These filters may also be used to create animated GIFs.

2. **Short-form videos**: Adding to the rise of visual content, the proliferation of short-form videos is a discernible trend within the social media domain (Wong, 2023). These brief video segments, typically less than one minute in length, have captured the interest of 66% of users (Wong, 2023). The combination of their brevity and veracity has made them particularly shareable, making them 2.5 times more engaging than their longer counterparts. Furthermore, 34% of the audience can relate to the sincere message these videos convey (Wong, 2023). TikTok videos have taken the internet by storm.

3. **Content adapted for mobile devices**: It is widely acknowledged that mobile devices are the most convenient way to access social media in general. The overwhelming majority, a remarkable 99%, utilize tablets or smartphones to interact with social platforms (Wong, 2023). Even

more remarkable is the fact that 78% of this group exclusively access social media via their mobile phones (Wong, 2023). The move toward mobile video platforms is more pronounced, particularly within the demographic age group ranging from 18 to 34 years old. As younger audiences shift away from traditional mediums such as TV, advertisers are rethinking their tactics and putting more of an emphasis on mobile-centric content. This transition necessitates the development of video content that is suitable for mobile devices, as well as material that is easily accessible and adaptable across a variety of platforms for companies.

4. **Social media influencers**: Social media influencers appear to wield considerable sway over the millennial demographic in terms of endorsements. 50% of millennials trust these influencers' product recommendations more than traditional celebrity endorsements, which have a trust quotient of 38% (Wong, 2023). The necessity to cultivate relationships with key influencers has also emerged as a direct result of the proliferation of social media. Increasingly, video bloggers or vloggers make up a sizeable portion of influencers. Furthermore, when it comes to influencing content on social media platforms, the focus has recently switched to micro-influencers, defined as those who have 100,000 followers or less. With the democratization of information, it is notable that the engagement rates of micro-influencers are greater than those of persons who are better recognized, which is one of the advantages of utilizing them in a campaign—it lends a greater sense of genuineness to content. Moving forward, the use of influencers in social media campaigns will be geared toward the use of multiple micro-influencers and finding influencers that will generate genuine engagement between your brand and its audience. This will be the case in the future use of influencers in social media campaigns.

5. **Advancements in AR and VR**: Using specialized software and hardware, virtual reality (VR) creates immersive environments, whereas AR enhances real-world imagery. These parallel-evolving domains have recently experienced increased momentum and accelerated growth trajectories. The global market for VR and AR is expected to grow significantly, according to projections. According to some estimates, the valuation of the VR industry is projected to increase from just under 12 billion US dollars in 2022 to more than 22 billion US dollars by 2025 (Alsop, 2023). According to experts in the field, these innovations will equip consumers with immersive prepurchase product interactions, which could translate promotional efforts into tangible sales. In addition, these innovations

provide avenues for integrating print media with the digital realm and leveraging real-time data to provide customized, impactful experiences to clients.

12.2 Future Developments in Social Media Analytics

It is clear that social media analytics tools enable organizations and businesses to acquire consumer insights, given the large number of users who actively participate on social media platforms and readily reveal personal data and preferences. Over the years, analytics that are specifically specialized for social media have grown, becoming a fundamental component of the digital marketing plans of many businesses. According to PR Newswire (2023), it is anticipated that the market value of the social media analytics industry will reach a staggering 43.25 billion USD by the year 2030.

Several factors contribute to this growth trajectory, including the rising use of social media channels for entertainment, e-commerce, brand promotion, and online purchasing, as well as an increased awareness of competitive dynamics and market trends (PR Newswire, 2023). There is an observable increase in the number of organizations integrating social media analytics due to its ability to decode audience preferences, increase engagement levels, identify and prevent potential challenges, and highlight emergent trends.

We are heading into an age where online content is increasingly personalized. From the perspective of marketers and social media managers, data-enabled analytics makes the personalization of marketing campaigns easier and refines the methods that companies use to improve client engagement and outreach. With the help of social media analytics, businesses can zero in on the specific goods, services, or pieces of information that their target audience is looking for. In addition, using these technologies gives marketers the ability to forecast the course of their efforts and avoid possible pitfalls that are inherent to the expansive domain of big data.

The increasing prevalence of video content on these platforms highlights the need for video analytics. Various tools are becoming available for social media analytics professionals to examine video content, decipher consumer behaviors, evaluate engagement metrics, and optimize video-centric marketing strategies.

Arguably, the most profound change in the world of social media analytics will be through artificial intelligence (AI). AI is a rapidly expanding field that has the potential to dramatically enhance the operations of organizations and bring useful insights and efficiencies. AI has been utilized by the most successful and largest businesses to enhance their operations and acquire a competitive advantage. In the following sections, we will take a deeper dive into the world of AI.

12.3 AI Insights

The field of AI encompasses a wide range of fields, ranging from psychology to computer science. AI is a subfield of computer science that aims to simulate human cognitive skills like learning, reasoning, and problem-solving by utilizing increasingly complex computer systems and programming techniques (Boden, 1996). Access to AI has been democratized through innovations such as ChatGPT, Dall-E, and Bing, empowering even people with only basic computing abilities.

The historical and philosophical context around AI is a topic of significant scholarly interest. In the 1940s, John Von Neumann introduced a revolutionary computer architecture that was crucial to the development of neural networks. Alan Turing introduced the Turing Test in the 1950s, establishing a standard for the capabilities of AI (Muggleton, 2014). This era, which spanned the 1950s and 1960s, was characterized by significant advances in AI, with substantial government and corporate support. The Dartmouth Symposium of 1956 marked the beginning of the modern era of AI studies (Kline, 2010). In the 1990s, breakthroughs in multiple disciplines, including Deep Blue's chess victory and Watson's victory in Jeopardy, signified the resurgence of AI (Vardi, 2012). Today, AI's footprint extends from autonomous transportation to healthcare, highlighting its profound impact on contemporary society.

The National Artificial Intelligence Initiative Act of 2020 describes AI as "a machine-based system that can, for a given set of human-defined objectives, make predictions, recommendations or decisions influencing real or virtual environments" (NAIIA, 2023, p. 2). This definition is consistent with the views of forerunners such as John McCarthy and Alan Turing, as it emphasizes the role of machines in simulating human intelligence.

The operational mechanism of AI primarily involves the identification and analysis of patterns within extensive datasets. For example, by employing meticulous data analysis techniques, an algorithm for image recognition may be effectively taught to detect and classify various objects seen in images accurately. The programming of AI relies on three core cognitive abilities, namely learning, reasoning, and self-correction (Jaber, 2022). The process of learning encompasses the gathering of data and the construction of algorithms, while the capacity to self-correct represents the progressive evolution and flexibility of AI.

Within the field of AI, machine learning and deep learning have emerged as crucial domains, with deep learning being a subset of machine learning. To have a comprehensive understanding of the broader area of AI, it is crucial to accurately perceive and differentiate the subtle distinctions across these specific subfields. Machine learning, as evident from its name, enables computers or machines to learn from data to improve their performance.

While the advent of AI has significantly influenced several technical domains, machine learning has assumed a major position in the field of social media analytics (Kanagavalli & Priya, 2022; Roy et al., 2020). The integration of AI with social media analytics has resulted in improved consumer interactions, more accurate data analysis, and increased marketing results (PR Newswire, 2023). The growing dependence on AI-based techniques, such as predictive analytics and sentiment analysis, has yielded significant insights for businesses, leading to a transformation in the manner in which brands communicate and interact with their target audience.

AI has established itself as an indispensable component across a wide range of industries, where it helps streamline operations and improves user experiences (Burgess, 2018). In the medical field, technology such as IBM Watson employs natural language processing to assist in diagnosis and better comprehend pandemics (Karađuzović-Hadžiabdićet al., 2021), while AI-driven virtual assistants such as ChatGPT help make administrative work easier (George & George, 2023). In the business world, AI is used to get consumer insights through analytics and chatbots. In the education sector, AI can create individualized learning experiences and automate grading (Chen et al., 2020; Malik et al., 2023). While law firms employ AI for document analysis and predictive analytics (Burgess, 2017), the finance sector utilizes it for individualized advice and efficient trading. In the manufacturing industry, multitasking robots are used for collaborative activities, while in the banking industry, AI-driven chatbots and virtual assistants are used to improve customer service and comply with regulations (Singh, 2020). In the field of transportation, AI helps to improve traffic management and forecast flight delays. Last but not least, the security industry uses AI to identify prospective cyber dangers to provide early warnings against unique assaults.

12.4 Applications of AI in Social Media

The application of AI is crucial to the development of contemporary social media platforms. AI improves both the user experience and the marketing techniques that can be implemented on sites such as TikTok, Snapchat, and Facebook. Social media platforms employ AI to personalize user content, identify instances of platform abuse, and boost engagement metrics (Gregory et al., 2021).

The applications of AI range from recommending information to users, as X does with its posts, to providing real-time customer service through chatbots that are powered by AI. In addition, more advanced forms of machine learning aid in the optimization of advertising techniques, which in turn assists firms in more successfully targeting their respective audiences (Kaponis & Maragoudakis, 2022).

In addition to improving customer service with chatbots, AI helps with demographic targeting, advertising, and data analysis, therefore reimagining how businesses interact with their target demographics. In addition, AI's capacity to do real-time analysis of massive data sets is proving to be of great use in emergency circumstances (Vaishya et al., 2020). These scenarios need businesses to draw from user-generated material on social media to respond to emergencies efficiently.

AI has also transformed social media content creation through the automation of post generation, optimization, and personalization to enhance audience engagement. Advanced AI solutions, including ChatGPT, Copy.ai, and Jasper, employ natural language processing and machine learning to generate engaging captions, posts, and video scripts that correspond with brand voice and audience preferences.

12.5 AI in Social Media Analytics

In today's information-driven society, the application of AI to the analysis of data gleaned from social media platforms is an absolute necessity. Social media users generate enormous volumes of data daily, and it is nearly impossible for human analysts to go through every byte of this data without the assistance of AI technologies such as machine learning (Nunavath & Goodvin, 2018). The combination of AI and analytics offers the opportunity for greater insights into user behaviors, preferences, and interactions with brands, which in turn enables businesses to fine-tune their marketing campaigns more successfully. Artificial intelligence has the potential to greatly increase the accuracy and effectiveness of social media analytics, which would provide businesses with greater insights into their target audiences and how those audiences interact with their brand.

12.5.1 AI for Discovery

In the context of the DAV (Discovery, Analysis, Visualization) Framework, AI's capabilities in data discovery are especially pronounced in the domains of automated data processing and complex pattern recognition. This automation significantly reduces the time traditionally spent on preprocessing.

1. **Automated data processing**: Artificial intelligence can automate processes such as data cleaning or refinement, preparation, and transformation, which formerly required a significant amount of time and human participation. For example, AI has the ability to automatically recognize and deal with outliers and missing values in a dataset. Furthermore, analysts may aggregate product mentions of a brand across social media platforms. AI can automate the data cleaning process by removing duplicate mentions, rectifying misspelled brand names, and completing lacking timestamps or user demographic information.

2. **Recognition of complicated patterns**: Machine learning, a subfield of AI, excels in locating complex patterns hidden within big datasets. Through the use of algorithms, it can identify connections or irregularities in the data that could be invisible to human analysts. For example, an analyst can employ an AI tool whose algorithm might detect, within TikTok data, emergent trends or challenges by analyzing its video content and correlating it with spikes in related hashtag usage, even before these trends become ubiquitous.

12.5.2 AI for Analysis

The application of AI has the potential to radically transform data analysis by delivering improved capabilities, increased speed, and new insights (Kaponis & Maragoudakis, 2022). The following is a description of the various ways in which AI makes the field of data analysis more accessible and transformative in all three areas within the DAV framework:

1. **Real-time analysis of data**: Artificial intelligence is capable of processing and analyzing data in real-time. This feature is necessary for applications, such as fraud detection in banking, that demand instant action depending on the results of the study. For example, if a brand introduces a new product and there is a sudden increase in negative sentiment on Twitter, real-time analysis can detect this sentiment shift, allowing the brand to address concerns or potential PR crises immediately.

2. **Predictive analytics**: Artificial intelligence can make predictions about future events or trends by analyzing past information. For instance, it may forecast how the stock market will move, how customers will

behave, or how equipment will break down. For example, by assessing past engagement metrics on a YouTube channel in terms of previous video views, comments, and likes, AI can forecast a future video's potential reach and engagement. This can inform content creators about the best themes, video durations, or publishing schedules to maximize viewership.

3. **Sentiment analysis**: Sentiment analysis, which utilizes natural language processing, has become a vital instrument within the field of social media analytics. Through the utilization of AI, these techniques can effectively extract emotions, themes, and even particular entities from extensive quantities of textual data. For example, an organization may utilize natural language processing techniques to analyze Reddit conversations, therefore assessing the prevailing public mood toward a recently launched product. For example, sentiment analysis powered by AI may be employed to assess the sentiments expressed in captions and comments on Instagram. AI has the potential to enhance the accuracy level of traditional sentiment analysis, encompassing not just basic emotions such as pleasure and sadness but also more complex and subtle expressions like sarcasm and comedy. This enhanced understanding enables businesses to develop strategies that better align with their intended target audiences.

4. **AI for image and video analytics**: When it comes to the field of social media analytics, the function that AI plays in picture identification is equally important. It is not sufficient for companies to just grasp data that is based on words in this visually driven digital age; there is an urgent need to analyze the content and context of shared photographs and videos. Image identification software that is powered by AI can examine visual input in great detail, identifying individual objects, locations, and even facial expressions. Take for example a firm that is introducing a fresh assortment of sunglasses. The use of AI to search social media sites for photographs of consumers wearing these sunglasses can provide crucial information regarding the product's popularity and reception.

5. **AI for identifying influencers in a social network**: Artificial intelligence is set to radically alter how corporations locate and work with social media influencers. Tools driven by AI can sift through massive quantities of user data to identify people who not only have a large number of followers but also have significant interactions with their audience and wield real influence within their respective industries. For example, a skincare company may utilize AI to discover beauty influencers who consistently create high

engagement rates, so paving the road for the possibility of partnerships that resonate genuinely with their target audience.

12.5.3 AI for Visualization

AI can significantly improve data visualization by transforming inert graphs into dynamic, interactive, and incisive visual narratives. AI facilitates and transforms data visualization in the following ways:

1. **Automated visualization selection**: AI can examine the characteristics of the data and automatically suggest the most suitable form of display. AI can determine which sort of data visualization, such as a bar graph, scatter plot, heat map, or any other type of visualization, most accurately portrays the features of the data. For instance, if an AI system were provided with time-series data on the number of times Facebook posts were engaged, it may recommend the use of a line chart to illustrate how patterns evolved over time. We may already see examples of various visualization selection options and recommended visualization in tools such as Excel and Tableau, however, advanced AI can take the guesswork out of the visualization mix and offer enhanced options to the users.

2. **Interactive and exploratory visualizations**: AI has the potential to power interactive visualizations that respond to user questions. This enables users to go deeper into certain data points or patterns for a more in-depth examination. For instance, on a map depicting worldwide sales, a user might be interested in delving more into the sales in Europe. AI has the potential to provide a drill-down feature, which displays a more comprehensive map of Europe together with sales data unique to individual countries. Another example could be a visualization that shows Instagram followers and allows marketers to click on certain data points to uncover more in-depth demographic information or engagement metrics pertaining to a particular category.

3. **Predictive visualizations**: AI can do more than just convey current data; it can also foresee future trends and display these forecasts in visual representations, which can assist decision-makers in planning. Consider the following scenario: you want to see the predicted number of subscribers for your YouTube channel over the next year based on previous growth patterns.

4. **Pattern highlighting**: AI can identify and highlight patterns, correlations, or anomalies within a dataset or a visualization. This draws the viewer's

attention to significant insights that might otherwise be missed. As an illustration, AI might highlight clusters that indicate segments that have high conversion rates in a scatter plot that compares the number of website visits to the number of purchases made.

5. **Personalized visualization**: AI can modify representations based on a user's preferences, responsibilities, or previous interactions, which ensures that the most important data is constantly at the forefront. For instance, a Reddit administrator would receive visualizations centered on user interaction and flagged articles, whereas an advertiser might view visualizations linked to ad impressions and click-through rates.

The enormous power that AI brings to bear on social media analytics brings with it a whole new set of obligations. In every data-centric project, there is always the possibility of employing data in a way that is immoral, inaccurate, or both. As a consequence of this, businesses must prudently implement AI while also making certain that their procedures are transparent, fair, and accountable. Businesses will be able to harness the potential of AI in a manner that is both successful and respectful of user rights if they perform regular reviews of the tools used by AI and also have an ethical framework in place to guide their decisions.

12.6 Conclusion

As we draw to a close in this foundational book on social media analytics, it is important to think about on the shifts and developments that are still to come in the years ahead. Even though technological and methodological progress is unavoidable, the Discover, Analyze, and Visualize (DAV) Framework's fundamental principles offered in this book will continue to serve as a guidepost. This parsimonious trio serves as the foundation of our analytical efforts, ensuring that we can convey stories via our data consistently and efficiently.

At its core, social media analytics is a set of tools that helps one comprehend the complex web of relationships that exist between people. It is a mirror that reflects the digital zeitgeist, catching the behaviors, feelings, and attitudes that we as a community share. Since the birth of social media platforms, there has always been an innate need to understand the "who," "why," "how," and "when" of interactions between users. The development of increasingly sophisticated analytic tools and AI will, without a doubt, enable us to see more clearly and precisely in the future. This improvement will occur in tandem with the progression of technology.

On the other hand, even though we are on the verge of a data-driven future, we must realize the difficulties and ethical conundrums that lie ahead. While the digital era is rife with opportunities, it is also riddled with perils. False information in the form of misinformation and disinformation clouds our judgment, and as a result, it is necessary to have the discernment to separate real things from fake ones. Users need to be able to navigate the enormous internet expanse with clarity, and there is a growing demand for digital literacy to make this possible.

The existence of questions regarding the fairness and equity of algorithms compels us to develop more fair and equitable computing methods that do not perpetuate prejudices or isolate users. In addition, because dominant social media companies have immense power over our online interactions, there is an urgent need for regulatory frameworks and rules to govern the industry. These would guarantee supervision and put a stop to the unfettered power that these platforms currently exert, influencing the information that appears in our feeds and how our data is used.

To fully realize the power and promise of analytics for social media, we need to, first and foremost, be watchful stewards of this space. The objective is not only to gain an understanding; rather, it is to do it in a responsible, ethical, and altruistic manner while maintaining a dedication to the greater good. The road that lies in front of us promises to be just as illuminating as it is difficult. As we travel down this road, let us make it a point to check that our compass is constantly pointing toward the truth, transparency, and true human connection.

Chapter Summary

- Social media analytics exemplifies the continuous quest of learning, adapting, and innovating in the ever-changing digital landscape.
- The United States and China stand out as the leading players when it comes to major social networks.
- AI is a subfield of computer science that aims to simulate human cognitive skills like learning, reasoning, and problem-solving by utilizing increasingly complex computer systems and programming techniques.
- The combination of AI and analytics offers the opportunity for greater insights into user behaviors, preferences, and interactions with brands, which in turn enables businesses to fine-tune their marketing campaigns more successfully.
- In the context of the DAV (Discovery, Analysis, Visualization) Framework, AI's capabilities in data discovery are especially pronounced in the domains of automated data processing and complex pattern recognition.
- The application of AI has the potential to radically transform data analysis by delivering improved capabilities, increased speed, and new insights.

- AI can significantly improve data visualization by transforming inert graphs into dynamic, interactive, and incisive visual narratives.

Questions for Review

1. What are the major future trends in the realm of social media analytics?
2. What are the major applications of AI for social media?
3. In what way does AI impact Discovery, Analysis, and Visualization within the DAV Framework?

References

Adams, M., Makramalla, M., & Miron, W. (2014). Down the rabbit hole: How structural holes in entrepreneurs' social networks impact early venture growth. *Technology Innovation Management Review, 4*(9), 19–27.

Adaval, R., Saluja, G., & Jiang, Y. (2019). Seeing and thinking in pictures: A review of visual information processing. *Consumer Psychology Review, 2*(1), 50–69.

Ahn, Y. J., & Juraev, Z. (2024). Al-Birunis bleibende Beiträge zur kartografischen Wissenschaft. *Journal for Geography, 19*(2), 17–36. DOI: https://doi.org/10.18690/rg.19.2.3746

Ajao, O., Hong, J., & Liu, W. (2015). A survey of location inference techniques on Twitter. *Journal of Information Science, 41*(6), 855–864.

Al-Hassani, S. T. (2012). *1001 inventions: The enduring legacy of Muslim civilization.* National Geographic Books. ISBN: 1426209479.

Alsop (2023). Virtual reality (VR) - statistics & facts. https://www.statista.com/topics/2532/virtual-reality-vr/#topicOverview

An, J., Kwak, H., Jung, S. G., Salminen, J., & Jansen, B. J. (2018). Customer segmentation using online platforms: Isolating behavioral and demographic segments for persona creation via aggregated user data. *Social Network Analysis and Mining, 8*(1), 54.

Arnaboldi, M., Azzone, G., & Sidorova, Y. (2017). Governing social media: the emergence of hybridised boundary objects. *Accounting, Auditing & Accountability Journal, 30*(4), 821–849.

Arora, D., & Malik, P. (2015, March). Analytics: Key to go from generating big data to deriving business value. In *2015 IEEE first international conference on big data computing service and applications* (pp. 446–452). Redwoord City, CA: IEEE. DOI: 10.1109/BigDataService.2015.62.

Asif, A., Khatoon, S., Hasan, M. M., Alshamari, M. A., Abdou, S., Elsayed, K. M., & Rashwan, M. (2021). Automatic analysis of social media images to identify disaster type and infer appropriate emergency response. *Journal of Big Data, 8*(1), 83.

Avery, E. J. (2017). Public information officers' social media monitoring during the Zika virus crisis, a global health threat surrounded by public uncertainty. *Public Relations Review, 43*(3), 468–476.

Awan, M. J., Khan, M. A., Ansari, Z. K., Yasin, A., & Shehzad, H. M. F. (2022). Fake profile recognition using big data analytics in social media platforms. *International Journal of Computer Applications in Technology, 68*(3), 215–222.

Awange, J. L., Kyalo Kiema, J. B. (2013). Spatial analysis. In: *Environmental Geoinformatics: Environmental Science and Engineering* (pp. 225–236). Berlin, Heidelberg: Springer. https://doi.org/10.1007/978-3-642-34085-7_17

Balia, R., Barra, S., Carta, S., Fenu, G., Podda, A. S., & Sansoni, N. (2021). A deep learning solution for integrated traffic control through automatic license plate recognition. In *Computational Science and Its Applications–ICCSA 2021: 21st International Conference, Cagliari, Italy, September 13–16, 2021, Proceedings, Part III 21* (pp. 211–226). Springer International Publishing.

Barbier, G., & Liu, H. (2011). Data mining in social media. In C. C. Aggarwal (Ed.), *Social network data analytics* (pp. 327–352). Boston, MA, USA: Springer, 2011. https://doi.org/10.1007/978-1-4419-8462-3_12

Barde, B. V., & Bainwad, A. M. (2017, June). An overview of topic modeling methods and tools. In *2017 International Conference on Intelligent Computing and Control Systems (ICICCS)* (pp. 745–750). Madurai, India: IEEE. DOI: 10.1109/ICCONS.2017.8250563.

Barnes, S. J., & Rutter, R. (2019). A framework for facial image analytics using deep learning in social sciences research. In *Digital Economy. Emerging Technologies and Business Innovation: 4th International Conference, ICDEc 2019, Beirut, Lebanon, April 15–18, 2019, Proceedings 4* (pp. 315–320). Springer International Publishing.

Barros, C., Moya-Gómez, B., & Gutiérrez, J. (2020). Using geotagged photographs and GPS tracks from social networks to analyse visitor behaviour in national parks. *Current Issues in Tourism, 23*(10), 1291–1310.

Barthel, M., Fava, J. A., Harnanan, C. A., Strothmann, P., Khan, S., & Miller, S. (2015). Hotspots analysis: providing the focus for action. In G. Sonnemann & M. Margni (Eds.), *Life cycle management* (pp. 149–167). New York: Springer.

Batrinca, B., & Treleaven, P. C. (2015). Social media analytics: a survey of techniques, tools and platforms. *Ai & Society, 30*, 89–116.

Batt, S., Grealis, T., Harmon, O., & Tomolonis, P. (2020). Learning Tableau: A data visualization tool. *The Journal of Economic Education, 51*(3–4), 317–328.

Baur, A. W. (2017). Harnessing the social web to enhance insights into people's opinions in business, government and public administration. *Information Systems Frontiers, 19*, 231–251.

Bean, R., & Davenport, T. H. (2019). Companies are failing in their efforts to become data-driven. *Harvard Business Review, 5*, 5–8.

Bekmamedova, N., & Shanks, G. (2014, January). Social media analytics and business value: a theoretical framework and case study. In *2014 47th Hawaii international conference on system sciences* (pp. 3728–3737). Waikoloa, HI: IEEE. DOI: 10.1109/HICSS.2014.464.

Bendler, J., Ratku, A., & Neumann, D. (2014). Crime mapping through geo-spatial social media activity. In *International Conference on Information Systems* (pp. 12–15). doi:10.1080/08998280.2014.11929037

Benzaghta, M. A., Elwalda, A., Mousa, M. M., Erkan, I., & Rahman, M. (2021). SWOT analysis applications: An integrative literature review. *Journal of Global Business Insights, 6*(1), 55–73.

Biggs, N., Lloyd, E., & Wilson, R. (1986). *Graph theory, 1736–1936.* Oxford University Press. ISBN: 9780198539162

Blei, D. M., Ng, A. Y., & Jordan, M. I. (2003). Latent dirichlet allocation. *Journal of Machine Learning Research, 3*(Jan), 993–1022.

Boden, M. A. (Ed.). (1996). *Artificial intelligence.* Elsevier.

Bonacich, P. (1987). Power and centrality: A family of measures. *American Journal of Sociology, 92*(5), 1170–1182.

Borgatti, S. P. (2005). Centrality and network flow. *Social Networks, 27*(1), 55–71.

Borgatti, S. P., Everett, M. G., & Johnson, J. C. (2018). *Analyzing social networks.* Sage.

Boulos, M. N., & Geraghty, E. M. (2020). Geographical tracking and mapping of coronavirus disease COVID-19/severe acute respiratory syndrome coronavirus 2 (SARS-CoV-2) epidemic and associated events around the world: how 21st century GIS technologies are supporting the global fight against outbreaks and epidemics. *International Journal of Health Geographics, 19*(1), 1–12.

Bourne, L. M., & Weaver, P. (2018). The origins of schedule management: the concepts used in planning, allocating, visualizing and managing time in a project. *Frontiers of Engineering Management, 5*(2), 150–166.

Bovet, A., & Makse, H. A. (2019). Influence of fake news in Twitter during the 2016 U.S. presidential election. *Nature Communications, 10*(1), 7.

Braun, V., & Clarke, V. (2006). Using thematic analysis in psychology. *Qualitative Research in Psychology, 3*(2), 77–101.

Brentjes, S. (2008). Shams al-Dīn al-Sakhawi on Muwaqqits, Mu'adhdhins, and the Teachers of Various Astronomical Disciplines in Mamluk Cities in the Fifteenth Century. In E. Calvo, M. Comes, R. Puig, & M. Rius (Eds.), *A shared legacy: Islamic science East and West* (pp. 129–150). Universitat de Barcelona. ISBN 978-84-475-3285-8.

Britannica (2023a). Itinerarium, ancient Roman map. https://www.britannica.com/science/itinerarium-ancient-Roman-map

Britannica (2023b). Mathematics in the Islamic world (8th–15th century) https://www.britannica.com/science/mathematics/Mathematics-in-the-Islamic-world-8th-15th-century

Broucke, S., & Baesens, B. (2017). *Web Scraping for Data Science with Python*. CreateSpace Independent Publishing Platform. ISBN:1979343780.

Brown, T. (2009). *Change by design: How design thinking transforms organizations and inspires innovation*. New York, NY: Harper Collins Press

Brown-Hejazi, A. & Larsen, K., (2021). Mapping the Islamic World The Ottoman, Safavid & Mughal Empires. https://exhibits.stanford.edu/islamicworld/feature/mapping-the-heavens

Bruns, A., & Moe, H. (2014). Structural layers of communication on Twitter. *Twitter and Society, Digital Formations, 89*, 15–28.

Burgess, A. (2018). AI in Action. In *The Executive Guide to Artificial Intelligence: How to identify and implement applications for AI in your organization* (Ed. 1, pp. 73–89). Cham: Palgrave Macmillan. https://doi.org/10.1007/978-3-319-63820-1

Burt, R. S. (2004). Structural holes and good ideas. *American Journal of Sociology, 110*(2), 349–399.

Burt, R.S., (1992). *Structural holes*. Cambridge, MA: Harvard University Press.

Butts, C. T. (2008). Social network analysis: A methodological introduction. *Asian Journal of Social Psychology, 11*(1), 13–41.

Cahyadi, A., & Prananto, A. (2015). Reflecting design thinking: A case study of the process of designing dashboards. *Journal of Systems and Information Technology, 17*(3), 286–306.

Cambridge (2024). Meaning of value in English. Retrieved from https://dictionary.cambridge.org/us/dictionary/english/value

Chen, L., Chen, P., & Lin, Z. (2020). Artificial intelligence in education: A review. *IEEE Access, 8*, 75264–75278.

Chen, X., Vo, H., Wang, Y., & Wang, F. (2018). A framework for annotating OpenStreetMap objects using geo-tagged tweets. *GeoInformatica, 22*, 589–613. https://doi.org/10.1007/s10707-018-0323-8.

Chongwatpol, J. (2020). Operationalizing design thinking in business intelligence and analytics projects. *Decision Sciences Journal of Innovative Education, 18*(3), 409–434.

Clarke, K. C. (2013). What is the world's oldest map? *The Cartographic Journal, 50*(2), 136–143.

Clarke, S. (2022). Mapping the visual icon. *The Philosophical Quarterly, 72*(3), 552–577.

Colombo, G., Bounegru, L., & Gray, J. (2023). Visual models for social media image analysis: Groupings, engagement, trends, and rankings. *International Journal of Communication, 17*, 1956–1983.

Cooper (2013). The Surprising History of Twitter's Hashtag Origin and 4 Ways to Get the Most out of Them. https://buffer.com/resources/a-concise-history-of-twitter-hashtags-and-how-you-should-use-them-properly/

Cowan, R., Jonard, N., & Zimmermann, J. B. (2007). Bilateral collaboration and the emergence of innovation networks. *Management science, 53*(7), 1051–1067.

Crampton, J. W. (2009). Cartography: maps 2.0. *Progress in Human Geography, 33*(1), 91–100.

Crivellari, A., & Beinat, E. (2019). Identifying Foreign Tourists' Nationality from Mobility Traces via LSTM Neural Network and Location Embeddings. *Applied Sciences.* https://doi.org/10.3390/APP9142861.

Davenport, T. (2014). *Big data at work: Dispelling the myths, uncovering the opportunities.* Brighton, USA: Harvard Business Review Press. https://doi.org/10.15358/9783800648153

Davenport, T. H., & Harris, J. G. (2007). *Competing on analytics: The new science of winning.* Boston, MA: Harvard Business School Press.

Davenport, T., & Harris, J. (2017). *Competing on analytics: Updated, with a new introduction: The new science of winning.* Harvard Business Press.

Dent, B. D., Torguson, J. S., & Hodler, T. W. (2009). *Cartography: Thematic map design* (6th ed.). McGraw-Hill.

DiMaggio, P., Nag, M., & Blei, D. (2013). Exploiting affinities between topic modeling and the sociological perspective on culture: Application to newspaper coverage of US government arts funding. *Poetics, 41*(6), 570–606.

Dixon, S. (2023). Global social networks ranked by number of users 2023. https://www.statista.com/statistics/272014/global-social-networks-ranked-by-number-of-users/

Dixon, S., (2023). Number of social media users worldwide from 2017 to 2027. https://www.statista.com/statistics/278414/number-of-worldwide-social-network-users/

Dzyabura, D., El Kihal, S., & Peres, R. (2021). Image analytics in marketing. In C. Homburg, M. Klarmann, & A. Vomberg (Eds.), *Handbook of market research* (pp. 665–692). Cham: Springer International Publishing. https://doi.org/10.1007/978-3-319-57413-4_38

Eisenberg, H. (2014, September 15). Humans process visual data better. Thermopylae Sciences + Technology. http://www.t-sciences.com/news/humans-process-visual-data-better

Endert, A., Ribarsky, W., Turkay, C., Wong, B., Nabney, I., Blanco, I., & Rossi, F. (2017). The State of the Art in Integrating Machine Learning into Visual Analytics. *Computer Graphics Forum, 36.* https://doi.org/10.1111/cgf.13092

Ezhilraman, S. V., & Srinivasan, S. (2018). State of the art in image processing & big data analytics: issues and challenges. *International Journal of Engineering & Technology, 7*(33), 195–199.

Fan, W., & Gordon, M. D. (2014). The power of social media analytics. *Communications of the ACM, 57*(6), 74–81.

Fan, W., Wallace, L., Rich, S., & Zhang, Z. (2006). Tapping the power of text mining. *Communications of the ACM, 49*(9), 76–82.

Farris, P. W., Bendle, N. T., Pfeifer, P. E., & Reibstein, D. J. (2006). *Marketing metrics: 50+ metrics every executive should master.* Pearson Education.

Felt, M. (2016). Social media and the social sciences: How researchers employ Big Data analytics. *Big data & society, 3*(1), 2053951716645828.

Fitzpatrick, K. R., & Weissman, P. L. (2021). Public relations in the age of data: corporate perspectives on social media analytics (SMA). *Journal of Communication Management, 25*(4), 401–416.

Flake, G. (1994). Font Production in past and present. In *Font Technology: Methods and Tools* (pp. 59–76). Berlin, Heidelberg: Springer. https://doi.org/10.1007/978-3-642-78505-4_4

Furche, T., Gottlob, G., Libkin, L., Orsi, G., & Paton, N. W. (2016, March). Data Wrangling for Big Data: Challenges and Opportunities. In *Proceedings of the 19th International Conference on Extending Database Technology (EDBT)* (pp. 473–478). https://doi.org/10.5441/002/edbt.2016.44.

Gaida, M. (2016). Muslim women and science: The search for the "missing" actors. *Early Modern Women: An Interdisciplinary Journal, 11*(1), 197–206.

Gao, Y. (2018). Aligning social media goals with business goals: A study of Australian SMEs. *Journal of Small Business and Enterprise Development, 25*(4), 738–758.

Garlin, B. (2025). The Biggest Social Media Trends Shaping 2025, Retrieved https://www.forbes.com/councils/forbescommunicationscouncil/2025/02/03/the-biggest-social-media-trends-shaping-2025/

George, A. S., & George, A. H. (2023). A review of ChatGPT AI's impact on several business sectors. *Partners Universal International Innovation Journal, 1*(1), 9–23.

Gerlach, M., Peixoto, T. P., & Altmann, E. G. (2018). A network approach to topic models. *Science Advances, 4*(7), eaaq1360.

Gibbons, S., Overman, H., & Patacchini, E. (2015). Chapter 3 – Spatial Methods. In *Handbook of Regional and Urban Economics* (Vol. 5, pp. 115–168). https://doi.org/10.1016/B978-0-444-59517-1.00003-9.

Goh, D. H.-L., Ang, R. P., Chua, A. Y. K., & Lee, C. S. (2009). Why we share: A study of motivations for mobile media sharing. In J. Liu, J. Wu, Y. Yao, & T. Nishida (Eds.), *Active media technology* (pp. 195–206). Springer Berlin Heidelberg. Retrieved from http://link.springer.com/chapter/10.1007/9783-642-04875-3_23

Golbeck, J. (2013). *Analyzing the social web.* Newnes.

Grandjean, M. (2015). Social network analysis and visualization: Moreno's Sociograms revisited.

Granovetter, M. S. (1973). The strength of weak ties. *American Journal of Sociology, 78*(6), 1360–1380.

Gräve, J. F. (2019). What KPIs are key? Evaluating performance metrics for social media influencers. *Social Media+ Society, 5*(3), 2056305119865475.

Gregory, R. W., Henfridsson, O., Kaganer, E., & Kyriakou, H. (2021). The role of artificial intelligence and data network effects for creating user value. *Academy of Management Review, 46*(3), 534–551.

Gu, X., Wong, Y., Peng, P., Shou, L., Chen, G., & Kankanhalli, M. S. (2017, October). Understanding fashion trends from street photos via neighbor-constrained embedding learning. In *Proceedings of the 25th ACM international conference on multimedia* (pp. 190–198). https://doi.org/10.1145/3123266.3123441

Guellil, I., & Boukhalfa, K. (2015, April). Social big data mining: A survey focused on opinion mining and sentiments analysis. In *2015 12th international symposium on programming and systems (ISPS)* (pp. 1–10). Los Alamitos, CA: IEEE.

Gurel, E., & Tat, M. (2017). SWOT analysis: A theoretical review. *Journal of International Social Research, 10*(51), 994–1006.

Han, J. (2006). *Data mining concepts and techniques.* San Diego: Morgan Kaufmann.

Harrell, J. A., & Brown, V. M. (1992). The World's oldest surviving geological map: the 1150 BC Turin Papyrus from Egypt. *The Journal of Geology, 100*(1), 3–18.

Harrigan, P., Daly, T. M., Coussement, K., Lee, J. A., Soutar, G. N., & Evers, U. (2021). Identifying influencers on social media. *International Journal of Information Management, 56*, 102246.

Hassan Zadeh, A., & Jeyaraj, A. (2018). Alignment of business and social media strategies: insights from a text mining analysis. *Journal of Business Analytics,* 1–18. doi:10.1080/2573234x.2019.1602

Hassan Zadeh, A., & Jeyaraj, A. (2018). Alignment of business and social media strategies: insights from a text mining analysis. *Journal of Business Analytics, 1*(2), 117–134.

Healy, K. (2018). *Data visualization: a practical introduction.* Princeton University Press.

Hearst, M. (2003). What Is Text Mining?, Retrieved from: www.sims.berkeley.edu/~hearst/textmining.html.

Heer, J., Bostock, M., & Ogievetsky, V. (2010). Crowdsourcing graphical perception: Using mechanical turk to assess visualization design. In *Proceedings of the SIGCHI conference on human factors in computing systems* (pp. 203–212).

Hiatt, A. (2021). *Geography at the Crossroads" in Cartography between Christian Europe and the Arabic-Islamic World, 1100–1500*. Leiden, The Netherlands: Brill.

Hinds, J., Williams, E. J., & Joinson, A. N. (2020). "It wouldn't happen to me": Privacy concerns and perspectives following the Cambridge Analytica scandal. *International Journal of Human-Computer Studies, 143*, 102498.

Holsti, O. R. (1969). *Content analysis for the social sciences and humanities*. Reading, MA: Addison-Wesley (content analysis).

Hong, L., & Davison, B. D. (2010, July). Empirical study of topic modeling in twitter. In *Proceedings of the first workshop on social media analytics* (pp. 80–88). IEEE security and privacy (Vol. 3(1), pp. 26–33). https://doi.org/10.1145/1964858.1964870.

Hossain, N., & Househ, M. S. (2016, January). Using HealthMap to Analyse Middle East Respiratory Syndrome (MERS) Data. In *Stud. Health Technol. Inform.* (Vol. 226, pp. 213–216).

Hunter, D., & Evans, N. (2016). Facebook emotional contagion experiment controversy. *Research Ethics, 12*(1), 2–3.

Islam, A. (2011). The contribution of Muslims to science during the Middle Abbasid Period (750-945). *Revelation and science, 1*(01), 39–56.

Islam, M. M., Hasan, M., Athrey, K. S., Braskich, T., & Bertasius, G. (2023). Efficient movie scene detection using state-space transformers. In *Proceedings of the IEEE/CVF conference on computer vision and pattern recognition* (pp. 18749–18758), 2023.

Ittoo, A., Nguyen, L., & van den Bosch, A. (2016). Text analytics in industry: Challenges, desiderata and trends. *Computers in Industry, 78*, 96–107.

Jaber, T. A. (2022). Artificial intelligence in computer networks. *Periodicals of Engineering and Natural Sciences, 10*(1), 309–322.

Jajuga, K., Sokolowski, A., & Bock, H.-H. (2002). *Classification, clustering and data analysis: Recent advances and applications*. Springer-Verlag.

Jamali, M., & Abolhassani, H. (2006, December). Different aspects of social network analysis. In T. Nishida, Z. Shi, U. Visser, X. Wu, J. Liu, B. Wah, ... Y-M. Cheung (Eds.), *2006 IEEE/WIC/ACM International Conference on Web Intelligence (WI 2006 Main Conference Proceedings)(WI'06)* (pp. 66–72). Los Alamitos, CA: IEEE. http://dx.doi.org/10.1109/WI.2006.61

Janetzko, D. (2017). The role of APIs in data sampling from social media. In *The SAGE Handbook of Social Media Research Methods* (pp. 146–160). https://www.doi.org/10.4135/9781473983847

Kanagavalli, N., & Priya, S. B. (2022). Social networks fake account and fake news identification with reliable deep learning. *Intelligent Automation & Soft Computing, 33*(1), 191–205.

Kaponis, A., & Maragoudakis, M. (2022, September). Data Analysis in Digital Marketing using Machine learning and Artificial Intelligence Techniques, Ethical and Legal Dimensions, State of the Art. In *Proceedings of the 12th Hellenic Conference on Artificial Intelligence (SETN '22, September 07–09, 2022, Corfu, Greece)* (Article 15, pp. 1–9). Association for Computing Machinery. https://doi.org/10.1145/3549737.3549756

Karađuzović-Hadžiabdić, K., Spahić, R., & Tahirović, E. (2021). Evaluation of IBM Watson Natural Language Processing Service to predict influenza-like illness outbreaks from Twitter data. *Periodicals of Engineering and Natural Sciences, 10*(1), 122–137.

Karami, A., Lundy, M., Webb, F., & Dwivedi, Y. K. (2020). Twitter and research: A systematic literature review through text mining. *IEEE Access, 8*, 67698–67717.

Kelman, H. C. (1958). Compliance, identification, and internalization: Three processes of attitude change. *Journal of Conflict Resolution, 2*(1), 51–60.

Kenoyer, J. M. (1998). *Ancient cities of the Indus valley civilization*. Oxford University Press; American Institute of Pakistan Studies. ISBN: 0195779045

Khan, M. L. (2020) Big data and entrepreneurship. In L. M. Mahoney & T. Tang (Eds.) *Handbook of media management and business* (pp. 391–406). Lanham, MD: Rowman & Littlefield.

Khan, G. (2015). *Seven layers of social media analytics: Mining business insights from social media text, actions, networks, hyperlinks, apps, search engine, and location data.* CreateSpace Independent Publishing Platform. ISBN: 978-1507823200.

Khan, G. F. (2015). *Seven layers of social media analytics: Mining business insights from social media text, actions, networks, hyperlinks, apps, search engines, and location data.* Gohar Feroz Khan. ISBN: 9781507823200.

Khan, G. F. (2017). Social media analytics. Social Media for Government: A Practical Guide to Understanding, Implementing, and Managing Social Media Tools in the Public Sphere, 93–118.

Khan, L., & Malik, A. (2022). Researching YouTube: Methods, tools, and analytics. In A. Quan-Haase & L. Sloan (Eds.), *The SAGE handbook of social media research methods* (2nd Edition, pp. 651–663). Sage Publishing. ISBN: 9781529720969. https://us.sagepub.com/en-us/nam/the-sage-handbook-of-social-media-research-methods/book272098.

Khan, M. L. (2017). Social media engagement: What motivates user participation and consumption on YouTube? *Computers in Human Behavior, 66*, 236–247.

Khan, M. L., & Malik, A. (2022). Researching YouTube: Methods, tools, and analytics. In A. Quan-Haase & L. Sloan (Eds.), *The Sage handbook of social media research methods* (2nd ed., pp. 651–663). Thousand Oaks, CA: Sage Publishing.

Khan, M. L., Zaher, Z., & Gao, B. (2018). Communicating on Twitter for charity: Understanding the wall of kindness initiative in Afghanistan, Iran, and Pakistan, *International Journal of Communication, 12*, 25. http://ijoc.org/index.php/ijoc/article/view/7726.

Khan, M. Laeeq, & Malik, A. (2022). Researching YouTube: Methods, Tools, and Analytics. In A. Quan-Haase & L. Sloan (Eds.), *The SAGE handbook of social media research methods* (2nd Edition). Sage Publishing. ISBN: 9781529720969. https://us.sagepub.com/en-us/nam/the-sage-handbook-of-social-media-research-methods/book272098

Khan, M. Laeeq, Ittefaq, M., Pantoja, Y., Raziq, M., & Malik, A. (2021). Public Engagement Model to analyze digital diplomacy on Twitter: A social media analytics framework, *International Journal of Communication, 15*, 1741–1769, https://ijoc.org/index.php/ijoc/article/view/15698

Khan, M. Laeeq, Malik, A., Ruhi, U., & Al-Busaidi, A. (2022). Conflicting attitudes: Analyzing social media data to understand early discourse on COVID-19 passports, *Technology in Society, 68*, 101830. https://doi.org/10.1016/j.techsoc.2021.101830

Khder, M. A. (2021). Web scraping or web crawling: State of art, techniques, approaches and applicaion. *International Journal of Advances in Soft Computing & Its Applications, 13*(3), 145–168. https://doi.org/10.15849/IJASCA.211128.11

Khyani, D., Siddhartha, B. S., Niveditha, N. M., & Divya, B. M. (2021). An interpretation of lemmatization and stemming in natural language processing. *Journal of University of Shanghai for Science and Technology, 22*(10), 350–357.

Kietzmann, J. H., Hermkens, K., McCarthy, I. P., & Silvestre, B. S. (2011). Social media? Get serious! Understanding the functional building blocks of social media. *Business Horizons, 54*(3), 241–251.

King, D. (1996), Astronomy and Islamic society: Qibla, gnomics and timekeeping. In R. Rashed (Ed.), *Encyclopedia of the History of Arabic Science*, (Vol. 1, pp. 128–184 [153]). London and New York: Routledge.

King, D. A. (1998). Mamluk astronomy and the institution of the muwaqqit. In T. Philipp & U. Haarman (Eds.), *The Mamluks in Egyptian Politics and Society* (pp. 153–162). Cambridge University Press. ISBN 978-0-521-59115-7.

Kitchens, B., Dobolyi, D., Li, J., & Abbasi, A. (2018). Advanced customer analytics: Strategic value through integration of relationship-oriented big data. *Journal of Management Information Systems, 35*(2), 540–574.

Kline, R. (2010). Cybernetics, automata studies, and the Dartmouth conference on artificial intelligence. *IEEE Annals of the History of Computing, 33*(4), 5–16.

Knaflic, C. N. (2015). *Storytelling with data: A data visualization guide for business professionals.* John Wiley & Sons.

Knura, M., Kluger, F., Zahtila, M., Schiewe, J., Rosenhahn, B., & Burghardt, D. (2021). Using object detection on social media images for urban bicycle infrastructure planning: a case study of Dresden. *ISPRS International Journal of Geo-Information, 10*(11), 733.

Ko, T. Y., & Lee, S. H. (2020). Novel method of semantic segmentation applicable to augmented reality. *Sensors, 20*(6), 1737.

Köppen, E., Meinel, C. (2014). Empathy via design thinking: creation of sense and knowledge. In H. Plattner, C. Meinel, & L. Leifer (Eds.), *Design thinking research. Understanding innovation* (pp. 15–28). Cham, Switzerland: Springer. https://doi.org/10.1007/978-3-319-06823-7_2

Korherr, P., Kanbach, D. K., Kraus, S., & Mikalef, P. (2022). From intuitive to data-driven decision-making in digital transformation: A framework of prevalent managerial archetypes. *Digital Business, 2*(2), 100045.

Krippendorff, K. (2004). Reliability in content analysis: Some common misconceptions and recommendations. *Human Communication Research, 30*(3), 411–433.

Kumar, A. V., Chitumadugula, S., & Rayalacheruvu, V. T. (2022, December). Crime Data Analysis using Big Data Analytics and Visualization using Tableau. In *2022 6th International Conference on Electronics, Communication and Aerospace Technology* (pp. 627–632). Coimbatore, India: IEEE. https://doi.org/10.1109/ICECA55336.2022.10009119

Lankow, J., Ritchie, J., & Crooks, R. (2012). *Infographics: The power of visual storytelling.* John Wiley & Sons.

Laucuka, A. (2018). Communicative functions of hashtags. *Economics and Culture, 15*(1), 56–62.

Lepkowska-White, E., & Parsons, A. (2019). Strategies for monitoring social media for small restaurants. *Journal of Foodservice Business Research, 22*(4), 351–374.

Levi, G., & Hassner, T. (2015). Age and gender classification using convolutional neural networks. In *Proceedings of the IEEE conference on computer vision and pattern recognition workshops, June 2015* (pp. 34–42).

Li, D., Wang, S., & Li, D. (2015). *Spatial data mining.* Berlin, Heidelberg: Springer Berlin Heidelberg.

Li, X., Xu, M., Zeng, W., Tse, Y. K., & Chan, H. K. (2023). Exploring customer concerns on service quality under the COVID-19 crisis: A social media analytics study from the retail industry. *Journal of Retailing and Consumer Services, 70*, 103157.

Li, Z., Wang, C., Emrich, C. T., & Guo, D. (2018). A novel approach to leveraging social media for rapid flood mapping: a case study of the 2015 South Carolina floods. *Cartography and Geographic Information Science, 45*(2), 97–110.

Li, Z., Zhang, X., Müller, H., & Zhang, S. (2018). Large-scale retrieval for medical image analytics: A comprehensive review. *Medical Image Analysis, 43*, 66–84.

Liere-Netheler, K., Gilhaus, L., Vogelsang, K., & Hoppe, U. (2019). A literature review on application areas of social media analytics. In W. Abramowicz, & R. Corchuelo (Eds.), *BIS 2019: Business Information Systems; Lecture Notes in Business Information Processing.* Berlin/Heidelberg, Germany: Springer, 2019; Volume 354.

Lin, M. S., Liang, Y., Xue, J. X., Pan, B., & Schroeder, A. (2021). Destination image through social media analytics and survey method. *International Journal of Contemporary Hospitality Management, 33*(6), 2219–2238.

Liu, B. (2022). *Sentiment analysis and opinion mining.* Springer Nature.

Liu, B., & Liu, B. (2011). Social network analysis. *Web data mining: Exploring hyperlinks, contents, and usage data* (pp. 269–309).

Longley, P. A., Goodchild, M. F., Maguire, D. J., & Rhind, D. W. (2015). *Geographic information science and systems.* John Wiley & Sons.

Lund, B. D. (2022). The art of (data) storytelling. *The International Journal of Information, Diversity, & Inclusion, 6*(1/2), 31–41.

Lynn, T., Healy, P., Kilroy, S., Hunt, G., Van Der Werff, L., Venkatagiri, S., & Morrison, J. (2015, July). Towards a general research framework for social media research using big data. In *2015 IEEE International Professional Communication Conference (IPCC) 1–8.* https://doi.org/10.1109/IPCC.2015.7235843

Mahmud, J., Nichols, J., & Drews, C. (2014). Home location identification of twitter users. arXiv preprint arXiv:1403.2345.

Malagaris, G. (2020). *Al-Biruni.* Oxford: Oxford University Press.

Malik, A., Dhir, A., & Nieminen, M. (2016). Uses and gratifications of digital photo sharing on Facebook. *Telematics and Informatics, 33*(1), 129–138.

Malik, A., Khan, M. L., & Hussain, K. (2023). How is ChatGPT transforming academia? Examining its impact on teaching, research, assessment, and learning. *SSRN Electronic Journal.* https://doi.org/10.2139/ssrn.4413516

Malik, A., Khan, M. L., & Quan-Haase A. (2021). Public health agencies outreach through Instagram during COVID-19 pandemic: Crisis and emergency risk communication perspective, *International Journal of Disaster Risk Reduction, 61,* 102346, https://doi.org/10.1016/j.ijdrr.2021.102346

Malleson, N., & Andresen, M. A. (2015). The impact of using social media data in crime rate calculations: shifting hot spots and changing spatial patterns. *Cartography and Geographic Information Science, 42*(2), 112–121.

Mancosu, M., & Vegetti, F. (2020). What you can scrape and what is right to scrape: A proposal for a tool to collect public Facebook data. *Social Media+ Society, 6*(3), 2056305120940703.

Marder, M., Harary, S., Ribak, A., Tzur, Y., Alpert, S., & Tzadok, A. (2015). Using image analytics to monitor retail store shelves. *IBM Journal of Research and Development, 59*(2/3), 3–1.

Marin, A., & Wellman, B. (2011). Social network analysis: An introduction. In J. Scott & P. Carrington (Eds.), *The Sage handbook of social network analysis* (pp. 11–25). Thousand Oaks, CA: Sage.

Marine-Roig, E. (2019). Destination image analytics through traveller-generated content. *Sustainability, 11*(12), 3392.

Marjani, M., Nasaruddin, F., Gani, A., Karim, A., Hashem, I. A. T., Siddiqa, A., & Yaqoob, I. (2017). Big IoT data analytics: architecture, opportunities, and open research challenges. *IEEE Access, 5,* 5247–5261.

Marotta, T. (2024). Feeling, thinking, and not seeing: how images engage and disengage in an information-saturated world–a neurophenomenological perspective. *Media Practice and Education, 25*(1), 35–55.

Marres, N., Colombo, G., Bounegru, L., Gray, J. W., Gerlitz, C., & Tripp, J. (2023). Testing and not testing for coronavirus on Twitter: Surfacing testing situations across scales with interpretative methods. *Social Media+ Society, 9*(3), 20563051231196538.

Mazhar, T., Malik, M. A., Nadeem, M. A., Mohsan, S. A. H., Haq, I., Karim, F. K., & Mostafa, S. M. (2022). Movie reviews classification through facial image recognition and emotion detection using machine learning methods. *Symmetry, 14*(12), 2607.

McCann, M., & Barlow, A. (2015). Use and measurement of social media for SMEs. *Journal of Small Business and Enterprise Development, 22*(2), 273–287.

McGuirk, M. (2021). Performing social media analytics with brandwatch for classrooms: A platform review. *Journal of Marketing Analytics, 9*(4), 363–378. https://doi.org/10.1057/s41270-021-00128-5

McInerney, D., & Kempeneers, P. (2015). Raster Data Explained. In *Open Source Geospatial Tools: Applications in Earth Observation* (pp. 51–60). https://doi.org/10.1007/978-3-319-01824-9

McKitrick, M. K., Schuurman, N., & Crooks, V. A. (2023). Collecting, analyzing, and visualizing location-based social media data: review of methods in GIS-social media analysis. *GeoJournal, 88*(1), 1035–1057.

Mehmet, M., & Simmons, P. (2018). Kangaroo court? An analysis of social media justifications for attitudes to culling. *Environmental Communication, 12*(3), 370–386.

Micera, R., & Crispino, R. (2017). Destination web reputation as "smart tool" for image building: the case analysis of Naples city-destination. *International Journal of Tourism Cities, 3*(4), 406–423.

Moghadas, M., Fekete, A., Rajabifard, A., & Kötter, T. (2023). The wisdom of crowds for improved disaster resilience: a near-real-time analysis of crowdsourced social media data on the 2021 flood in Germany. *GeoJournal, 88*(4), 4215–4241.

Monaco, S. F. (2017). The Management of Settlements in Fourth Millennium BCE Mesopotamia (pp. 41–48).

Morrison, M. (2010). History of SMART objectives. Rapid Business Improvement. Retrieved from http://rapidbi.com/management/history-of-smart-objectives/.

Morstatter, F., Gao, H., & Liu, H. (2015). Discovering location information in social media. *IEEE Data Engineering Bulletin, 38*(2), 4–13.

Morstatter, F., Pfeffer, J., Liu, H., & Carley, K. (2013). Is the sample good enough? comparing data from twitter's streaming api with twitter's firehose. In *Proceedings of the international AAAI conference on web and social media* (Vol. 7, No. 1, pp. 400–408).

Muggleton, S. (2014). Alan Turing and the development of artificial intelligence. *AI Communications, 27*(1), 3–10. https://doi.org/10.3233/AIC-130579

Murray, A. T. (2021). Significance assessment in the application of spatial analytics. *Annals of the American Association of Geographers, 111*(6), 1740–1755.

NAIIA (2023). National Artificial Intelligence Initiative Act of 2020, Division E of Public Law. https://www.ai.gov/wp-content/uploads/2023/04/National-Artificial-Intelligence-Initiative-Act-of-2020.pdf

Nam, H., Joshi, Y. V., & Kannan, P. K. (2017). Harvesting brand information from social tags. *Journal of Marketing, 81*(4), 88–108.

Nasar, Z., Jaffry, S. W., & Malik, M. K. (2021). Named entity recognition and relation extraction: State-of-the-art. *ACM Computing Surveys (CSUR), 54*(1), 1–39.

Nelson, D. L., Reed, V. S., & Walling, J. R. (1976). Pictorial superiority effect. *Journal of Experimental Psychology: Human Learning and Memory, 2*(5), 523–528. https://doi.org/10.1037/0278-7393.2.5.523

Newberry, C. (2023). 34 Instagram Stats Marketers Need to Know in 2023. https://blog.hootsuite.com/instagram-statistics/

NewVantage Partners (2023). Data and analytics leadership annual executive survey 2023. Retrieved from: https://www.newvantage.com/_files/ugd/e5361a_247885043758499ba090f7a5f510cf7c.pdf

Nunavath, V., & Goodwin, M. (2018, December). The role of artificial intelligence in social media big data analytics for disaster management-initial results of a systematic literature review. In *2018 5th International Conference on information and communication technologies for disaster management (ICT-DM) Sendai, Japan, 2018* (pp. 1–4). doi: 10.1109/ICT-DM.2018.8636388.

O'Sullivan, D., & Unwin, D.J. (2003). *Geographic information analysis*. Hoboken, NJ: Wiley.

Ofoeda, J., Boateng, R., & Effah, J. (2019). Application programming interface (API) research: A review of the past to inform the future. *International Journal of Enterprise Information Systems (IJEIS)*, 15(3), 76–95.

Ojo, A., & Heravi, B. (2018). Patterns in award winning data storytelling: Story types, enabling tools and competences. *Digital Journalism*, 6(6), 693–718.

Otte, E., & Rousseau, R. (2002). Social network analysis: a powerful strategy, also for the information sciences. *Journal of Information Science*, 28(6), 441–453.

Pang, B., & Lee, L. (2008). Opinion mining and sentiment analysis. *Foundations and Trends in Information Retrieval*, 2(1–2), 1–135.

Park, S. B., Kim, J., Lee, Y. K., & Ok, C. M. (2020). Visualizing theme park visitors' emotions using social media analytics and geospatial analytics. *Tourism Management*, 80, 104127.

Parsons, P. (2021). Understanding data visualization design practice. *IEEE Transactions on Visualization and Computer Graphics*, 28(1), 665–675.

Pastuch, C. (2022). Al-Idrisi's Masterpiece of Medieval Geography. https://blogs.loc.gov/maps/2022/01/al-idrisis-masterpiece-of-medieval-geography/

Patil, D. J., & Mason, H. (2015). *Data driven: Creating a data culture*. Sebastopol, CA: O'Reilly Media Inc.

Peters, K., Chen, Y., Kaplan, A. M., Ognibeni, B., & Pauwels, K. (2013). Social media metrics—A framework and guidelines for managing social media. *Journal of Interactive Marketing*, 27(4), 281–298.

Petrosyan, A. (2024). Worldwide digital population 2024. https://www.statista.com/statistics/617136/digital-population-worldwide/

Plattner, H. (2011). Foreword. In H. Plattner, C. Meinel, & L. Leifer (Eds.), *Design thinking: understand - improve - apply* (pp. v–vi). Springer-Verlag, Heidelberg, Berlin.

Pomputius, A. (2019). Can you hear me now? Social listening as a strategy for understanding user needs. *Medical Reference Services Quarterly*, 38(2), 181–186.

PR Newswire (2023). *Social Media Analytics Market to Hit $43.25 Billion by 2030*. Grand View Research, Inc. https://finance.yahoo.com/news/social-media-analytics-market-hit-095000128.html

Prell, C. (2011). Social network analysis: History, theory and methodology. In *Social Network Analysis* (pp. 1–272). Thousand Oaks, CA: Sage. ISBN: 9781446254103.

Puschmann, C., & Burgess, J. (2014). Metaphors of big data. *International Journal of Communication*, 8, 1690–1709.

Ramage, D., Rosen, E., Chuang, J., Manning, C. D., & McFarland, D. A. (2009, December). Topic modeling for the social sciences. In *NIPS 2009 workshop on applications for topic models: text and beyond* (Vol. 5, No. 27, pp. 1–4).

Ramamonjisoa, D. (2014, March). Topic modeling on users's comments. In *Proceedings of the 2014 third ICT international student project conference (ICT-ISPC)* (pp. 177–180). Nakhonpathom, Thailand: IEEE, 26–27 March 2014.

Rattenbury, T., Hellerstein, J., Heer, J., Kandel, S., & Carreras, C. (2017). *Principles of data wrangling: Practical techniques for data preparation*. O'Reilly Media, Inc.

Reece, A. G., & Danforth, C. M. (2017). Instagram photos reveal predictive markers of depression. *EPJ Data Science*, 6(1), 15.

Ricov, F., & Pripuzic, K. (2022). Performance Evaluation of Java Serialization Frameworks on Geospatial Big Data. In *2022 7th International Conference on Smart and Sustainable Technologies (SpliTech), Split / Bol, Croatia, 2022* (pp. 1–6). IEEE. https://doi.org/10.23919/SpliTech55088.2022.9854334.

Rietveld, R., Van Dolen, W., Mazloom, M., & Worring, M. (2020). What you feel, is what you like influence of message appeals on customer engagement on Instagram. *Journal of Interactive Marketing*, 49, 20–53.

Rodrigues, J., Balan, A., Traina, A., & Traina, C. (2008). The Visual Expression Process: Bridging Vision and Data Visualization (pp. 207–215). https://doi.org/10.1007/978-3-540-85412-8_19

Rogers, E. M., Singhal, A., & Quinlan, M. M. (2014). Diffusion of innovations. In *An integrated approach to communication theory and research* (2nd Edition, pp. 432–448). New York, NY. ISBN: 9780203887011.

Rolandi, M., Cheng, K., & Pérez-Kriz, S. (2011). A brief guide to designing effective figures for the scientific paper. *Advanced Materials*, *23*(38), 4343–4346. doi:10.1002/adma.201102518

Roy, A., Nikolitch, K., McGinn, R., Jinah, S., Klement, W., & Kaminsky, Z. A. (2020). A machine learning approach predicts future risk to suicidal ideation from social media data. *NPJ Digital Medicine*, *3*(1), 78.

Rubin, R. S. (2002). Will the real SMART goals please stand up? *The Industrial-Organizational Psychologist*, *39*(4), 26–27.

Ruhi, U. (2014). Social media analytics as a business intelligence practice: Current landscape & future prospects. *Journal of Internet Social Networking & Virtual Communities*, *2014*. https://doi.org/10.5171/2014.920553

Ruhi, U. (2014). Social media analytics as a business intelligence practice: Current landscape & future prospects. *Journal of Internet Social Networking & Virtual Communities*, *2014*, 1.

Sabuncu, İ., & Atmis, M. (2020). Social media analytics for brand image tracking: A case study application for Turkish airlines. *Yönetim Bilişim Sistemleri Dergisi*, *6*(1), 26–41.

Saggi, M. K., & Jain, S. (2018). A survey towards an integration of big data analytics to big insights for value-creation. *Information Processing & Management*, *54*(5), 758–790.

Salloum, S. A., Al-Emran, M., Monem, A. A., & Shaalan, K. (2017). A survey of text mining in social media: Facebook and Twitter perspectives. *Advances in Science, Technology and Engineering Systems Journal*, *2*(1), 127–133.

Sandhiya, R., Boopika, A. M., Akshatha, M., Swetha, S. V., & Hariharan, N. M. (2022). A review of topic modeling and its application. In S. Bhattacharyya, P. K. Singh, & A. K. Kole (Eds.), *Handbook of intelligent computing and optimization for sustainable development* (pp. 305–322). Wiley. DOI: https://doi.org/10.1002/9781119792642.ch15

Sarikaya, A., Correll, M., Bartram, L., Tory, M., & Fisher, D. (2018). What do we talk about when we talk about dashboards?. *IEEE Transactions on Visualization and Computer Graphics*, *25*(1), 682–692. doi: 10.1109/TVCG.2018.2864903

Schulz, A., Hadjakos, A., Paulheim, H., Nachtwey, J., & Mühlhäuser, M. (2013). A multi-indicator approach for geolocalization of tweets. In *Proceedings of the International AAAI Conference on web and social media* (Vol. 7, No. 1, pp. 573–582).

Schwartz, H. A., & Ungar, L. H. (2015). Data-driven content analysis of social media: A systematic overview of automated methods. *The ANNALS of the American Academy of Political and Social Science*, *659*(1), 78–94.

Scott, J. (2011). Social network analysis: developments, advances, and prospects. *Social Network Analysis and Mining*, *1*, 21–26.

Seidel, V. P., & Fixson, S. K. (2013). Adopting design thinking in novice multidisciplinary teams: The application and limits of design methods and reflexive practices. *Journal of Product Innovation Management*, *30*, 19–33.

Shah, M., Pabel, A., & Martin-Sardesai, A. (2020). Assessing Google reviews to monitor student experience. *International Journal of Educational Management*, *34*(3), 610–625.

Sharma, R., Ahuja, V., & Alavi, S. (2018). The future scope of netnography and social network analysis in the field of marketing. *Journal of Internet Commerce*, *17*(1), 26–45.

Shevchenko, Y., & Reips, U. D. (2024). Geofencing in location-based behavioral research: Methodology, challenges, and implementation. *Behavior Research Methods*, 56(7), 6411–6439.

Singh, K. (2020). Banks banking on ai. *International Journal of Advanced Research in Management and Social Sciences*, 9(9), 1–11.

Singh, P., Dwivedi, Y. K., Kahlon, K. S., Sawhney, R. S., Alalwan, A. A., & Rana, N. P. (2020). Smart monitoring and controlling of government policies using social media and cloud computing. *Information Systems Frontiers*, 22, 315–337.

Sinha, V., Subramanian, K. S., Bhattacharya, S., & Chaudhary, K. (2012). The contemporary framework on social media analytics as an emerging tool for behavior informatics, HR analytics and business process. *Management: Journal of Contemporary Management Issues*, 17(2), 65–84.

Sparavigna, A. C. (2014). Al-Biruni and the Mathematical Geography. *PHILICA, Article*, 443.

Statista (2024). Most popular social networks worldwide as of October 2023, ranked by number of monthly active users. https://www.statista.com/statistics/272014/global-social-networks-ranked-by-number-of-users/

Statista (2024). Number of monthly active Facebook users worldwide as of 2nd quarter 2023. Retrieved from https://www.statista.com/statistics/264810/number-of-monthly-active-facebook-users-worldwide/

Statista (2025). Number of internet and social media users worldwide as of February 2025 (in billions). Retrieved from: https://www.statista.com/statistics/617136/digital-population-worldwide/

Steiger, E., Resch, B., & Zipf, A. (2016). Exploration of spatiotemporal and semantic clusters of Twitter data using unsupervised neural networks. *International Journal of Geographical Information Science*, 30, 1694–1716. https://doi.org/10.1080/13658816.2015.1099658.

Sterne, J. (2010). *Social media metrics: How to measure and optimize your marketing investment.* John Wiley & Sons.

Stieglitz, S., Dang-Xuan, L., Bruns, A., & Neuberger, C. (2014). Social media analytics: An interdisciplinary approach and its implications for information systems. *Business & Information Systems Engineering*, 6, 89–96.

Stieglitz, S., Mirbabaie, M., Ross, B., & Neuberger, C. (2018). Social media analytics – Challenges in topic discovery, data collection, and data preparation. *International Journal of Information Management*, 39, 156–168. https://doi.org/10.1016/j.ijinfomgt.2017.12.002

Stobierski, T. (2021). Data Wrangling: What it is and why it's important, Retrieved from: https://online.hbs.edu/blog/post/data-wrangling

Stoner, J., Hardy, R., & Bryant, C. (2023). Maps that Changed Our World, Geography & Map Division, Library of Congress, https://www.loc.gov/ghe/cascade/index.html

Szabo, G., Polatkan, G., Boykin, P. O., & Chalkiopoulos, A. (2018). *Social media data mining and analytics.* John Wiley & Sons.

Szukits, Á., & Móricz, P. (2024). Towards data-driven decision making: the role of analytical culture and centralization efforts. *Review of Managerial Science*, 18(10), 2849–2887. https://doi.org/10.1007/s11846-023-00694-1.

Taboada, M., Brooke, J., Tofiloski, M., Voll, K., & Stede, M. (2011). Lexicon-based methods for sentiment analysis. *Computational linguistics*, 37(2), 267–307.

Taherdoost, H., & Madanchian, M. (2023). Artificial intelligence and sentiment analysis: A review in competitive research. *Computers*, 12(2), 37.

Tam, L., & Kim, J. N. (2019). Social media analytics: how they support company public relations. *Journal of Business Strategy, 40*(1), 28–34.

Thelwall, M. (2016). Sentiment analysis for small and big data. In N. G. Fielding, R. M. Lee, & G. Blank (Eds.), *The SAGE handbook of online research methods* (pp. 344–355). SAGE Publications.

Thelwall, M. (2018). Social media analytics for YouTube comments: Potential and limitations. *International Journal of Social Research Methodology, 21*(3), 303–316.

Thelwall, M., Buckley, K., & Paltoglou, G. (2011). Sentiment in Twitter events. *Journal of the American Society for Information Science and Technology, 62*(2), 406–418.

Tian, X., He, W., Tang, C., Li, L., Xu, H., & Selover, D. (2020). A new approach of social media analytics to predict service quality: evidence from the airline industry. *Journal of Enterprise Information Management, 33*(1), 51–70.

Tobler, Waldo (1973). Choropleth Maps Without Class Intervals? *Geographical Analysis.* 5(3): 262–265. doi:10.1111/j.1538-4632.1973.tb01012.x

Tollner, T., Zehetleitner, M., Gramann, K., & Müller, H. J. (2011). Stimulus saliency modulates pre-attentive processing speed in human visual cortex. *PLoS One, 6*(1), e16276.

Tornberg, A., & Tornberg, P. (2016). Muslims in social media discourse: Combining topic modeling and critical discourse analysis. *Discourse, Context & Media, 13,* 132–142.

Trafton, A., (2014, January). In the blink of an eye MIT neuroscientists find the brain can identify images seen for as little as 13 milliseconds. MIT News. https://news.mit.edu/2014/in-the-blink-of-an-eye-0116

Tsou, M. H. (2015). Research challenges and opportunities in mapping social media and Big Data. *Cartography and Geographic Information Science, 42*(sup1), 70–74.

Tsvetkova, R. (2023). 99 Amazing Social Media Statistics and Facts. https://www.brandwatch.com/blog/amazing-social-media-statistics-and-facts/

Tsvetovat, M., & Kouznetsov, A. (2011). *Social network analysis for startups: Finding connections on the social web.* O'Reilly Media, Inc.

Tufte, E. R. (1983). *The visual display of quantitative information,* 2nd edition, Cheshire, CT: Graphics Press.

Tukey, J. W. (1977). *Exploratory data analysis.* Reading, MA: Addison-Wesley.

Vaishya, R., Javaid, M., Khan, I. H., & Haleem, A. (2020). Artificial Intelligence (AI) applications for COVID-19 pandemic. *Diabetes & Metabolic Syndrome: Clinical Research & Reviews, 14*(4), 337–339.

Valente, T. W., & Pitts, S. R. (2017). An appraisal of social network theory and analysis as applied to public health: challenges and opportunities. *Annual Review of Public Health,* 38, 103–118.

Valyaeva, A. (2021). Look This Way: 9 Visual Content Options to Consider. https://contentmarketinginstitute.com/articles/visual-content-examples-boost-engagement/

Van Der Meer, T. G. (2016). Automated content analysis and crisis communication research. *Public Relations Review, 42*(5), 952–961.

Vardi, M. Y. (2012). Artificial intelligence: past and future. *Communications of the ACM, 55*(1), 5–5.

Vayansky, I., & Kumar, S. A. (2020). A review of topic modeling methods. *Information Systems, 94,* 101582.

Vegas, J., Crestani, F., & Fuente, P. (2007). Context representation for web search results. *Journal of Information Science,* 33, 77–94. https://doi.org/10.1177/0165551506067123.

Verhoef, P., Kooge, E., & Walk, N. (2016). *Creating value with big data analytics: Making smarter marketing decisions.* Routledge.

Verma, T., Renu, R., & Gaur, D. (2014). Tokenization and filtering process in RapidMiner. *International Journal of Applied Information Systems, 7*(2), 16–18.

Vogel, D. R., Dickson, G. W., & Lehman, J. A. (1986). Persuasion and the role of visual presentation support: The UM/3M study.

Vu, H., Li, G., Law, R., & Ye, B. (2015). Exploring the travel behaviors of inbound tourists to Hong Kong using geotagged photos. *Tourism Management, 46*, 222–232. https://doi.org/10.1016/J.TOURMAN.2014.07.003.

Waller, L. A. (2022). Building the analytic toolbox: From spatial analytics to spatial statistical inference with geospatial data. In Faruque, F. S. (Ed.) *Geospatial technology for human well-being and health* (pp. 29–35). Cham: Springer International Publishing. https://doi.org/10.1007/978-3-030-71377-5_2

Wang, Z., & Ye, X. (2018). Social media analytics for natural disaster management. *International Journal of Geographical Information Science, 32*(1), 49–72.

Ware, C. (2019). *Information visualization: perception for design.* Morgan Kaufmann.

Warwick, C., Terras, M., & Nyhan, J. (Eds.). (2012). *Digital humanities in practice.* Facet Publishing. ISBN: 9781856047661.l.

Wasserman, S., & Faust, K. (1994). Social network analysis: Methods and applications.

Watson, H. J. (2014). Tutorial: Big data analytics: Concepts, technologies, and applications. *Communications of the Association for Information Systems, 34*(1), 65.

Watts, D. J. (2004). *Six degrees: The science of a connected age.* New York: W. W. Norton & Company.

Weber, R. P. (1990). *Basic content analysis* (Vol. 49). Sage.

Wexler, S., Shaffer, J., & Cotgreave, A. (2017). *The big book of dashboards: visualizing your data using real-world business scenarios.* John Wiley & Sons.

Whittingham, N., Boecker, A., & Grygorczyk, A. (2020). Personality traits, basic individual values and GMO risk perception of twitter users. *Journal of Risk Research, 23*(4), 522–540.

Wieneke, A., & Lehrer, C. (2016). Generating and exploiting customer insights from social media data. *Electronic Markets, 26*, 245–268.

Wiktionary (2024). Πλῆθος. Retrieved February 17, 2024, from https://en.wiktionary.org/wiki/%CF%80%CE%BB%E1%BF%86%CE%B8%CE%BF%CF%82

Williams, J. (2024, December 3). *The difference between social media monitoring vs. social media listening.* Sprout Social. Retrieved from: https://sproutsocial.com/insights/listening-vs-monitoring/

Wilmot Li, A. L., & Berthouzoz, F. (2011). Design principles for visual communication. *Communications of the ACM, 54*(4), 60–69. https://doi.org/10.1145/1924421.1924439

Wong, B. (2023). Top Social Media Statistics and Trends Of 2023. https://www.forbes.com/advisor/business/social-media-statistics/

Xiang, Z., Schwartz, Z., Gerdes Jr, J. H., & Uysal, M. (2015). What can big data and text analytics tell us about hotel guest experience and satisfaction? *International Journal of Hospitality Management, 44*, 120–130.

Zachlod, C., Samuel, O., Ochsner, A., & Werthmüller, S. (2022). Analytics of social media data–State of characteristics and application. *Journal of Business Research, 144*, 1064–1076.

Zhan, L., Cheng, M., & Zhu, J. (2024). Progress on image analytics: Implications for tourism and hospitality research. *Tourism Management, 100*, 104798.

Zhang, S., & Metaxas, D. (2016). Large-scale medical image analytics: recent methodologies, applications and future directions. *Medical Image Analysis, 33*, 98–101.

Index